BOOKS BY NORMAN BEIM

NOVELS
Hymie and The Angel

PLAYS
Six Award Winning Plays
Plays At Home And Abroad
My Family The Jewish Immigrants
Giants Of The Old Testament
Infamous People
Comedy Tonite!
Women Laid Bare
Three Dark Comedies
Six Ironic Comedies
The Wrath Of God, Plus 5 Additional Dramas

PRAISE FOR "HYMIE AND THE ANGEL"

PUBLISHERS WEEKLY
"Beim authentically evokes a time and place with ironic humor and a fine ear for dialogue...a lightheartedly entertaining look at loss, guilt and the will to live"

THE MIDWEST BOOK REVIEW
*"Hymie And The Angel" is Norman Beim's debut novel in which he showcases **unforgettable characters** in a story that is part suspense, part memoir and totally fascinating from first page to last."*

DETROIT JEWISH NEWS
News & Reviews: Alice Burdick Schweiger
*"A powerful novel. A record of places and a life that no longer exists. Beim skillfully crafts the plot as Hymie faces his moral dilemma...The result, the **heartwarming story** of " Hymie and the Angel."*

THE JEWISH JOURNAL OF THE SOUTH
Dr. Morton I. Teicher, Dean Emeritus, University of North Carolina
*"There is also a tragic element that goes back to ancient death and resurrection ceremonies. Most of all, the book is **a buoyant amusement;** an effervescent entertainment."*

THE WRATH OF GOD
Plus 5 Additional Dramas

NORMAN BEIM

NEW CONCEPT PRESS
425 West Street   Suite 2J
New York, NY 10019
212-265-6284
fax: 212-265-6659
newconpres@aol.com

CAUTION: These plays are fully protected in whole, in part, or in any form under copyright laws and are subject to royalty. All rights, including professional, amateur, motion pictures, radio, television, recitation and public readings are strictly reserved.

All inquiries for performance rights should be addressed to:
Samuel French, Inc.
45 West 25th Street
New York, New York 10010
212-206-8990

Library of Congress Control Number: 2009912248

Beim, Norman
   Plays: the wrath of god, plus 5 additional dramas/Norman Beim
       p.   cm.
   Contents: The Wrath of God-Labor of Love-The Establishment-Buck Jarvis-The Haircut-The Dark Corner of an Empty Room

ISBN: 0-931231-16-7 / 978-0-931231-16-2   (Alk. paper)

1. Drama   I. Title: The Wrath Of God, Plus 5 Additional Dramas

812'.54-dc22

Special thanks to LARRY ERLBAUM, FRANK BARA, MARVIN HAYES and last, but not least MARTY BEIM.

Printed in the United States of America
10 9 8 7 6 5 4 3 2 1

TABLE OF CONTENTS

The Wrath Of God	Page 1
Labor Of Love	Page 81
The Establishment	Page 180
Buck Jarvis	Page 250
The Haircut	Page 345
The Dark Corner Of An Empty Room	Page 415

THE WRATH OF GOD

CAST OF CHARACTERS

Tim Rafferty, A Cop

Helen Rafferty, His Sister-in-Law

Moira Rafferty, His Mother

Jason Rafferty, His Brother

Doc MacGregor, The Family Doctor

SCENE
Living room of a tenement flat on the East Side of Chicago

TIME
1933

STYLE
The dialogue is sometimes accompanied by the spoken thoughts of the characters. The thoughts are shown in italics. Care should be taken to prevent the thought speeches from impeding the physical action and causing the scene to become static.

ACT ONE

(The combination living room and dining room of a simply furnished flat. The back wall has two windows. The shades are more than half way down to block the morning sun. Upstage left and downstage left are doors leading to two bedrooms. Upstage right is a door leading to the kitchen. Downstage right is a door leading out to the hallway. There is a table, stage right, with four chairs. The song "I'll Take You Home Again, Kathleen" leads into the show. The song fades as the lights come up, and the sound of a clock ticking can be heard. DOC MACGREGOR enters from the bedroom downstage left.)

DOC: *Waiting, waiting, waiting. It seems to me one spends ones life waiting.* (HE wanders upstage and looks out the window.) *The first snow of the season. How fresh and clean it looks, like a new born baby. Such white innocence. But then, this is the beginning of winter. My sixty-third, to be exact. Sixty three years. Thirty years of medical practice and still the miracle of birth seems as fresh to me as the day I first encountered it.*
It was here, here in this very flat that I delivered my first baby. The Raffertys, Moira and Frank, fresh from the Old Sod. They're gone now, Moira and Frank, God rest their souls, gone with their dreams of a new life.
Dreams and reality, how unhappily they warred within the heart of their first born, Jason. Such a remarkable boy, such promise. Unfortunately there was his dark side, headstrong and defiant, fighting for his space at a time when space was at a premium; and his younger brother, Timmy, a sweet, gentle nature. Timmy, upright, and straight forward.

(The lights come down. When they come up again, it's summer, late morning, seven months earlier. TIM RAFFERTY, wearing the uniform of a police officer, enters from the outside, lost in thought as he closes the door.)

TIM: *The world's at sixes and at sevens, and yet me heart is singing, crazy fool that I am.* (HE walks absentmindedly toward the table, removes his hat, tossing it on the table, and then his jacket, hanging it on a chair.) *It's a hot and humid August day. Me brother, Jason, the man I used to idolize, has broken out of prison. Oh, I knew that he would, but not so soon. Not now, when me poor dear mother, lies in bed, her left arm paralyzed by a stroke from which she barely recovered. He's bound to come here, unless they catch him first. He's bound to come here to claim his wife. But she's mine now, Jason. Helen's mine, with her crooked smile and her sad brown eyes.*

(HELEN RAFFERTY enters from the bedroom.)

HELEN: You're home.

TIM: I just got in. How is she?

HELEN: She's resting.

(HE kisses her.)

HELEN: I'll never get used to your hours.

TIM: Neither will I. (HE caresses her cheek.) *Just to be near her. I never thought I could be this happy. My feet never touch the ground, my big flat feet.*

HELEN: (SHE pats his face and breaks away.) *Like an overgrown boy, but he's not a boy. He's Jason, Jason the way I*

THE WRATH OF GOD

saw him in my mind, gentle, strong and clean, and burdened by that harridan.

TIM: Is there anything wrong?

HELEN: Your mother. She can be trying at times. Did you have a hard night?

TIM: Same old grind. **(HE approaches her and puts his arm around her waist.)** *Her tiny feet, her lovely breasts. Her soft, warm belly. The miracle, the miracle of love. I've been on my legs all night and I feel wide awake. Oh, sweet, sweet Jesus!* **(HE kisses her, caresses her cheek, then stops.)** *But how will she feel when she finds out?*

HELEN: I think we ought to tell her.

TIM: What's that?

HELEN: About us. Timmy...

TIM: What?

HELEN: I think we ought to tell her about us.

TIM: This is not a good time. *And when the time comes, if the time comes, who will she choose?*

HELEN: **(SHE sits wearily.)** *Must I live forever in the shadow of that banshee? Powerless...I've always been powerless, always the outsider. Two grown men in the clutches of that tyrant, that wretched, scrawny tyrant.*

TIM: You look tired.

THE WRATH OF GOD

HELEN: *Why don't I leave all this behind? Why don't I go back to where I came from? Jason in prison is as good as dead. The child is dead. What is there for me here?* It's too much for me. You don't know what it's like.

TIM: *Those lovely dark eyes.*

HELEN: She knows, and she knows that I know she knows, and both of us pretending. It's ridiculous and awkward and...

TIM: What do you want me to do?

HELEN: I want you to tell her. Tell her that I'm planning to divorce Jason, and that you and I are planning on getting married.

TIM: Doc MacGregor says she shouldn't be excited.

HELEN: I see. Have you changed your mind?

TIM: No, of course not. Let me talk it over with the Doc first.

> *(MOIRA RAFFERTY appears in the bedroom doorway. SHE stands studying the two lovers.)*

MOIRA: *Here I am in this old familiar room, in this old familiar doorway. And look at them, the two of them. The Judas and the whore. Why did that woman come into our lives, to steal my Jason from me, and now my Timmy? What were they whispering about before I came in? Words of love, no doubt. Now wonder I had a stroke.*

TIM: If it isn't Mother McCree!

HELEN: You shouldn't be out of bed.

THE WRATH OF GOD

MOIRA: **(MOIRA starts toward the table.)** *Oh, don't mind me, my dears. Go on with your filthy coupling.*

(HELEN moves to help her.)

MOIRA: It's me arm that's crippled, not me legs. *He didn't even come into the room to wish me good morning, he's so besotted. Look at him, the fool. The fool and the whore.* **(SHE sits at the table.)** Have ye had yer breakfast, dear?

TIM: Is that what you've got to worry about?

MOIRA: Who else is there to look after you?

HELEN: Doc MacGregor said you should be resting.

MOIRA: I am resting. I'm sitting here and I'm resting.

TIM: *How wasted she looks; bony and wasted with those deep sunken eyes.*

MOIRA: What are you staring at?

TIM: The prettiest lady in Christendom.

MOIRA: "The prettiest lady in Christendom. That's what you are, my dear, the prettiest lady in Christendom." Poor dear Frank. I hope you're happy, wherever you are, with your bottle beside you. "I'm a bottle baby, my dear." That's what you were, my dear, my bottle baby. So handsome when you were young. So bloated when they carried you out.

TIM: *It breaks my heart to see her like this.*

THE WRATH OF GOD

HELEN: *The two of them, like two love birds.* I'll get your breakfast. **(SHE goes into the kitchen.)**

MOIRA: Your brother came to visit me last night.

TIM: *His name is Jason, goddamnit. And, yes, I'm fucking his wife. I'm fucking my brother's wife.* What did you dream?

MOIRA: He came to wish me Godspeed.

TIM: You're going on a journey?

MOIRA: Could be.

TIM: *He's all she thinks about, all she cares about. Her husband, my father, drank himself to death. Did she weep? Oh, no. But when dear Jason was sentenced to prison...Oh, the buckets and buckets of tears.*

MOIRA: You wrote him about me stroke, didn't ye? Well...

TIM: Well, what?

MOIRA: He came to visit me.

TIM: In your dreams.

MOIRA: It was more than a dream.

TIM: I see.

MOIRA: *You're not half the man your brother is. You belong to your father...dreamers, the two of you.*

THE WRATH OF GOD

TIM: *What a handsome couple they made! And how it broke my heart to see them grow old; to see him drink himself to death, and to see her grow cold and bitter.*

MOIRA: *If I could only go back home, where the sky is blue and the trees and the grass are green, and the air smells fresh. Why did we come here? To die in this coffin, this dreary city with the traffic and the noise. And now who's left to hold a wake? Who's left to mourn me?* Has the mail come yet?

TIM: It doesn't come till noon. You know that. *There won't be a letter from Jason, Mother dear. There may, God help us, be a visit though.*

MOIRA: *There was that old beggar woman. "I'll put a curse on you," she croaked. "Go ahead. Put a curse on me. See if I care." "You'll care, my beauty, when you're plagued with the wrath of God. The wrath of God."* The wrath of God.

TIM: What was that?

MOIRA: Nothing. I was just remembering.

TIM: You ought to be in bed.

MOIRA: I'll be there soon enough.

TIM: Now what is that supposed to mean?

MOIRA: *It's the wrath of God, that drove dear Frank, to drink. It's the wrath of God that made a gangster out of Jason. It's the wrath of God that made a brother testify against his brother and then steal his wife.*

THE WRATH OF GOD

(TIM picks up his hat and jacket and goes into the upstage bedroom. HELEN enters with silverware and napkin, places them on the table and goes back off.)

MOIRA: *I knew she was trouble, the minute I laid eyes on her. An Irish girl wasn't good enough for my Jason. He had to pick an "eyetalian." "Ma, this is Helen, the girl I'm gonna marry." Just like that. "Are ye now?" I should have said. "How nice for you!" And she was the one. She was the one that turned my Jason into a gangster. "Where'd you get the money to buy a fur coat?" I asked him. "You want one, too?" he asked. "That's not what I asked you?" "I'm a business man, my dear?" What sort of business?" "Never you mind." But I did mind, and so did the law.*

(HELEN reenters with a glass of orange juice which she places on the table.)

MOIRA: *That Thomasino, he was an eyetalian, too. He was the one that led my boy astray.*

(TIM reenters and sits at the table.)

HELEN: Would you like some oatmeal, Mother?

MOIRA: I've had me breakfast.

HELEN: It was quite a while ago, and you didn't eat very much.

MOIRA: **(Mimicking)** *You didn't eat very much. As if she cared.* All right, all right. I'll go back to me coffin.

TIM: Now, is that the way to talk?

THE WRATH OF GOD

MOIRA: What would ye have me say? Maybe I've lived too long, as it is. Oh, go drink your orange juice.

(SHE rises, starts for the bedroom and stumbles. HELEN rushes to help her.)

MOIRA: Leave me be.

(MOIRA goes off to bedroom, slamming the door behind her. HELEN follows her off, closing the door behind her. TIM picks up the orange juice, then sets it down and sits lost in thought.)

TIM: *Who am I really? And how did I get to be who I am? The youngest son of immigrant parents, Frank and Moira Rafferty, come over from the Old Sod to escape the famine and the poverty. Frank was a dreamer and a blowhard. He kept getting fired, going from one job to another. And Moira... Moira, too, was a dreamer, strong and ambitious. Two baby boys to take care of, and odd jobs she could manage at home, washing, sewing. And then there was Jason, Jason, whom she adored, and Frank was afraid of.* **(HE takes a sip of the orange juice.)** *And then there was me, little Timmy who worshipped his older brother until one day... "You mustn't do that, Jason?" "Don't be such a pussy." "But that's stealing, Jason." "Stealing is when you get caught. Read your Bible. God helps those who help themselves."* **(HE finishes his the orange juice.)**

MOIRA: **(Offstage)** Go on, go on. Leave me be. I don't need your help.

(HELEN reenters, closing the door behind her.)

TIM: What's gotten into her?

THE WRATH OF GOD

HELEN: She's been like that all day. She keeps talking about Jason.

(TIM moves the glass away, looking uneasy.)

HELEN: What is it? Timmy, what is it?

TIM: He's escaped.

HELEN: **(SHE sits)** *Why doesn't that surprise me? All morning long I've had this premonition. Maybe it was Moira that put it there, rattling on about how Jason paid her a visit, how he'd be coming here to bid her a fond farewell. And all morning long I've felt Jason all around me, his arms, his mouth, his body.*

TIM: Did you hear what I said?

HELEN: Yes, I heard you.

TIM: There's nothing to worry about. They've got the building surrounded, and your building as well.

HELEN: And you think that'll stop him? **(SHE rises, picks up the juice glass and goes into the kitchen.)**

TIM: *Ah, yes. Jason Rafferty. My older brother, my hero. He isn't a man; Jason's a myth. When Frank couldn't come up with the rent, there was Jason, fifteen years old. "There you are, me boyo. Here's the money for the rent," said Jason. "Where'd you get that money, Jason?" asked Dad. "I worked for it," said Jason, and that shut old man up for a moment, and then he said, as fatherly as he could, which was not very fatherly, "I don't like that crowd you're hanging out with." "Don't ye now?" said Jason. "Well, maybe when*

THE WRATH OF GOD

you sober up, you'll like 'em better." Frank slammed the door on the way out, on the way out to the corner bar.

(HELEN enters with a bowl of oatmeal.)

HELEN: Is he alone?

TIM: What's that?

HELEN: Jason? Was he alone when he escaped?

TIM: No, there were three of them. **(HE eats the oatmeal.)**

HELEN: *(SHE sits.)* "Where are you going?" I asked. "You don't want to know," said Jason. "When will you be back?" "I love ya, baby. Just sit tight." "Jason..." And he was gone, for three long months. I didn't know what to think. That was the first time, and that was the first time I turned to Timmy, for some sort of reassurance, for some sort of comfort. Dear, sweet, upright, Timmy. He blushed when I pushed the hair out of his eyes. And I teased him mercilessly. It was all so innocent, so innocent. I never realized how dangerous it was until it was too late. **(SHE rises, takes the oatmeal bowl and goes into the kitchen.)**

TIM: *He'll try to take her back, of course. They're still man and wife. "Father, I don't know what to do. I can't testify against me own brother." "You've got to tell the truth, Timmy. If your brother committed a crime, he's got to pay for it." "But me own brother." "There are no buts." "What will people think of me? How can I live with meself?" "I'm your priest. You came to me for advice. The rest is up to you."*

(HELEN reenters with a plate of ham and eggs and toast which she places on the table. TIM digs in.)

THE WRATH OF GOD

HELEN: When did he get out?

TIM: The night before last.

HELEN: When did you find out about it?

TIM: This morning. At the station. I don't know if it's hit the newsstands yet, or the radio.

(TIM continues to eat. There's a knock at the door. TIM looks up at HELEN.)

HELEN: That must be the doc. Shall I open it?

(SHE hesitates, then opens the door. DOC MACGREGOR enters, carrying a small black bag.)

DOC: Why does everyone live on the second floor?

TIM: Have a seat, Doc.

HELEN: Would you like some lemonade?

DOC: You took the words right out of my mouth.

(HELEN goes off to the kitchen.)

TIM: This is my breakfast, Doc. Excuse me.

DOC: Go right ahead, Son.

(TIM continues to eat.)

DOC: **(HE sits.)** *How quickly they grow. Little Timmy, now a big,*

THE WRATH OF GOD

strapping cop. Of all the little ones I brought into this world, I think this one is the one I'm proudest of. How's the patient?

TIM: She won't stay put.

DOC: *Good old Moira. Made of steel that woman is.*

(HELEN reenters with a glass of lemonade.)

DOC: Thank you, Helen.

(HELEN returns to the kitchen.)

DOC: It's mighty hot out there. **(HE drinks the lemonade.)**

TIM: *Good old Doc. He used to bound up those steps, and there was always that big, hearty greeting. And always that ominous black bag. "What are you gonna do to me, Doc?" "I'm gonna make you better, Son." "Will it hurt?" "A little. But it'll be worth it, Son, 'cause you won't feel as bad as you do now. Frank, Moira, I want you to hold this boy down. He mustn't move. You hear me? He mustn't move." And here on this very table he slit open the back of my ear to let it drain.*

(HELEN reenters with a mug of coffee.)

DOC: I guess you've heard the news.

TIM: What's that, Doc?

DOC: They've caught Jason. It just came over the radio. They've caught all three of them.

TIM: Are you sure, Doc?

THE WRATH OF GOD

DOC: Why don't you turn on the radio?

TIM: It's broken. I've been meaning to get it fixed.

HELEN: Why don't I go upstairs to the Oleary's? **(SHE goes off.)**

TIM: How's the wife, Doc?

DOC: Thank you for asking, son. Ironic, isn't it? I can help all my patients, but I can't even help my own wife.

TIM: Is it serious?

Doc: It's her heart. There's nothing to be done about it, and there's no pain or anything. She just keeps getting weaker, just fading away. A rather poetic way to die, isn't it? Like Mimi in La Boheme? You like opera, Son?

TIM: I don't know much about it?

DOC: It's the arias. They can tear you apart. That's what art can do for you, you know. It's called catharsis. Better than most medicines. I better get in there and see how my patient is doing.

> **(DOC goes into the downstage bedroom. TIM finishes his coffee, picks up the dishes and goes into the kitchen. After a moment or two the door is opened cautiously and JASON RAFFERTY enters, closing the door softly behind him.)**

JASON: *Empty. No one here to greet the prodigal son? Where's me mother ready to throw her arms around her favorite? And Timmy, dear old Timmy. My Judas and my darlin' little brother all*

THE WRATH OF GOD

rolled into one. Why aren't they here? This moment I've been dreaming about. What a letdown!

(TIM reenters from the kitchen. The TWO BROTHERS stand silently face to face. TIM eyes JASON apprehensively. JASON moves towards his brother. HE throws his arm around him, then stands with his hands on TIM's shoulders.)

JASON: Well, say it.

TIM: What?

JASON: What the hell am I doing here? Why don't I stay buried?

TIM: They said you'd been caught.

JASON: Who said?

TIM: It came over the radio.

JASON: No such luck.

TIM: Doc MacGregor's in the bedroom with Mom.

JASON: How she doin'?

TIM: She seems to be coming along. Do you think it wise? For Doc to see you here?

JASON: Why? Do you think he'd give me away?

TIM: I don't know.

THE WRATH OF GOD

JASON: How's Helen? Have you seen her lately?

TIM: She's been taking care of Mom.

JASON: Is she here?

TIM: She's upstairs.

JASON: *Two strangers. This man isn't my Timmy. This man's the cop I used to see on the corner. The arm of the law I used to be so wary of.*

TIM: *Two strangers. This isn't Jason. He's one of those hoods you see in the movies. He's Edward G. Robinson. He's Humphrey Bogart.*

JASON & TIM: *Two strangers.*

TIM: How'd you manage to get out?

JASON: You don't really wanna know, do you?

TIM: This building's surrounded, you know.

JASON: I'm sure it is.

TIM: How'd you manage to get in?

JASON: They forgot about that cellar door, the one in the back that's blocked off.

TIM: I thought it was locked?

JASON: Apparently not.

THE WRATH OF GOD

TIM: Where do you go from here?

JASON: To a new life, Timmy boy, a new life. How's Helen? How's my lovely wife?

TIM: She's okay, I guess.

JASON: What do you mean, you guess? Why don't you get rid of the Doc.

TIM: Jason...

JASON: I'll wait in the kitchen.

> **(JASON goes into the kitchen. TIM sighs, hesitates then opens the bedroom door. After a moment DOC enters. TIM closes the door.)**

TIM: How she doing?

DOC: She keeps talking about Jason. You sure she hasn't heard anything?

TIM: I'm positive.

DOC: Well, now that he's been captured I'd make sure she doesn't know about it. She's much too excited. I could use some more of that lemonade, by the way.

TIM: Ah...sure.

> **(TIM takes the empty glass and goes off to the kitchen. DOC sits with a sigh.)**

THE WRATH OF GOD

DOC: *If only my Fanny had the stamina of that woman in there. Dear, Fanny, she never complains. "Sit down and talk to me," says Fanny. "What would you like to talk about?" I say, and I sit, reluctantly, because my mind is elsewhere. How cruel of me! How selfish! There's only another year or so, if we're lucky. But, the fact of the matter is, I can't help dear Fanny, but I can help those others, all those others depending on me.*

(TIM enters with the glass of lemonade.)

TIM: Here you are, Doc.

DOC: Thank you.

TIM: You look tired.

DOC: There seems to be no rest for the weary, Son. And the heat doesn't help. **(HE drinks some lemonade.)** I'm proud of you, Timmy.

TIM: Why?

DOC: You've had a lot to overcome, and you've done nobly. You oughta find yourself a nice Irish girl and raise a family. I think you'd make a great father. **(HE finishes the lemonade.)** Well, I'd better be going. Don't let that mother of yours get too rambunctious.

TIM: Thank you, Doc. Don't we owe you something?

DOC: Five dollars would help.

TIM: It must be more than that.

THE WRATH OF GOD

DOC: If you could make it ten, that would be fine.

TIM: Here you are, Doc. **(HE hands him a bill.)**

DOC: I'll write you out a receipt. **(HE opens his bag, takes out a receipt book and writes out a receipt, which he hands to TIM.)**

TIM: Thank you.

DOC: Make sure she eats regularly. You have the list I gave you. I'll drop by on Thursday, and if anything changes give me a call.

TIM: Right.

(The outside door is opened and HELEN enters looking distraught.)

TIM: What is it? What's wrong?

HELEN: They say he's been shot.

DOC: I hate to say it, but maybe it's for the best. I can't see Jason spending his life in a cage.

TIM: They could be mistaken.

HELEN: It just came over the news. They captured two of the men, and the third tried to run away, and he was shot. They think it was Jason.

TIM: *The myth continues.*

DOC: Take it easy, Helen. Here. Have a seat.

THE WRATH OF GOD

HELEN: **(SHE sits.)** I can't believe he's dead.

TIM: He hasn't been identified, has he?

HELEN: I don't know.

TIM: It wasn't him.

HELEN: What makes you so sure?

TIM: Because Jason never runs away, that's why.

DOC: **(To HELEN)** I've got this prescription for Moira. It's something she should be taking regularly. As a matter of fact, why don't you run down and have it filled?

HELEN: Right now?

DOC: I think it's a good idea...if you're up to it, that is.

HELEN: Yes, of course.

TIM: I wouldn't worry about that news. They always get things mixed up.

DOC: Just a minute. Let me take your blood pressure. **(HE takes out his instrument and gauges her blood pressure.)** It's a little high.

HELEN: I'll be all right.

DOC: I don't want two strokes on my hand.

HELEN: I'll be fine. Will this take long, do you think?

THE WRATH OF GOD

DOC: I don't think so. I'd wait for it though.

HELEN: Okay. **(SHE takes the prescription and goes off.)**

DOC: I'm worried about that girl. She's not taking care of herself.

TIM: You think I ought to take a leave of absence? I mean, somebody's got to look after my mother.

DOC: Let's wait a day and see. You have any reason to believe that man wasn't Jason? I mean, you haven't heard from him, have you?

TIM: Excuse me, Doc. **(HE picks up the coffee cup and goes into the kitchen.)**

DOC: *Ah yes, Jason was something special. One knew it the minute he was born. "Well, now, Moira, you've produced a miracle," said I. "He wears a caul," said Moria. "Now how did you know that?" I asked. "Because he's special. I knew it all along. I'm going to call him Jason. Jason who guarded the Golden Fleece." Ay, Moira, Moira. Didn't you know that Jason stole the Golden Fleece?*

(TIM reenters with the coffee cup refilled.)

DOC: Does your mother still have that caul?

TIM: What's that?

DOC: The caul. The caul that Jason was born with?

TIM: It's wrapped in tissue paper, and kept in a drawer next to our birth certificates.

THE WRATH OF GOD

(MOIRA opens the bedroom door and stands in the doorway.)

DOC: And where do you think you're going, young lady?

MOIRA: I don't want any of your blarney. I wanna know what's goin' on.

DOC: What do you think is going on?

MOIRA: I don't know, but I intend to find out.

TIM: You're not going to get any better wandering around like this.

MOIRA: And stop giving me orders. You're not a policeman here. The Doc said I should be getting some exercise. Didn't you, Doc? And I can't just lay there all day and all night, without even a radio to listen to.

TIM: You'll have your radio tomorrow. They promised me.

MOIRA: Then I'm going upstairs to the Oleary's. I'd like to listen to the news.

TIM: Why don't you wait until Helen comes back? She'll go upstairs with you.

MOIRA: What do I need Helen for?

DOC: Now, Moira.

MOIRA: Where she gone to?

TIM: She gone to get you your medicine. She'll be right back.

THE WRATH OF GOD

MOIRA: Then I'll sit and wait.

(SHE walks to the table and sits. HELEN enters.)

HELEN: They're way behind. It's going to take at least an hour.

TIM: Mother wants to go upstairs to the OLeary's. She wants to listen to the radio.

HELEN: There's no one there right now. Maggie just went out shopping. I'll read to you, if you like.

MOIRA: I'm not a child.

HELEN: Then why don't you read the book I brought you?

MOIRA: *If only I could get my thoughts together. Everything keeps whirling around. Oh, Frank, how handsome and darling you were, when you came acourtin', full of jokes and games. "No more farm work for you, me girl. Your pretty hands won't be milking cows and feeding chickens, and digging in the dirt."*

HELEN: Moira?

MOIRA: Yes? What is it?

HELEN: Would you like a cup of tea?

MOIRA: I'd like some fresh air, that's what I'd like.

DOC: You won't find it outside, I'll tell you that? It's hot and it's humid. And at least you've got a fan in your room.

MOIRA: **(SHE rises and walks toward the bedroom.)** *"In*

THE WRATH OF GOD

America you'll be wearing silks and eating chocolates, me girl. We'll be taking taxis and going to the opera." "The opera! You've never been to an opera." **(SHE goes off.)**

DOC: It's a good thing you don't have the radio, with all this conflicting news.

HELEN: Have you heard anything more?

TIM: No.

(HELEN follows MOIRA off.)

MOIRA: *(Offstage)* And close that door. I don't want any of that hot air in here.

(HELEN slams the bedroom door shut.)

DOC: I'm sure Jason must be aware of the fact that they've got people watching this place.

TIM: I suppose so.

DOC: You be careful, Tim. You hear me?

TIM: Aren't I always?

(DOC picks up his bag and goes off.)

TIM: **(Mutters.)** Careful.

(JASON enters munching on the remains of a sandwich, a bottle of beer in the other hand.)

THE WRATH OF GOD

JASON: Good old Doc. He's just as feisty as ever.

TIM: What did you hope to accomplish by coming here?

JASON: What kind of a greeting is that from a loving brother?

TIM: I'm serious, Jason. You're putting us all in danger.

JASON: Danger? With a big, strapping cop to protect us? And besides, you heard the news. I'm dead, me boyo.

TIM: What do you hope to accomplish?

JASON: Well, since my brother never came to visit me, I just thought that maybe I ought to pay him a visit.

TIM: I didn't know if I'd be welcome, but I have been praying for you, Jason.

JASON: And did you light a candle for me, too?

TIM: Yes.

JASON: Well, that oughta clinch it. Is Mom gonna make it?

TIM: She's on the mend, but she is still fragile. And she doesn't know about your getting out.

JASON: And you think that'll upset her?

TIM: What do you think?

JASON: I think she'll be happy to see me. A tonic for her tired old eyes. Or you think she'll be happier with me locked up. Is that it?

THE WRATH OF GOD

Ah, what happened to my bright little brother? *What happened to those big shiny eyes, that eager little face?*

TIM: *What happened to that wise, intelligent man I used to look up to? So sure of where he was going and how he was going to get there.*

JASON & TIM: *If that's what we look like now, what will we look ten years from now?*

JASON: *If I'm still alive.* **(After a moment)** How about Helen?

TIM: What about her?

JASON: How has she been holding up?

TIM: You'll have to ask her.

JASON: She spends a lot of time here I gather.

TIM: Taking care of Mom.

JASON: You never see her? You never talk to her?

TIM: Of course, I see her. Of course, I talk to her.

JASON: Well?

TIM: She's having a hard time. How do you think she feels, losing a child, losing her husband?

JASON: Okay, okay. I'll make it up to her.

TIM: And how are you going to manage that?

THE WRATH OF GOD

JASON: I'm out, ain't I? And I'm gonna stay out. What are you shaking your head for?

TIM: Jason, they've got people watching this place.

JASON: I got in, didn't I? And I'll get out. You have no faith, me boyo. **(HE drinks his beer.)**

TIM: *"But Jason, why do you have to steal? Why can't you get a decent job?" "Because we need the money, that's why? Look, kid, how do you think this country got started? I'll tell you how. We took it away from the Indians. That's how. God helps those who help themselves. But you're gonna go to college, kid."*

(There is a knock at the door.)

JASON: **(HE sets the bottle on the table.)** Are you expecting anyone?

TIM: No.

(The knock is heard again.)

JASON: You better answer it.

(JASON goes into the kitchen. TIM opens the door. DOC enters, glancing around the room.)

TIM: Is there anything wrong?

DOC: No, no, no. I passed by the drug store. Moira's prescription was ready and I thought I'd better bring it up. She oughta start on it right away. **(HE sets his bag on the table and produces a bottle which he hands to TIM.)**

THE WRATH OF GOD

TIM: Thank you, Doc. That was very thoughtful of you.

DOC: You're drinking kind of early, aren't you?

TIM: What's that? Oh, yeah. Got kind of thirsty all of a sudden.

DOC: Where is he?

TIM: Who?

(JASON enters.)

JASON: Morning, Doc.

DOC: Ah, Jason, Jason.

JASON: That's me.

DOC: You'll never learn, will you?

JASON: Apparently not.

DOC: Well, I will say this for you. You don't look any the worse for wear.

JASON: They feed you good in prison, Doc. Nothing fancy, mind you. I mean there's no caviar, and there's no champagne.

DOC: You know, of course, they've got this place surrounded.

JASON: I'm here, ain't I?

DOC: Well, getting out, may not be that easy.

THE WRATH OF GOD

JASON: You're not gonna give me a hard time, are you, Doc?

DOC: You don't need me for that.

JASON: You know what I mean.

DOC: And if I did make a fuss. What are you going to do, Jason? Shoot me?

JASON: Come on, Doc.

DOC: So what are you gonna do, fight your way out?

JASON: Nobody knows I'm here, except you and Timmy. And nobody's gonna see me leave. **(HE drinks his beer.)**

DOC: **(HE sits with a sigh.)** *"How'd you get this, Jason?" "It's just a scratch, Doc." "Don't tell me that a scratch. That's a bullet wound, Jason." "Now Doc, you don't think I'm stupid enough to be hit by a bullet." "Okay, Jason. I'll patch it up this time. But the next time, I've got to report it."*

JASON: We're pals, Doc, aren't we?

DOC: **(HE laughs.)** I'm not your pal, Jason. I'm a law abiding citizen.

JASON: Okay, okay. So you wanna turn me in.

DOC: You know I wouldn't do that. But I wish you'd do it yourself.

JASON: I never meant to kill that guy, Doc.

THE WRATH OF GOD

DOC: But you did.

JASON: Okay, okay.

DOC: He was a human being, with a family.

JASON: It was an accident, Doc.

DOC: So you have no regrets.

JASON: Of course, I have regrets. I'm sorry it ever happened, but accidents happen.

DOC: Does your mother know you're here?

JASON: No.

DOC: She's recovering from a stroke, you know. And, as far as I know, she doesn't know that you've escaped. Why don't you go back, Son, and serve your time?

JASON: Another twenty two years. No, thank you, Doc.

DOC: Okay, Jason, okay. But you've got two women in this flat, and neither of them are doing too well.

JASON: What's wrong with Helen?

DOC: Mostly nerves. And she should be taking better care of herself.

JASON: I'll take care of her.

THE WRATH OF GOD

DOC: Okay, Jason. Okay, boy. **(HE zips up his bag and prepares to leave.)**

JASON: I can count on you, Doc.

DOC: Haven't you always, Son? And I sometimes wonder if I've done you a favor. **(HE goes off.)**

JASON: Now don't start.

TIM: I wasn't gonna say a thing.

JASON: You want me to go back? Is that what you want? You want me to go back and die?

TIM: No, Jason, I don't want you to die.

JASON: 'Cause that's what it's like. It's death. So tell me, what do you want me to do?

TIM: **(HE chokes back the tears.)** *I want you to give me back my brother. That's what I want you to do. I want you to be the Jason that I loved, the Jason that I looked up to, the Jason I wanted to please. That's what I want you to do.* **(HE sighs.)** You do what you have to do, Jason. You always have. I've been up all night. I wanna get out of this uniform and take a shower.

> **(TIM goes off to the room upstage right. JASON sits, then rises and paces about, as the lights come down.)**

ACT TWO

(The action is continuous. JASON is seated, lost in thought.)

JASON: *I should have sent for her, that's what I should have done. Of course, it has been months since she paid me a visit, and you hear all sorts of stories. But she did write, didn't she? We are man and wife. Aren't we? Till death do us part?* **(After a moment)** *"How many years you been in here, Sam?" "Ten." "What's your secret?" "There's only one way to survive in this joint." "And what might that be?" "By facing the facts. You are dead, Buddy. As far as them out there are concerned you are dead, and you are in hell."* **(HE rises.)** I think I need another beer.

(JASON goes off to the kitchen. A moment later HELEN enters, closing the door behind her. SHE looks about.)

HELEN: Tim?

(JASON reenters, holding a bottle of beer. HELEN sees him, freezes and falls to the floor in a faint.)

JASON: Oh, Jesus! **(HE sets the bottle on the table and rushes over to her.)** Helen? Baby? **(HE pats her cheek.)** Honey?

(HE lifts her up and seats her on a chair. HE picks up the bottle of beer and holds it against her face. SHE pushes it away and looks up.)

HELEN: You're alive.

JASON: Apparently.

THE WRATH OF GOD

HELEN: They said on the radio that you'd been killed.

JASON: How many times have I told you, don't believe what you hear on the radio?

HELEN: How did you get in?

JASON: I'm here, Baby. That's all that matters, isn't it?

HELEN: Oh, Jason.

JASON: That's me.

HELEN: Why couldn't you wait?

JASON: Wait? For what?

HELEN: You'll be up for parole eventually.

JASON: Eventually? In another year and a half? And then what? You never get a parole the first time up. (**He runs his fingers over her face.**) *She's lost weight. And that worried look, that line between the eyes.*

HELEN: I look awful, I know. It hasn't been easy.

JASON: Those sons of bitches. They wouldn't even let me come to the funeral. Did the kid suffer much?

HELEN: Not really, no. It came so sudden. He had a fever, that night, but it wasn't that high. And when I called Doc in the morning, it was too late. It was pneumonia.

JASON: "The wrath of God."

34

THE WRATH OF GOD

HELEN: What's that?

JASON: That's what Mom keeps muttering. She said this beggar woman put a curse on her back in Ireland. And it's followed us here. How she doin'?

HELEN: She doesn't know anything about you getting out.

JASON: I think seeing me will be good for her. Don't you think?

HELEN: Not under these conditions, Jason.

JASON: Can she get around?

HELEN: She's still weak, and her left arm is paralyzed, but she's as cantankerous as ever.

JASON: That's my Mom.

HELEN: And she keeps dreaming about you.

JASON: Does she now?

HELEN: *The same old Jason. "Everything's gonna be fine, Honey." "But they could send you to jail." "I've been through this before. It's a piece of cake." "I didn't know." "What?" "That you were a thief." "Hey, Honey, take it easy."*

JASON: How are you doin'?

HELEN: You must be hungry. Have you eaten anything?

JASON: I'm fine. Did you miss me?

THE WRATH OF GOD

HELEN: Oh, Jason, what do you want me to say? You show up, a fugitive, a fugitive from justice. They're out there hunting for you. And you want us to play Romeo and Juliet?

JASON: Okay, okay. Apparently you're not very glad to see me.

HELEN: Look, Jason, let's not play games. What do you intend to do?

JASON: I intend to go on with my life, our life.

HELEN: I see. And how are you going to manage that?

JASON: We'll move to another town, some small town in another state...and I have the name of a plastic surgeon.

HELEN: You're going to change your face?

JASON: Take it easy. It's not that big a deal. It's like when you go to the beauty parlor. I'll be handsomer than ever. You think that's funny?

HELEN: No, Jason. I don't think that's funny.

JASON: We can start all over again. It'll be like it was in the beginning. Remember?

HELEN: Jason, the building's surrounded by police. How are you going to get out of here?

JASON: The same way I came in. I'll wait till it gets dark, and it's a piece of cake. And as soon as I get settled, I'll send for you.

THE WRATH OF GOD

HELEN: You're a wanted man, Jason. Is that the way you want to spend the rest of your life, as a fugitive?

JASON: It's better than being dead, Honey. What?

HELEN: Does that mean...?

JASON: What?

HELEN: We'd have to cut ourselves off from everyone? From our family, from our friends?

JASON: Maybe, at first.

HELEN: I see.

JASON: We'd have each other, Honey. Things'll be different now. I'll settle down. I promise you.

(TIM reenters, wearing his own clothes.)

JASON: There he is! My little brother. There was some cop in here a little while ago. I don't know where he came from.

TIM: The same place you came from.

JASON: That's my little Timmy. Always quick on the draw. That's a nice shirt. You make enough as a cop to pay for that shirt?

TIM: Apparently.

JASON: I think I oughta say hello to Mom.

HELEN: She's sleeping right now.

THE WRATH OF GOD

JASON: **(To TIM)** I'd like to get out of these clothes. Can I borrow some of yours?

TIM: Help yourself.

(JASON goes off.)

TIM: What did he have to say for himself?

HELEN: He expects me to join him.

TIM: I see.

HELEN: He wants to live in some small town somewhere, and he's planning to see a plastic surgeon.

TIM: Good Lord!

HELEN: "And this is my handsome brother, Timmy. Look at him blush. You can kiss her, brother. She won't bite." "Jason, leave him alone." And he leaned over and kissed me on the cheek...and my heart beat a little faster.

TIM: "Wait till you meet her, Timmy. Real class." "For a change?" "What is that supposed to mean?, you little fuck." "Where'd you find her, Jason?" "In church. She's from New York. I'm gonna show her the city." "Is that all?" "Watch your tongue." I love you, Helen. You know that, whatever you decide.

HELEN: *So proper. So upright.*

TIM: What do you plan to do?

HELEN: *If I had the courage, I know what I would like to do. I*

38

THE WRATH OF GOD

would like to get rid of these impossible burdens: a tyrannical old harpy, a selfish, unprincipled, demanding brute, the ghost of a child who never had a chance, and an innocent, bumbling lamb who longs for my love, a love I no longer have to give. I know what I would like to do. I would like to lay down and sleep...peacefully.

TIM: Helen?

HELEN: What?

TIM: What are you going to do?

(MOIRA enters.)

HELEN: What's wrong?

MOIRA: That's what I'd like to know. You're readin' to me, and then you stop.

HELEN: You fell asleep.

MOIRA: I was not asleep. I just closed me eyes. **(SHE walks toward the chair and sits.)** *Oh, wait till Jason comes home. He'll give the two of you what for.*

HELEN: I've got to go downstairs and get a prescription. Doc wants you to have this medicine.

MOIRA: What for?

HELEN: To calm you down.

THE WRATH OF GOD

MOIRA: I don't need nothin' to calm me down. **(Indicating the bottle on the table.)** What's that?

HELEN: What?

TIM: That's your medicine. Doc brought it up.

MOIRA: Well, why didn't you say so?

TIM: **(HE studies the bottle.)** You need to swallow it with a glass of water.

MOIRA: Makes sense to me.

TIM: I'll get you some. **(HE goes off to the kitchen.)**

MOIRA: You stopped just when it was getting interesting.

HELEN: I thought you were asleep.

MOIRA: *How did I get to be a grumpy old lady? Where's the young girl that came here to Chicago full of hopes and dreams? And Frank so full of jokes and funny stories. "I'm going to run for president." "You can't run for president, Dad." And why not, may I ask?" "You've got to be a natural born citizen?" "Well, Timmy, me boy, I was the most natural born baby you ever saw."*

(TIM reenters with a glass of water.)

MOIRA: *Dear, dear Frank, you were such a charming man, such a foolish man. How often you made us laugh, and how often you made us cry.*

TIM: Here you are, me girl.

40

THE WRATH OF GOD

(HE hands her the glass, opens the bottle, takes out a pill and hands it to her. SHE swallows pill and washes it down.)

HELEN: Would you like me to read you more of the story?

MOIRA: What else is there to do?

HELEN: We could play checkers.

MOIRA: Checkers! A game for idiots. Chess is the game.

HELEN: We don't have a chess set.

MOIRA: I know that. Me father did though. He was a good chess player. "That's the game," he would say, "for the mind."

TIM: You never told me he played chess.

MOIRA: There are lots of things I never told you. On second thought, I think I'd like to make meself presentable, for when Jason gets here. *(To TIM)* And let me know as soon as he arrives.

(HELEN and TIM exchange looks. MOIRA goes off. HELEN follows her off, closing the door behind her.)

TIM: *"Your brother's in trouble." "Jason's always in trouble, Mom" "This time it's serious. I feel it in me bones." "Yes, I know. It's the wrath of God." "You're not a believer, son, I know. But there are powers beyond us, Timmy. How do you explain the radio? How do you explain the universe?"*

(TIM picks up the glass and goes into the kitchen. A

THE WRATH OF GOD

moment later JASON reenters in different clothes. Seeing no one about, he sits at the table, lost in thought.)

JASON: *What a magical feeling, sitting on a toilet, in private! Taking a shower in private! Walking about in a civilized room. Childhood mementos lying about. Timmy's graduation picture, framed, on the wall. A snapshot of Timmy and me. I must have been about eighteen. He must have been twelve. Our arms about one another, and he has that silly grin on his face. The pair of boxing gloves I bought him, hanging on a nail in the closet. Mementos of days gone by, of a way of life almost forgotten.*

(TIM enters with a cup of coffee.)

TIM: Would you like some coffee?

JASON: No. No, I'm fine.

(JASON sits. The men are lost in thought.)

JASON & TIM: *It's 1933, and here we sit, two brothers waiting for a god of wrath to decide our fate. Here we sit, the evil spell cast by an Irish beggar-woman hanging over us. Our Dad, the dashing Frank Rafferty, struck down by the curse of drink. Our little boy...*

JASON: *My son.*

TIM: *My nephew.*

JASON & TIM: *His little lungs filled with water, struck down by the curse of pneumonia. Our Mom, the lovely Moira Rafferty, now*

THE WRATH OF GOD

drawn and fragile, weak and crippled by the curse of a stroke. And what fate awaits us now, the two of us?

TIM: *I survived a stray bullet fired during a feuding teen age gang battle.*

JASON: *I survived a battle with a prison bully with just a couple of broken ribs.*

JASON & TIM: *It's 1933, and here we sit, two brothers on the East Side of Chicago, the brawling heart of America.*

TIM: *On the West Side the glorious World's Fair, The Century of Progress Exposition.*

JASON: *On the radio the Lone Ranger roams the West, saving ranchers and other people in distress.*

TIM: *Our new president, Franklin Delano Roosevelt is going take us out of the Great Depression.*

JASON: *And we can now drink liquor legally because prohibition has come to an end.*

(TIM drinks his coffee.)

JASON: What's wrong with Helen?

TIM: What do you mean?

JASON: She's not herself. It's as if something died inside of her.

TIM: What do you expect? She's been through hell.

THE WRATH OF GOD

JASON: Okay, okay. What does she do with herself, aside from looking after Mom?

TIM: Not very much.

JASON: Doesn't she go out. Doesn't she do something to relax?

TIM: She reads. She goes to a movie occasionally.

JASON: Alone?

TIM: **(HE looks away.)** Sometimes I go with her.

JASON: Maybe I would like that cup of coffee?

TIM: Right. **(HE goes off to the kitchen.)**

JASON: *"Don't you like my wife, Timmy?" Of course, I like her." "Every time you come over the house, you act so strange. Another thing, kid, when are you gonna settle down?" "When I find the right girl."*

(TIM reenters with a cup of coffee, which he hands to JASON.)

JASON: Thanks. **(HE sips the coffee. After a moment.)** What have you got against Helen?

TIM: What the hell you talking about? Of course, I like Helen. I've always liked Helen. As a matter of fact, I never thought that you were good enough for her.

JASON: Oh, really?

THE WRATH OF GOD

TIM: Yes, really. You've put her through hell and now, I understand, you're going to continue.

JASON: What the fuck you talking about? And how do you know what I'm gonna do?

TIM: She told me. You want her to come and live with you in some small town somewhere, cut off from everyone. I can't believe it.

TIM: What?

TIM: After all she's been through.

JASON: What are you, her father?

TIM: If you really loved her, you would let her go.

JASON: Is that what she told you? I'm asking you. Is that...

TIM: No.

JASON: Then mind your own fucking business. You want me to go back to that stinking hole? Is that what you're saying? You want me to crawl up and die?

TIM: How can you possibly make a life for yourself, and for her with things the way they are?

JASON: That's my affair.

TIM: How? If you get out of here alive, and that's a big "if," you're gonna spend the rest of your life on the run. Is that what you want for her, and for yourself?

THE WRATH OF GOD

JASON: **(After a moment.)** Have you got the hots for Helen? Jesus! What's been going on while I've been gone? Have you been screwing my wife?

TIM: Jason, you've got to let her go.

JASON: I asked you something. Have you been screwing my wife?

TIM: We're in love.

JASON: "You mean to tell me my little brother's a virgin?" "What's wrong with that?" "You're not queer, are you?" "Who knows?" "Look, I know a nice girl. I'll pay for it." "No." "Why not?" "Because I want the first time to be with a girl I love." You have, haven't you?

TIM: I'm sorry.

JASON: You're sorry?!

TIM: She seemed so lost, so unhappy. Jason, you were sentenced for twenty five years. Twenty five years. What is she supposed to do? Stop living?

JASON: You godamned son-of-a-bitch!

(The bedroom door is opened and MOIRA enters. SHE wears a nice dress and some makeup.)

JASON: Well, well, well. Look who we have here.

MOIRA: I knew it.

THE WRATH OF GOD

(MOIRA extends her right arm. JASON approaches her and THEY embrace. HELEN enters.)

MOIRA: **(To HELEN)** What did I tell you?

HELEN: **(Eyeing TIM and JASON)** *Something's happened.*

JASON: And they told me you were sick.

MOIRA: You're free. I knew it, I just knew it.

JASON: Yes, indeedy, here I am.

MOIRA: **(To HELEN)** Why didn't you tell me?

HELEN: Obviously there was no need.

MOIRA: I knew it was a mistake. Those lawyers you had. They were good for nothin'.

JASON: *If we've got to grow old, why can't we grow old gracefully? Why do we have to wrinkle and wither?*

MOIRA: **(To HELEN)** We've got to make a welcome home dinner.

HELEN: Yes, of course.

JASON: The prodigal son has returned, old girl.

MOIRA: Oh, Jason. You're a wicked, wicked boy.

JASON: But you love me all the same. Are you all right?

THE WRATH OF GOD

MOIRA: All this excitement. I'm a little light headed.

JASON: Well, have a seat, me beauty. Be my guest.

(HE helps her to a chair.)

MOIRA: Well now, I hope you've learned your lesson.

JASON: Oh, that I have.

MOIRA: From now on, no more trouble. You're going to find yourself a good job, and give me another grandson.

JASON: All at the same time?

MOIRA: I'm serious. The family's going to be together again. Timmy's going to find himself a wife. Aren't you, Timmy?

HELEN: **(To MOIRA)** It's time for your lunch. Jason?

JASON: No, no. I'm fine.

(HELEN goes into the kitchen.)

MOIRA: As soon as I'm strong enough, I'm going to make you a dinner with all the trimmings.

JASON: Are ye now?

MOIRA: And you're not going to be seeing anymore of that gang of yours.

JASON: Is that a fact?

THE WRATH OF GOD

MOIRA: I'm serious. And as soon as you find a job, you'll be going back to school and get your diploma. You've a good mind, Jason, and it's time you put it to use.

JASON: The same old tyrant.

MOIRA: Maybe you can join Timmy on the police force. And why not? You can be very useful. You know enough about crime. What do you think, Timmy.

TIM: Oh, yes.

MOIRA: Do you think you might be able to put in a good word for your brother, Timmy?

JASON: Let's not rush things, me beauty.

MOIRA: Oh, it does me good to see you, my dear. Even though you and your father never saw eye to eye, he always said that you had a lot of good in you, and you could go far, if you only put your mind to it.

JASON: Is that what he said?

MOIRA: And I want you to go to church this Sunday. And I'll go with you. I don't care what the Doc says.

TIM: Jason may have other plans, Mom.

MOIRA: Like what?

JASON: There are things I've gotta tend to.

MOIRA: Like what?

THE WRATH OF GOD

JASON: Nothing for you to worry your pretty head about.

MOIRA: Your parole officer?

JASON: Among other things.

TIM: He might want to take a little vacation, before he settles down, that is.

JASON: Exactly.

TIM: *Here we sit, playing games. Hide and seek. Guess the secret. Secrets we hide from one another. Secrets we hide from ourselves.*

MOIRA: *He looks different somehow. I don't remember those hard lines around the mouth. Those circles under the eyes.*

TIM: *What does this woman really think of her sons, this woman, whose every dream has been shattered? The husband she loved, drowned in alcohol. The son she adored, a common criminal. The grandchild she fussed over, not two years old, lying in his little grave. Does she still have faith? Does she go on deceiving herself?*

(HELEN enters with a bowl of soup and a slice of bread which SHE places on the table in front of MOIRA, who proceeds to eat.)

TIM: *And you, Timothy Rafferty, what do you think of this family that's falling apart? Is there any love left in you, now? The woman who bore you, raised you; the woman you respected and loved, in whose heart you never ranked first. What do you feel for her now? And the brother you adored, the idol who turned out to be made of clay. What's left of the worship you held for him? And his lovely wife, the fragile flower you longed for all those years? Do you long*

THE WRATH OF GOD

for her now, now that her husband's come back to claim her, the husband to whom she rightfully belongs?

HELEN & TIM: *Go back, Jason. Go back and leave us alone.*

MOIRA: You'll want to visit the grave site, Jason, the grave of our dear little Michael. He's resting next to your father.

JASON: Resting is he?

MOIRA: How your father adored that child. Well, now he has him all to himself.

JASON: They're in heaven, you think?

MOIRA: Where else would they be?

JASON: That's a good question.

MOIRA: You mustn't speak like that. That's been the source of all your trouble.

JASON: And what might that be?

MOIRA: You have no respect for the church.

JASON: I have the greatest respect for the church. Mother dear. I've yet to see a skinny priest, or a picture of the pope, without all his finery.

MOIRA: You start going to church, and you'll see how your luck'll change. Look at Timmy. He's been promised a promotion to sergeant. Isn't that so, Timmy?

THE WRATH OF GOD

TIM: It's been mentioned.

JASON: And how did you earn this great honor, Timmy?

TIM: By doing my job.

MOIRA: Now, Jason, you're not gonna bring that up again. Timmy had no choice. Perjury is a serious crime.

JASON: *He took my life away from me, and now he wants to take my wife.*

HELEN: Time for your nap.

MOIRA: Me nap? I've been nappin' all day and all night.

JASON: Now be a good girl.

MOIRA: You watch your tongue. I'm not a little child. *(SHE gets up.)* Will you be here when I get up?

JASON: Now where would I want to be, except near me own mother?

MOIRA: You will be good from now on, Jason.

JASON: I'll do me best.

MOIRA: Welcome home.

(SHE kisses him, caresses his cheek and goes off, accompanied by HELEN.)

JASON: How long has she been like that?

THE WRATH OF GOD

TIM: About a month or so, though it's been coming on gradually.

JASON: *She used to take pride in her appearance, She used to carry herself like a queen. Even when she was washing clothes, or cooking or cleaning, there was always something special about her, something regal, royalty, married to a clown.* Forget about Helen.

TIM: Jason, what kind of a life can you offer her?

JASON: What's between me and my wife is none of your business.

TIM: For your information, if it weren't for me, you would have no wife.

JASON: What are you talking about?

TIM: She tried to kill herself.

JASON: When was this?

TIM: A month or so after the baby died. She was depressed.

JASON: Why was she depressed?

TIM: Why the fuck do you think? Everything was closing in on her.

JASON: Okay, okay. Take it easy. It's just that...

TIM: What?

JASON: That's not like Helen. It must have been something else, something more.

THE WRATH OF GOD

TIM: Look, Jason, she's been through hell, and if you really loved her, you would let her go.

(HELEN reenters.)

JASON: What's going on between you and my brother?

HELEN: We're in love.

JASON: Really? You're in love. Just like that.

HELEN: It wasn't just like that.

JASON: How was it then?

HELEN: Our marriage was over, even before you went to prison.

JASON: Over? You mean God came down and said, "Helen, you're free. Your word doesn't mean anything anymore." You are my wife, till death do us part. Remember?

HELEN: I thought you didn't believe in God.

JASON: This has nothing to do with God. This has to do with commitment. Or don't you think there is such a thing? You think it's been easy for me? I never looked at another woman. What you and I have is sacred.

HELEN: Would you want me, knowing that I don't love you?

JASON: Love?! What the fuck is love? Love is for kids. For ditsy young girls. Love! Maybe I don't go to church, but what's between us, what's between a man and a wife is holy. Don't you talk to me about love.

THE WRATH OF GOD

TIM: Your wife's feelings don't matter. Is that it?

JASON: Feelings? You little wimp. What do you know about feelings? Where would you be, if I worried about my feelings? How about responsibility? Huh? I didn't worry about my feelings when I realized that somebody in this family had to see to it that there was bread on the table. Feelings? Where was that cripple we called a father? He had feelings. He was full of feelings. He reeked with feelings. You could smell him a mile away. And you have feelings, too. You're holier than thou. You loved your brother so much you sent him to prison.

TIM: I did not send you to prison.

JASON: You didn't testify against me?

TIM: You would have gone to prison whether I testified or not, and you know it.

JASON: You put the nail in my coffin.

TIM: Come on, Jason. Don't play the martyr with me. You enjoyed what you did. You got a thrill out of it. Making your own rules. Bucking Society, you called it. You could have got a regular job just like anyone else. But, no. You had to show off how tough you were.

JASON: Get a regular job, as if it was as easy as that. Did you ever try to get a regular job. No. You didn't have to. Get a regular job. People standing in line for hours hoping for a job any kind of a job, and then turned away. People standing in line for a free cup of soup and a crust of bread. Business men selling apples on the corner. I did what I did, because I had to, because there was no one else to step up to the plate.

THE WRATH OF GOD

TIM: You did what you did, because you wanted to do it, and don't blame anyone else.

JASON: I'm not blaming anybody, but there is such a thing as respect. There is such a thing as honor. Or don't they teach you that in church?

TIM: You took a man's life, Jason.

(MOIRA enters.)

MOIRA: What's all the shoutin' about?

JASON: Go back to bed.

MOIRA: I want to know what's goin' on?

JASON: Nothin's going on.

MOIRA: Then what are you shoutin' about? As if I didn't know.

JASON: What's that supposed to mean?

MOIRA: You'd have to be blind not to see it.

TIM: You don't know what you're talking about.

MOIRA: Your own brother's wife. I'm ashamed of you, ashamed. I warned you, Jason. I warned you from the very beginning. She's not right for you. She's not our kind. She with her know-it-all ways. I told her to call the doctor that night.

HELEN: You did no such thing.

THE WRATH OF GOD

MOIRA: I knew the child was ailing. Didn't I say that? "That child doesn't look too good," I said. Didn't I say that?

HELEN: You said lots of things. And if there was any trouble between me and Jason, you were the one that caused it.

MOIRA: That's right, blame it on me. When you know that Jason ended up in jail because of you. You had to have this, and you had to have that. You had to have your baby in a fancy hospital. Much good it did that poor little thing.

JASON: All right, Mom, butt out of this.

MOIRA: I will not butt out. If you'd listened to me in the first place...

JASON: I said, butt out. Now go back to bed.

MOIRA: Try and put me there.

TIM: Mom, you're not helping things any.

MOIRA: I'll tell you what'll help things. Send that woman back to New York, where she came from, with all her fancy ideas. She was never good enough for you, I told you that.

JASON: I'm telling you for the last time, butt out. **(To HELEN)** I can understand. You were lonely, and he took advantage of you, my loving brother.

HELEN: It wasn't that way at all.

MOIRA: Of course, it wasn't.

THE WRATH OF GOD

HELEN: Oh, shut up. Everyone shut up. Look, I tell you what. Why don't the three of you sit down and have a family meeting. Talk it over between the three of you, and let me know what you decide. **(SHE picks up the plate and silverware from the table and goes into the kitchen.)**

JASON: Look, there's no use getting all worked up. We all make mistakes. Helen's always been a good wife. She had a moment of weakness, and that's understandable. Ain't it?

MOIRA: You talkin' to me, or are you talkin' to yourself?

JASON: Mom, you never made her feel welcome.

MOIRA: Is that what she told you?

JASON: She didn't need to tell me. You had your heart set on me marrying Bridget what's-her-name, a nice Irish girl you approved of.

MOIRA: Nonsense.

JASON: You resented her because you didn't choose her for me.

MOIRA: That's not true.

TIM: You never accepted her, Mom.

MOIRA: Who asked you, you adulterer.

JASON: We're gonna forget this ever happened. As soon as I get settled I'm gonna send for Helen, and I'm gonna make a home for her.

THE WRATH OF GOD

MOIRA: What's wrong with the home you have now?

TIM: You might as well tell her. Jason wasn't released. He escaped.

JASON: Thanks a lot.

MOIRA: You escaped? You mean they might be looking for you?

TIM: Exactly.

MOIRA: Why did you do that? Why? I don't understand.

JASON: Don't worry about it. I'm gonna work things out.

MOIRA: How? How are you gonna work things out? You're a fugitive. They'll keep after you until they find you.

JASON: They're not gonna find me.

MOIRA: Oh, Jason, Jason. How could you be so stupid?

JASON: Look, I said I'm gonna work things out. I got a plan.

MOIRA: What sort of plan?

JASON: What difference does it make? I said I've got a plan.

MOIRA: You've said a lot of things, my dear.

TIM: Look, there's no use getting excited.

MOIRA: Who's excited?

THE WRATH OF GOD

TIM: Doc said you should take it easy.

MOIRA: Don't you worry about me, son. I'm perfectly fine. Your brother's the one that's got the problem. **(SHE stalks off.)**

JASON: You stupid son of a bitch. What the fuck do you think you were doing?

TIM: She had to know some time.

JASON: I could have thought of something. You didn't have to spring it on her, just like that.

TIM: That's right. The fault's all mine. Jason, give yourself up.

JASON: You'd like that wouldn't you?

TIM: I'm thinking of you.

JASON: And Helen.

TIM: Yes, and Helen.

JASON: Look, there comes a time when enough is enough. You've been more like a son to me than a brother. But, so help me God, Timmy boy, if you lay a finger on my wife again, no matter where I am, I'll come back and I'll kill you.

(A sound of a crash is heard coming from the kitchen.)

JASON: What was that?

(TIM rushes off to the kitchen.)

THE WRATH OF GOD

JASON: **(HE goes toward the kitchen.)** What is it? What happened?

(TIM reenters a moment later.)

TIM: She cut her wrists. Call the Doc.

(TIM goes back into the kitchen. JASON hesitates then walks quickly to the phone as the lights come down.)

ACT THREE

(A few hours later. It is dusk. TIM is seated at the table. JASON is pacing. A rumble of thunder is heard.)

JASON: I don't know what's taking him so long. She didn't lose that much blood, did she? Did she? *That's right. Sit there and blame it on me. Mealy mouthed son-of-a-bitch. How could I have been so mistaken? I loved that kid. I would have killed for him. It was that damned priest. The priest and the church. They took the man out of him. And Mom. Yes, Mom... "You got away from me, but I learned my lesson. It'll be different with your brother. I'll see to that.*

TIM: What are you muttering about?

JASON: Nothing. What time do you go on duty?

TIM: Eleven.

JASON: You're such a good cop, how come you got such a shitty shift?

TIM: It's not so bad. Not in the section I'm in. **(After a moment.)** Jason...

JASON: What?

TIM: Never mind.

JASON: Well, say it.

TIM: I never meant to hurt you. Getting on that stand...it killed me. And when Helen and I... I know it doesn't mean a thing to you, but I pray for you. I pray for you every day. I know you meant well,

THE WRATH OF GOD

and I know you'll never forgive me, and I'll have to live with that, but I love you, Jason. You've always meant the world to me. No matter what happens.

JASON: Big deal.

(DOC enters from the downstage bedroom.)

JASON: How is she?

DOC: She's okay. She lost some blood, of course, but you caught it in time. I'm worried about your mother though. All this excitement.

JASON: She seemed fine.

DOC: She's okay right now. But your coming here didn't help matters any. And, by the way, how, exactly do you plan to get out of here?

JASON: Piece of cake, Doc.

DOC: Don't get smart with me, Son. I'd just as soon turn you in. **(After a moment)** It might interest you to know, the both of you...

TIM: What?

DOC: Helen's pregnant.

(JASON sinks into a chair.)

TIM: Is the child okay?

DOC: Offhand, I'd say so, yes.

THE WRATH OF GOD

JASON: What month is she in?

DOC: It's not yours.

JASON: I didn't ask you whose it was?

DOC: Second, I'd say. I don't think she knew.

JASON: She knows now, doesn't she?

DOC: Yes, she knows now. I'm sorry.

JASON: What are you sorry about?

DOC: I know how much you loved your little boy.

JASON: *(A little too cavalierly)* It's all in the family, Doc. What the hell!

DOC: I can make it easy for you, Jason. I can speak to the men they've got watching the building. We can arrange for you to leave quietly.

JASON: I intend to leave quietly, Doc. And thank you, but no thanks.

DOC: I brought you into this world, son. I'd like to see you leave peacefully.

JASON: Peacefully. That's a way of life I've never been acquainted with.

(TIM starts for the bedroom.)

THE WRATH OF GOD

DOC: I wouldn't go in there right now. She's resting.

(MOIRA enters.)

DOC: Where do you think you're going, young lady?

MOIRA: What's the matter with Helen?

DOC: She had an accident.

MOIRA: What kind of an accident?

DOC: She cut her wrist.

MOIRA: Is she pregnant?

DOC: Yes.

MOIRA: I'm not sayin' a word. **(SHE starts for the kitchen.)**

DOC: Where you going?

TIM: You want something, Ma? I'll get it for you. What would you like?

MOIRA: A glass of beer.

(TIM looks at DOC, who nods. TIM goes into the kitchen.)

MOIRA: **(SHE sits at the table.)** To celebrate. Now that poses an interesting question. Would you consider the child a bastard, Doc?

JASON: That's not funny.

THE WRATH OF GOD

MOIRA: I think it's hilarious. If your father were alive, he'd sing a song about it.

JASON: I think you're losin' it.

MOIRA: Me? I'm not the one that's losin' it. If you'd listened to me, none of this would have happened. You can leave Christ, you can leave God, but he'll never leave you.

JASON: What are you talkin' about?

(TIM enters with a glass of beer which he places on the table in front of MOIRA.)

MOIRA: I'm talkin' about the devil. I'm talkin' about Satan. I'm talkin' about the wrath of God. Once you tempt fate you are lost. What's that?

TIM: You said you wanted some beer?

MOIRA: What are you, crazy? I'm a sick, old lady. What would I do drinkin' beer? Give some of that beer to that whore of yours.

JASON: Watch it!

MOIRA: You watch it! **(SHE takes a sip of the beer.)**

TIM: I thought you didn't want any beer.

MOIRA: I changed me mind. A woman's got a right to change her mind, hasn't she, me boyo?

DOC: Okay, Moira. Let's calm down.

THE WRATH OF GOD

MOIRA: *What am I doin' here? Why am I sitting here, in this room all alone? I must have fallen asleep. Colin, are you awake? Why is your hand so cold? Oh, mother of God. He's dead, and its all my fault. You wicked girl. You fell down on the job, and you let your brother die of the cholera. Oh, Colin, Colin, dear sweet Colin.*

DOC: Moira?

MOIRA: What?

DOC: Let me take your pulse.

(SHE offers her hand and DOC feels her wrist.)

MOIRA: I'm not dead yet.

DOC: What day is it?

MOIRA: Don't be an idiot. I lost track of the days a long time ago.

(TIM goes off to the downstage bedroom, closing the door behind him. JASON approaches the table.)

MOIRA: What's he doing here? He's supposed to be in prison.

JASON: **(To Doc)** Is she putting on an act, or what?

DOC: Moira's fine. She's just a little confused, that's all.

MOIRA: Ha! Confused! I'm the only sane one in this family. **(SHE plays with the glass.)** "He's a fine lookin' boy, Mrs. Rafferty, a fine lookin' boy." "And why shouldn't he be? He's mine, isn't he? And he's going places, that one is. He's going to be a lawyer, or

THE WRATH OF GOD

maybe a senator. Or maybe even a priest? I wouldn't rule that out."

(HELEN, her left wrist wrapped in a bandage, enters from the bedroom, accompanied by TIM. HE escorts her to the table. SHE comes face to face with JASON. HE looks at her and walks away. SHE sighs and sits at the table. JASON stands observing his family members.)

JASON: *What I did, did I do it for myself, or did I do it for them? Or did I do it to prove what a weakling that father of mine was? Or did I do it to prove what a man I was?*

(TIM goes into the kitchen.)

DOC: I'd like to call my wife.

JASON: Go ahead and call her.

(DOC picks up the phone and dials.)

JASON: *And now there's no one, no one to do anything for. I was a son. I was a brother. I was a father. I was a husband. What am I now?*

DOC: (On the phone) Fanny, dear. I should be home shortly. Don't bother. I'll fix something when I get home. I'll see you soon, dear. (HE hangs up.)

JASON: How's the wife doin', Doc?

DOC: Not too good, Son. Thank you, for asking.

JASON: She's a nice lady.

THE WRATH OF GOD

DOC: There's a lot of nice people in this world.

JASON: And I'm not one of them.

DOC: I've always been fond of you, Jason. You were my first, you know. Jason...

JASON: No, thank you, Doc! I can take care of myself. You think that's funny?

DOC: What do you think? We all need help, Son, in one way or another; at one time or another. Self respect is one thing. Pride...well, that's another thing.

JASON: You think I'm too proud.

DOC: Maybe it runs in the family.

JASON: You're not talking about my father, are you?

DOC: No, Son. I'm not talking about your father. I don't know. Maybe sometimes we expect too much out of life. And maybe sometimes we're in too much of a rush. The pace in this country is not a leisurely one.

JASON: What did you think of my father, Doc?

DOC: You were pretty hard on him, Son. So was your mother.

MOIRA: You think so, do you?

DOC: Not all of us are full of spunk and vinegar, Moira. Some of us need a little coddlin' now and then.

THE WRATH OF GOD

MOIRA: You think I was hard on him, do you?

DOC: Well, you didn't exactly inspire him, Moira. As a matter of fact, there were times when it was downright embarrassing, the way you treated him.

(TIM enters with a bowl of soup which he places on the table in front of HELEN.)

TIM: That's true, Mom. You did shame Dad in front of people, made a fool of him.

MOIRA: Your father lived in a dream world, and he expected everything just to come to him. Who do you think saved this family? I did, and your brother did.

HELEN: You were mean and you were cruel.

MOIRA: Who the hell's asking you? You with your fancy ways. Miss know-it-all.

HELEN: If anyone's responsible for Jason ending up, the way he's ended up, it's you. When he started to steal did you try to stop him?

MOIRA: Of course, I did.

HELEN: Did you, really? That first time? Did you ask him to return those groceries he stole. Did you?

MOIRA: You weren't here. What the hell do you know?

JASON: Leave her alone. No one's to blame for anything. And what the hell difference does it make?

THE WRATH OF GOD

(The phone rings. Everyone freezes as the phone continues to ring.)

TIM: Are you expecting a call, Doc?

DOC: Not really, no.

TIM: I guess I'd better answer it. It might be for me. **(HE picks up the phone and listens, then hangs up.)**

JASON: Who was it?

TIM: I don't know, but they asked for you.

JASON: You should have answered it.

TIM: Well, I didn't.

JASON: It was probably the police. But why would they ask for me? Nobody knows that I'm here.

DOC: Don't look at me. I never said a word.

JASON: Then how do they know?

DOC: Maybe they don't. Maybe they're just guessing.

JASON: You should have answered it.

TIM: Well, I didn't. It took me by surprise.

MOIRA: Give yourself up. Jason, please.

JASON: Then they still don't know I'm here.

THE WRATH OF GOD

DOC: I think they do now.

TIM: They may call again.

MOIRA: Jason, give yourself up.

JASON: Relax, Mom. I got in here in broad daylight, didn't I? And now that it's getting dark, I can get out easy.

MOIRA: And then what?

HELEN: *I'm no longer his wife. The bond has been severed. My loyalty is to the child, the child that I'm carrying, the child that isn't his. And isn't it odd?! I can actually feel compassion for him now.*

TIM: I think they'll call again.

JASON: Meanwhile why don't you fix me up a sandwich, and wrap it up in some wax paper.

TIM: What kind of a sandwich?

JASON: What the fuck difference does it make? And heat up some soup.

(JASON goes off to the upstage bedroom. TIM hesitates and goes off to the kitchen.)

MOIRA: *Mother of God, have mercy on my son. Have pity on my Jason. Spare him his life. Oh, Mother of God, spare my Jason's life.*

HELEN: *I haven't been a good Catholic. I seldom go to*

THE WRATH OF GOD

communion. But dear Jesus, have pity on the man I loved. He was led astray, but he tried to follow what was good in his heart. He tried, dear Jesus.

>**(TIM enters with a plate of soup, which he places on the table, and then goes back into the kitchen.)**

MOIRA: *He was a good husband, and a good father to the little one. He's sinned, I know, but forgive him, please.*

>**(JASON reenters wearing Tim's uniform, including the gun the belt, with the gun in the holster. HE sits at the table and eats the soup. HE looks at HELEN and smiles.)**

JASON: Just like old times, isn't it? The family, sitting down for dinner.

MOIRA: You would have made a fine officer, my dear.

JASON: Woulda, coulda.

MOIRA: You've still got a chance, if you give yourself up.

HELEN: Your mother's right.

JASON: That baby's mine, no matter who gave it to you. Is that understood? If he's a boy, that is.

>**(TIM reenters with a sandwich wrapped in wax paper.)**

TIM: What do you think you're doing?

JASON: What does it look like?

THE WRATH OF GOD

TIM: You'll never get away with it.

JASON: That remains to be seen, does it not?

TIM: Those men out there know what I look like.

JASON: It's dark isn't it? Incidentally, can't we turn on a light here?

(TIM turns on a lamp.)

TIM: Jason, don't be a fool. **(After a moment)** You woulda made a good cop.

JASON: That seems to be the consensus. This soup is good. **(HE looks at HELEN.)** You haven't lost your touch.

HELEN: Thank you.

JASON: I missed your cooking...among other things. We did have a good thing going...for a while, didn't we?

(SHE nods.)

JASON: I had a lot of time to think about the good times. Actually that's all I thought about, when I had time to think.

HELEN: It was a mistake, you and me.

JASON: I don't think so. You and me, that is. I made the mistakes. The only thing is my mistakes were small. That was the mistake. It's the big mistakes, those are the ones you can get away with. Size matters, you see. **(HE smiles and winks.)** Ain't that right, Timmy. That's one thing the Rafferty's were blessed with.

THE WRATH OF GOD

MOIRA: Mind your tongue.

JASON: And I want you to know, that I never broke my marriage vow, never. Never.

(HELEN turns away.)

JASON: That's right. When I reach the pearly gates, I can say to Saint Peter, "Saint Peter, I made a vow to God, and I never broke that vow." That may give me some points. What do you think?

MOIRA: You were always a good boy, Jason.

JASON: What is it?

MOIRA: Why are you dressed like that?

JASON: It's Halloween, my dear. It's time to dress up.

MOIRA: That's Timmy's clothes. That's his uniform. Why are you wearing Timmy's uniform?

JASON: I'm just trying it on for size.

(The phone rings. JASON turns to TIM.)

JASON: Answer it, and do as I say.

(TIM stands hesitantly. The phone continues to ring.)

JASON: I said, answer it. **(HE pulls the gun out from the holster.)**

DOC: They know you're here, Jason.

THE WRATH OF GOD

JASON: That remains to be seen. Are you gonna answer it, or aren't you?

(TIM walks to the phone and picks it up.)

JASON: If they ask for me, I'm not here.

TIM: **(On the phone)** Hello? Who is this? This is Tim Rafferty. Yes, Bob. Yes, I picked it up before. I thought it was some crank calling. No, he's not here. I will. Thanks, Bob. **(HE hangs up.)**

JASON: What'd he say?

TIM: He said to take care. Incidentally, Bro, that gun isn't loaded.

(JASON examines the gun.)

TIM: Sometimes we have the kids here from upstairs, and sometimes they go poking around.

JASON: Where do you keep the bullets?

TIM: Jason, don't be a fool.

JASON: Where do you keep the bullets?

MOIRA: Don't give 'em to him.

JASON: I'm leaving here, with an empty gun, if I have to.

(TIM goes off to his room.)

DOC: You really think you can get out of here alive?

THE WRATH OF GOD

JASON: They can't kill me, Doc.

DOC: How's that?

JASON: Did you ever try to kill a corpse?

(TIM reenters and hands JASON the bullets. JASON proceeds to load the gun.)

JASON: Do you know what it's like to be a number, Doc? To be nobody? Do you know what it's like to live without hope? To live with other zombies to whom life means nothing?

MOIRA: If you'd only reach out to the Lord.

JASON: I am the Lord, Mom. In my own little gang, I am the Lord.

MOIRA: You mustn't talk like that. It's sacrilegious.

JASON: It's all a crap shoot, my dear. And I lost. I put up a fight, and I lost.

TIM: I don't know what you've got to be proud of? You're a criminal, Jason. You're a murderer.

JASON: I'm sorry I took a life, but it was an accident. A casualty of war. Lots of people are killed in a war.

HELEN: Jason, I'm sorry I failed you, but you still have a life ahead of you. You have so much to offer. Turn yourself in.

JASON: And if it's a boy. Jason Junior.

THE WRATH OF GOD

(HELEN weeps.)

JASON: Save your tears. You may need them in the years to come. Everyone seems to think that I'm not gonna make it. Maybe they know something I don't know. Well, whether I make it or not, kids, it's been quite a ride.

(Bright lights shine through the part of the window not covered by the shade.)

JASON: I'll send you all a postcard from...wherever. **(HE puts the sandwich in his pocket and starts for the door.)**

TIM: Jason, they may have people out there in the hallway.

JASON: Maybe they have, and maybe they haven't. But the light in that hallway is pretty dim, and you told them that I'm not here.

TIM: There are men out there that know me.

JASON: I guess I'll just have to take my chances.

HELEN: Jason, don't.

(HE opens the door and steps back. HE then steps out the door, closing it softly behind him. After a few moments a volley of shots is heard. There is silence. The door is opened slowly and JASON reenters. Closing the door behind him HE leans against it.)

JASON: I was mistaken.

(HE falls to the floor. Blood seeps through the jacket.)

THE WRATH OF GOD

HELEN: Jason!

(**TIM rushes to his brother and raises his head.**)

JASON: Sorry I messed up your jacket, kid.

(**JASON shudders several times, and is silent. As the lights slowly come down the sound of a clock ticking can be heard. When the lights come up again, it's seven months later. As in the opening, it is morning and DOC is discovered waiting, and looking out the window at the falling snow. A groan is heard coming from HELEN in the bedroom. TIM enters.**)

TIM: I think it's time, Doc.

(**DOC goes into the bedroom. TIM paces about. HE looks out the window. Cries of pain can be heard from HELEN.**)

TIM: *Oh, please, please, make it all come out right. Father in heaven be kind to my dear wife.*

(**The wailing of an infant can be heard. TIM hesitates and starts toward the bedroom door. DOC reenters, wiping his hand with a towel.**)

DOC: Mother and child are doing fine.

TIM: Thank you, Doc. (**HE starts off.**)

DOC: Incidentally...

TIM: Yes? What is it?

THE WRATH OF GOD

DOC: It's a girl.

TIM: Oh? Do you think we can still call her Jason?

DOC: I don't think she'd be very happy about it. I mean that little girl. And, of course, there is your mother to consider.

TIM: That was her last request, wasn't it? I guess we'll call her Moira

> **(TIM goes into the bedroom. DOC walks to the window and looks out at the falling snow. As the lights come down we hear "I'll Take You Home Again, Kathleen.")**

LABOR OF LOVE

CAST OF CHARACTERS

Oscar Zeller, a labor leader

Dorothy Zeller, his wife

Esther Zeller, his daughter

Carl Newman, a newspaper man, his friend

John Sebastian III, a socialite

SCENE
The living room Oscar Zeller's suite in one of the best hotels in Washington, DC.

TIME
The fall of 1941

ACT ONE

(iving room of Oscar Zeller's hotel suite, oval shaped and opulent. A double door upstage center leads to the hotel corridor. A door downstage right leads to a study. A door upstage right leads to OSCAR's bedroom. A door downstage left leads to a sitting room, now CARL'S bedroom, and a door upstage left leads to another bedroom.
It is late in the afternoon of a brisk day, early September 1941. The outer door is opened and JOHN SEBASTIAN III is ushered in by CARL NEWMAN. JOHN is a pleasant faced, weary looking man in his early thirties. CARL is a short, dapper, pugnacious man about fifty.)

CARL: Opulent, eh what? Offhand what sort of a man would you say lived in a place like this? A duke? An emperor? King Louis the fifteenth? Just feel this rug. Go ahead. Feel it. I get sea-sick every time I walk across this floor. And the furniture. Come here. You see that spot? An Egyptian prince pissed right there. That's nothing to laugh at, young man. 'T'was a royal predicament. And those pictures. They were once quite fashionable. Strange, isn't it, how fashions change, and taste?

JOHN: Not if you go back far enough.

CARL: You have breeding. I can tell. Something Oscar Zeller would give anything for, and myself. Don't shake your head. I'm crude and uncouth. Only I'm not ashamed of it.

JOHN: And Mr. Zeller is?

CARL: Did I say that? How old did you say you were? Never mind. It doesn't matter. In the ways of the world, the political world, that is, you are an infant. Now, why do you think I brought you up here? You must have some idea. Is it because of your mind, your body, your spirit?

LABOR OF LOVE

JOHN: I really don't know.

CARL: In your thirty odd years on earth, you must have formed some sort of philosophy that you live by.

JOHN: Do unto others have as you would have them do unto you?

CARL: The motto of Christ and of myriad Hebrew prophets before him. It's never been tried. But even so it would never have worked.

JOHN: And why is that?

CARL: It's based on a premise that everyone's taste is the same. For example. If I like Roquefort cheese, and you despise it, it would not be very gracious of me to insist on serving it to you, in hopes of your serving it to me. *(JOHN sighs.)* What a sigh! It's the ginger ale you've been drinking. When I see a man at a bar drinking ginger ale, I think one, this man is ill; or two, he's afraid to drink anything else.

JOHN: I'm an alcoholic.

CARL: That's quite all right. We all have weaknesses. I talk too much. It's compulsive. Today the fashion is to find out why. Have you been through analysis? Save your money. It's very expensive. You belong to Acholic Anonymous.

JOHN: It's been seven months. I woke up one morning in the gutter, and I said to myself, "This is ridiculous." What made you undergo analysis?

CARL: I never said that I did.

JOHN: You said it was expensive.

LABOR OF LOVE

CARL: That would never hold up in court.

JOHN: I have no intention of taking you to court.

CARL: Have you ever been to court? Now that's the place to study human nature. The astounding brilliance of the human mind, alongside its unmitigated depravity. As a reporter, I've spent a good deal of my life in court. I assume you have read my column. Never mind. I see by that looks of apology on your face that you haven't. I'm not exactly Walter Winchell, but I do have my following, in the business world that is. But of course, that's never interested you, up until recently that is.

JOHN: That's not entirely true.

CARL: You're quite right to be distrustful. Mutual distrust is the only sound basis for any human relationship. If only I could say what I really thought in one of my columns.

JOHN: Have you ever tried?

CARL: Once, when I was drunk. It never appeared in print. I've still got a copy of it. I'll show it to you sometime.

JOHN: I doubt if you ever will.

CARL: You're probably right. However, one never knows. We may become bosom buddies. I'm a man in search of a son. You may be a man in search of a father. I never had a son. Are you religious?

JOHN: Not formally. Are you?

CARL: I pay lip service, just in case. I'm a skeptic or, you might say, a hypocrite. They're one and the same, are they not? A man

LABOR OF LOVE

who stands on the fence, unwilling, or afraid to take sides. You're not even curious as to why I've brought you up here.

JOHN: You want some sort of a favor in return for your getting me in to see Mr. Zeller.

CARL: Actually I'm giving you the opportunity to contribute to a tremendous work I'm preparing, a biography of Oscar Zeller.

JOHN: I've never met Mr. Zeller.

CARL: Ah, but you know his wife, his current wife, that is.

JOHN: Dottie? Don't you think a biography is rather premature. I'd say Mr. Zeller is at the zenith of his career.

CARL: On the contrary. I think a biography, a truthful biography, at this time, would be invaluable.

JOHN: What do you want to know?

CARL: Weren't you two engaged at one time?

JOHN: It didn't work out.

CARL: Are you still in love with her?

JOHN: If you're really in love with someone, you never really fall out.

CARL: Why haven't you asked Dottie for help?

JOHN: I don't think it's cricket to take advantage of our past relationship. Besides her father asked me not to.

LABOR OF LOVE

CARL: Why did Mr. Vickers object to the marriage?

JOHN: You may know more about that than I do.

(There is a knock at the door.)

CARL: Excuse me.

(CARL opens the door and ESTHER ZELLER is discovered. She is a slim, dark, rather intense looking girl in her early twenties.)

ESTHER: I'm a day early.

(THEY fall into each others arms.)

CARL: Welcome home.

ESTHER: *(SHE kisses him on the cheek.)* Where's Papa?

(ESTHER comes into the room, as CARL picks up her bag and closes the door.)

CARL: He went out for a drive with his new wife. This is John Sebastian, the Third. Meet Esther Zeller, Oscar's daughter.

JOHN: How do you do.

ESTHER: *(SHE nods.)* Who pays for all this?

CARL: The union, my dear. Who else? You've lost weight. And that suit!

ESTHER: In London, at the moment, this suit would be considered

LABOR OF LOVE

the height of elegance. It's a amazing. Everything here seems so bright and new. It's as if there was no war going on. And you look wonderful, so healthy and prosperous.

JOHN: Perhaps I'd better leave.

ESTHER: Oh, no, please. You were probably talking business, and I'd like to unpack and get settled.

(The phone rings.)

CARL: That'll be Myrna, about next week's column. This will only take a minute. Excuse me, please. *(HE goes off, downstage left.)*

JOHN: Would you care for a cigarette?

ESTHER: Thank you, but I don't smoke. In London, however, they're a great luxury now.

JOHN: Were you born there?

ESTHER: Oh, no. I was born in New York. I have relatives there.

JOHN: You do have an accent, you know.

ESTHER: So I've discovered. I've been there for over three years.

JOHN: It seems to suit you.

ESTHER: Thank you. Are you a friend of Carl's?

JOHN: We just met this afternoon.

LABOR OF LOVE

ESTHER: Beware of Carl. He's the sweetest man in the world, but completely ruthless when it comes to his work. What sort of work do you do?

JOHN: I'm...in business. It must be pretty rough over there.

ESTHER: It can't go on much longer...unless, of course...

JOHN: We come in.

ESTHER: It's inevitable.

JOHN: It's funny how unimportant everything gets to be at the prospect of war.

ESTHER: Do you know my father?

JOHN: No. However, I'm looking forward to meeting him. I have great respect for the work he's been doing.

ESTHER: You just gave yourself away.

JOHN: What did I say?

ESTHER: It's not what you said, it's the way you said it. Labor has become so respectable, it's difficult to tell the difference between it and Capital, until one speaks. My father is respected by Capital. Labor either worships him or fears him.

JOHN: I've been in Washington just one week, and I hate it already. Not the city. I mean the politics.

ESTHER: You'll find politics everywhere.

LABOR OF LOVE

JOHN: Yes, but here in Washington, it's considered respectable. There's even a so-called gentleman in the White House.

ESTHER: You're a Republican. That's quite all right. I have many Republican friends.

JOHN: I feel rather awkward. This is your father's suite. And and I haven't really been invited.

ESTHER: Carl lives here, too, and he's invited you, I gather. In Washington it's considered an honor to be able to come through the back door.

JOHN: That's what I mean. It's all so sneaky.

ESTHER: Oh, dear. You are a little lamb. How did you ever get mixed up in all of this?

JOHN: It's much too sordid a tale for your young and gentle ears.

ESTHER: These young and gentle ears have lain awake nights listening to the screech of rockets and bombs. Nothing, I can assure you, is as sordid as that.

(CARL re-enters.)

CARL: I'm sorry. You must want to get settled.

ESTHER: That would be nice. When will Oscar be back?

CARL: He should be back soon. You're in here. We share the bath.

ESTHER: Excuse me.

LABOR OF LOVE

JOHN: Certainly.

ESTHER: Will I see you again?

CARL: Shameless hussy!

ESTHER: I just meant...

CARL: Come along, come along.

> *(CARL, holding ESTHER's suitcase ushers her in the room upstage left. JOHN wanders about the room, eyeing the bar. CARL reenters.)*

CARL: She's charming, isn't she? But terribly intellectual. It would take an Einstein to suit her.

JOHN: Or an Oscar Zeller. May I stay and meet him now?

CARL: Why not? Oscar's always on display. As a matter of fact, he needs an audience to function. You've never met him? He'll remember if you have.

JOHN: I was never really introduced to him. I did hear him speak at a dinner once.

CARL: Where was this?

JOHN: In Boston. It was several years ago.

CARL: Nothing escapes him. He has a mind like a steel trap.

JOHN: I haven't seen Dottie for quite some time, and I may not be able to give it to you...the information you're looking for.

LABOR OF LOVE

CARL: Don't worry about it, my boy. Have some ginger ale.

(CARL pours two drinks and hands the ginger ale to JOHN.)

CARL: A toast...to labor and love.

JOHN: I'll drink to that.

(The door is opened as THEY drink, and DOROTHY ZELLER enters. She is a fair, attractive girl in her late twenties.)

CARL: Dottie, my sweet.

DOROTHY: Hello, John. I didn't know you were in town.

JOHN: I've been meaning to call you. And then I ran into Mr. Newman, and he invited me up here.

CARL: We ran into each other at the bar. How was your drive?

DOROTHY: Very pleasant, thank you.

CARL: Where is our dollar-a-year man?

DOROTHY: He was cornered by reporters in the lobby. You look well, John. But then, you always do.

JOHN: This is ginger ale.

CARL: It is, I assure you. I understand you two are old friends.

LABOR OF LOVE

DOROTHY: John and I were engaged to be married, at one time. How long have you been back from California?

JOHN: A year or so.

DOROTHY: Have you been well?

JOHN: I belong to A. A..

DOROTHY: I'm glad to hear it. I'd like to freshen up. Will you excuse me? I hope you'll stay and meet Oscar. *(SHE goes off upstage right.)*

JOHN: One look at me, and they all run to freshen up. Would you believe it? She used to tremble when I came into the room. Tempus, tempus...and good, hard liquor. It's painful to see her like this, so cold, so unfeeling.

CARL: You think she's unhappy?

JOHN: That marriage was nothing more than another form of self destruction.

CARL: We mustn't get too emotional about this.

JOHN: I have no intention of getting emotional. Not with Oscar Zeller. "Reason and moderation. These are the weapons of progress."

CARL: You know our man.

JOHN: Maybe I ought to meet him at another time.

CARL: Suit yourself.

LABOR OF LOVE

JOHN: I'm grateful for your interest, Mr. Newman. Really I am. You're the first person that's been kind to me here, except for some relatives, and they look upon me as some sort of freak. Which I am. I need a father, badly.

CARL: Don't we all, my boy.

(The outer door is opened and OSCAR ZELLER, a distinguished looking, well tailored man in his middle fifties, appears in the doorway.)

OSCAR: *(Addressing someone in the corridor.)* Thank you. Thank you very much.

CARL: Uh oh! Too late, I'm afraid.

OSCAR: *(HE closes the door.)* If you're a reporter...

CARL: He's a friend of mine.

OSCAR: I didn't mean to be rude, young man. But the fourth estate, invaluable as it is, has very bad manners.

JOHN: That's quite all right.

OSCAR: As Carl here will tell you, I've always done my best not to offend the press. And that takes some doing. What is it about newspaper men?

CARL: They're under pressure, like everyone else.

OSCAR: You were never like that.

LABOR OF LOVE

CARL: I was worse, and you know it. I still am, except with you, of course. Esther's here.

OSCAR: When did she get in?

CARL: A short while ago.

OSCAR: How does she look?

CARL: Thin, and a little tired.

OSCAR: At least she's safe. The sleepless nights I've spent; Goldie pointing her finger at me, accusing me, "Why did you send her over there?"

CARL: You didn't send her over. She went of her own free will.

OSCAR: I've neglected her shamefully, and you know it. If you ever have a family, young man, make sure there's time for them. That's the enemy, you know. It's not the Germans or the Japanese or the Italians, it's time. Aren't you going to introduce me to your friend? Though his face looks awfully familiar. We've met somewhere. I'm sure of it. Boston. It was in the Spring, at a dinner given by the N.A.M.

CARL: What did I tell you?

JOHN: We were never really introduced.

OSCAR: I'm greatly relieved. I couldn't think why the name escaped me.

JOHN: Sebastian. John Sebastian, the third.

LABOR OF LOVE

OSCAR: Oh.

JOHN: Ah...yes, sir.

OSCAR: Dottie didn't tell me that you were in town. I thought you were in California.

JOHN: I've soaked up enough sunshine to last me for the rest of my life.

OSCAR: What brings you to Washington?

CARL: Now, Oscar, this is Saturday evening. You've sent away your staff, and tomorrow is Sunday, a day of rest.

OSCAR: Will you be in town for long?

JOHN: That all depends.

OSCAR: Have you spoken to Mr. Vickers lately?

JOHN: Yes, sir.

OSCAR: Did he mention Dorothy and myself?

JOHN: At length.

OSCAR: I suppose he still feels the same.

JOHN: He's a very bitter man, and not too well.

OSCAR: So he gave us to understand, time and again. What is it really that he holds against me? That I represent labor?

LABOR OF LOVE

JOHN: You took his daughter away from him.

OSCAR: Someone was bound to, eventually.

JOHN: No one is good enough for Dottie. You're a father. You must have some idea how he feels.

OSCAR: I love my daughter dearly, but never for one moment, have I ever felt that she was my exclusive property.

JOHN: But then, Mr. Zeller, you're not president of Vickers Motor Company.

OSCAR: How long ago did Esther arrive? I should have met her in New York.

CARL: Then you wouldn't have been in Chicago.

OSCAR: The story of my life. I'm never where I want to be.

CARL: You want to be where you're needed the most.

OSCAR: That's not always easy to tell.

(ESTHER enters.)

ESTHER: Hello, Papa.

(SHE kisses him and HE embraces her.)

OSCAR: You look so pale.

ESTHER: And you look tired. Don't you get any sleep?

LABOR OF LOVE

CARL: What a question to ask a newly married man!

OSCAR: How is Aunt Zelda?

ESTHER: So, so. She hasn't been the same since Myron was reported lost.

OSCAR: Has there been any word from Europe? No letters?

ESTHER: They must have been caught by the Germans.

OSCAR: Miriam and all of them? I'm sure those stories about the camps must be exaggerated. What do you think, Carl?

CARL: Who knows?

OSCAR: And the children?

CARL: They're still in the country. I saw them before I left. They need everything.

OSCAR: I've been sending packages regularly.

ESTHER: I know, I know.

OSCAR: I'm so glad you're safe, my little one.

ESTHER: Oh, Papa. Isn't it ridiculous? This is a fine time to cry. What will Mr. Sebastian think of us?

CARL: Delicate ladies of gentility are supposed to shed a tear in times of stress. Just make sure your eyes don't get too red.

LABOR OF LOVE

OSCAR: There are times, Carl, when your cynicism is just a little too much.

ESTHER: Now, Papa, he was just joking.

OSCAR: Exactly.

CARL: No, your father's right.

ESTHER: On the contrary. Of we lose our sense of humor, we've lost everything. You can't imagine what it's like. They need us, Papa. We've got to come in. It's our war, too.

JOHN: What do you mean by **our** war?

ESTHER: Humanity's. I suppose the president doesn't talk to you about the war.

OSCAR: Yes, of course, he does. But I'm not a soldier. I'm not a politician.

CARL: Don't be so modest.

OSCAR: I'm a labor leader. I've never claimed to be anything else. Your godfather here has been giving me a hard time of late. He's writing my biography. Anything you want to know about your father, go to Mr. Newman. Even things you may not want to know. or anyone else, for that matter.

CARL: Don't underestimate the curiosity of the human race. Aside from sustenance and sex, the desire to know stands uppermost in the mind of the human animal. And I believe in the truth.

OSCAR: The truth, dear Carl, is a two edged sword.

LABOR OF LOVE

CARL: It's a sword that takes courage to wield.

ESTHER: Your not accusing Papa of lacking courage, are you?

CARL: Who, in his right mind, would do that?

OSCAR: I've been called a coward before, among other things.

CARL: Not by me.

OSCAR: There are other things more important than the truth.

CARL: Like what?

OSCAR: Like Labor, for one.

CARL: Labor. That's a word. What does it mean, Labor?

OSCAR: Those who work with their hands for pay. Like your father did, and mine.

CARL: Your father was a Capitalist.

ESTHER: You mustn't take this seriously, John. This has been going on for as far back as I can remember. Papa's father was a shoemaker in Russia, and he had his own shop. The family always had shoes, but they often went hungry.

OSCAR: I wish I knew you were coming in today. We could have met you at the airport. Dottie's very nervous about meeting you. Does she know you're here?

CARL: I don't think so.

LABOR OF LOVE

OSCAR: I'd better let her know. She'll want to look her best.

ESTHER: And so will I. I'd like to change, and I haven't even finished unpacking.

OSCAR: There's no rush. I've reserved the entire week-end for my family. It's been a long time since I've been so happy, Liebchen. Even Carl approves of Dottie, and you know what a misogynist Mr. Newman is.

CARL: I am not a misogynist. I distrust women, it's true, but no more so than I do my fellow man.

OSCAR: Don't listen to him. Go change.

(ESTHER kisses OSCAR and goes off.)

OSCAR: She's so thin.

CARL: So we'll fatten her up.

OSCAR: I guess I'm lucky to get her back. But I'm worrried about the rest of the family.

CARL: Maybe the president...

OSCAR: No. He isn't God, you know. And he has enough to worry about. I wish I were a religious man, instead of a hypocrite like you.

CARL: Oscar, do me a favor. For one night forget that you're Atlas. Pretend, just pretend that you're an ordinary human being.

OSCAR: I don't need to pretend. *(HE goes off.)*

LABOR OF LOVE

CARL: Now that you've met the great man, what do you think of him? A little pompous, perhaps. A little impressed with his own importance. I met Oscar on his second day in this country. He was not a very impressive figure. Thin, a little round-shouldered, and looking somewhat lost. But not for long. Oscar Zeller always knew where he was going. He came from nowhere...the wilds of Russia...and now he tells big business what to do.

JOHN: The relationship between you two is...well, rather puzzling, to say the least. I suppose you might say friendly enemies.

CARL: Enemies: Oscar and I? Oscar and I are the best of friends, and that's what we've been since his second day in America. That's something I would think you'd understand, since it is typically American. Where else does "son of a bitch" mean "comrade," and "you bastard" mean "brother?"

JOHN: Is Dottie happy with him, not that it's any of my business.

CARL: Then why do you ask?

JOHN: Curiosity, I suppose. Vanity. Pride. All the things that matter the most, and are considered too petty to be of any importance. Well? What next?

CARL: You're joining us for dinner, of course. Unless you have something better to do. Don't look so apprehensive.

JOHN: I don't want to cash in on my relationship with Dottie.

CARL: You have a job to do, and if you're going to be that fussy, you'll never get it done.

JOHN: I'd like very much to get that government contract. It would

LABOR OF LOVE

mean a great deal to me. A new life, perhaps. God knows, the old one wasn't very much, but I do have certain principles.

CARL: You don't want to hide behind a woman's skirt.

JOHN: Especially Dottie's. She doesn't owe me a thing. As a matter of fact, I wish I could make up for all the unhappiness I've caused her. I have no illusions about why I got this job. Old man Vickers knows I'm still carrying the torch for Dottie, and he knows I'll give him an accurate report about her. And, as far as the contract is concerned there are two vice presidents behind me with all the facts and figures. All I've got to do is arrange a meeting, and my part of the job is done.

CARL: How were you going to manage that without seeing her?

JOHN: You think I'm a little ridiculous.

CARL: No, no, no. Though I don't pretend to understand. I was raised in the jungle of the lower East Side in New York. If you want something, you go after it. If you're too fussy, you get crushed in the stampede. And if you're too honest, you sometimes pay with your life, like my father did.

JOHN: He must have been a very fine man.

CARL: He was a saint. You'll join us for dinner. I'll handle it. Relax.

JOHN: I think I ought to change. Don't you? At least a dark suit.

CARL: How long will it take.

JOHN: Twenty minutes or so. I'm at the Statler.

LABOR OF LOVE

CARL: We'll wait for you.

JOHN: Thank you, Mr. Newman.

CARL: Don't thank me yet.

JOHN: I'll be right back.

(JOHN goes off. CARL picks up the phone and dials.)

CARL: Hello, Myrna. What did you find out? No, he's not here. I can talk freely. I see. Type it up and drop it off at the front desk. And have a nice week-end. Sunday then. Oh, Myrna...

(DOROTHY enters dressed for the evening. CARL hangs up.)

DOROTHY: Has John left already?

CARL: He'll be back.

DOROTHY: You two seem to have hit it off pretty well.

CARL: He's a charming fellow.

DOROTHY: Oh, yes. He was always that. The Fourth of July and New Years Eve all rolled into one. Was that really ginger ale he was drinking?

CARL: Oh, yes. You two were engaged for quite some time.

DOROTHY: I kept hoping for a miracle, which never materialized.

CARL: You're back much earlier than I expected.

LABOR OF LOVE

DOROTHY You know how difficult it is to get Oscar to relax. I used to think that marriage was the answer to everything. You said "I do" and the rest was a fairy tale. What's your secret, Carl? You're the only one I know whose life seems to go along in a straight line. You're never flustered. You're never at a loss for words.

CARL: A newspaperman has to be glib.

DOROTHY: Glib and rude. I'm not referring to you.

CARL: Oscar's an important public figure. He's news.

DOROTHY: Then they ought to show him some respect. I'm realy concerned about him. How long can he keep up this pace?

CARL: He's been at it for over thirty years.

DOROTHY: Exactly.

CARL: Nonsense. He thrives on too much to do.

DOROTHY: Has John said anything about my father?

CARL: He spoke of him, yes.

DOROTHY: You're not keeping something from me, are you?

CARL: Now why would I do that?

DOROTHY: I worry about him continually. He's not well, and he's all alone in that big house.

CARL: Your aunt is with him, isn't she?

LABOR OF LOVE

DOROTHY: They never see each other, except at dinner. Besides, they don't get along very well.

CARL: Does anyone get along with your father? I'm sorry.

DOROTHY: Oh, no. It's true. He's a very unhappy man. It seems that everyone he put his faith in has let him down. My brother escaped a long time ago, but not from himself. And now I've let him down.

CARL: He may come around.

DOROTHY: Oh, no. Not Daddy. I've written to him every week since I've been married. I'm sure he hasn't opened any of my letters. But I'll continue writing them.

CARL: What's the point?

DOROTHY: Aunt Mary reads them and, in case he should permit her to talk about me, she'll know what I've been up to.

CARL: He's a tyrant, your old man.

DOROTHY: Who isn't, at one time or another.

CARL: You're much more tolerant than I am, and I suspect just as cynical.

DOROTHY: Let's just say that I'm not as idealistic as my husband is.

CARL: Women seldom are. That's what I admire about your sex. I'd sooner have a man as my enemy than the sweetest of the so-called gentler sex. And I am not a misogynist.

LABOR OF LOVE

DOROTHY: Why haven't you married?

CARL: The fact of the matter is I'm much too fond of women to punish any one of them by marrying her.

DOROTHY: I understand you're very fond of Esther.

CARL: As her godfather, I knew her when she was completely helpless. You can't fight that.

DOROTHY: Why do you find it necessary to fight all your natural feelings?

CARL: My dear child, if one were to investigate ones natural feelings, what do you think one would find?

DOROTHY: What, pray tell?

CARL: Murder, incest and rape, among other things. We all carry about Pandora's box. And few of us are sensible enough to keep the lid tightly closed.

DOROTHY: Except for my husband. You don't agree. Now Carl, even you must admit that Oscar is perfect. Stop scowling. I'm only joking.

CARL: I know Oscar's worth better than anyone.

DOROTHY: Of course, you do. And he thinks highly of you. Otherwise I doubt if he'd permit you to write his authorized biography. Will Esther like me, do you think? I don't make friends with woman very easily.

LABOR OF LOVE

CARL: You don't have to make friends with her. You're her mother.

>(OSCAR *re-enters.*)

OSCAR: Isn't she out yet? Now, now, there's nothing to be nervous about.

DOROTHY: Meeting a step-daughter who is almost as old as you are?

OSCAR: She can't help but like you. Now what are our plans for the evening? Shall we have our dinner sent up here, or what?

DOROTHY: Why don't we go out somewhere? Actually, we could go downstairs. The room is charming and that trio is very pleasant. You'll join us, won't you, Carl?

CARL: I'd like that very much, but I promised John I'd have dinner with him.

DOROTHY: Bring him along. You don't mind, do you, dear?

OSCAR: No, of course not.

>(ESTHER *enters, wearing a new dress.*)

DOROTHY: *(After a moment)* I'm Dorothy.

>(SHE *goes to kiss* ESTHER, *who extends her hand, and they shake hands.*)

ESTHER: How do you do.

LABOR OF LOVE

DOROTHY: You're very much like your father.

ESTHER: Not really.

DOROTHY: How was your trip?

ESTHER: It was all right. I came by plane.

DOROTHY: Yes, I know. I'm sorry we didn't get to meet you. That's a very pretty dress.

OSCAR: Except for the price tag.

DOROTHY: Here, let me.

ESTHER: I'm not into clothes. I mean...

DOROTHY: Yes, I know what you mean.

CARL: What are you looking for?

ESTHER: The man that I just met...

CARL: He'll be back. He's joining us for dinner. If you'll excuse me. Myrna is dropping something off on her way home. I want to see if I can catch her. I'll be back in a few minutes. *(HE goes off.)*

ESTHER: He hasn't changed a bit, has he? The two of you are so much alike, it's frightening.

DOROTHY: I don't think they're alike at all.

OSCAR: In what way are we different?

LABOR OF LOVE

DOROTHY: With Carl, it's a crusade.

OSCAR: And with me?

DOROTHY: It's your life's work. Carl acts like the constant bridegroom.

OSCAR: You make him sound like a romantic.

DOROTHY: He is, in his attitude, I mean.

OSCAR: I wouldn't tell him that. He'd consider it an insult.

DOROTHY: He insults you continually.

OSCAR: It's just part of his crusade.

DOROTHY: We were so sorry you couldn't be here for the wedding.

OSCAR: Well, she'll be here for the anniversary. Won't you, liebchen?

DOROTHY: It all looks so hopeless, the war, I mean.

OSCAR: Not tonight. Not on her first day back. I want her to relax, and I want to fill out those cheeks of hers.

ESTHER: You can't ignore it, Papa. I can't understand why we haven't come in before this.

OSCAR: There are many people here that feel the war isn't ours. The President doesn't feel that way, and we're preparing for it, slowly but surely. That's why I'm here. We're almost geared for wartime production.

DOROTHY: Your father has done a magnificent job. Things were in a mess before you took over.

OSCAR: There were too many people with too much to say. Now that there are only two of us, we can act more quickly. And, if war should come, and it probably will, there may be only one in charge, and it won't necessarily be me. And it wouldn't be any tragedy. After fighting for the underdog all my life, it's been rather ticklish appearing to be on the side of the bosses, especially since Capital has never considered me part of the family.

DOROTHY: Oscar, please.

OSCAR: I'm sorry. Dottie's father has never accepted me or our marriage, and he won't have anything to do with her, as long as she's my wife.

DOROTHY: It's not that he dislikes Oscar personally. Actually he has great admiration and respect for Oscar.

OSCAR: As an enemy.

DOROTHY: As you can see, Esther, the odds are against us. I told your father that from the very beginning. Who ever heard of a labor leader marrying into the Vickers family?

OSCAR: On the contrary. What worker doesn't dream about marrying the boss's daughter? Your step-mother has a very tragic view of life. Her favorite opera is "Tristan And Isolde."

DOROTHY: Only because you proposed to me that night.

LABOR OF LOVE

OSCAR: What else could I do? You looked so sad.

DOROTHY: Do you like opera?

OSCAR: She's like me. She's only interested in Labor.

ESTHER: I do have other interests, Papa.

DOROTHY: Do you play tennis?

ESTHER: Not too well.

OSCAR: Poor Dottie! She can't find anyone to play tennis with. Isn't it strange, John Sebastian popping up like that. What do you suppose he wants?

DOROTHY: It might have been a coincidence. John has never planned anything in his life.

OSCAR: Carl seldom asks someone he's just met to dinner.

DOROTHY: Since he is a friend of the family, so to speak, it doesn't seem strange at all.

ESTHER: Do you know him?

DOROTHY: We were engaged at one time.

ESTHER: Oh?

DOROTHY: We haven't seen each other in almost three years. He's really very charming. Too charming, as a matter of fact, for his own good.

LABOR OF LOVE

OSCAR: He's not for you.

DOROTHY: Oscar!

OSCAR: What did I say?

DOROTHY: Well, if you don't know.

ESTHER: That's all right. He meant well.

DOROTHY: My father means well, too.

OSCAR: Now what did I say? Esther isn't really interested in him, romantically that is.

DOROTHY: Then what was the point of that remark?

OSCAR: Do you think John is the kind of man that Esther should date?

DOROTHY: That's not the point.

OSCAR: What do you want me to do, apologize?

DOROTHY: Would that be so terrible?

ESTHER: That's quite all right. Really it is.

DOROTHY: You're the most stubborn man I've ever known.

OSCAR: Except for your father.

DOROTHY: As a matter of fact, I don't see any difference.

LABOR OF LOVE

ESTHER: Please.

(The telephone rings.)

OSCAR: That's for me. I'll take it in my study.

DOROTHY: Don't bother. *(SHE goes off.)*

OSCAR: You'll give yourself a headache.

ESTHER: That wasn't necessary.

OSCAR: It's true. She works herself up like this and then she stuffs herself with aspirins. Excuse me. That call is very important. Go to her, please.

(OSCAR goes off to his study. After a moment the phone stops ringing. ESTHER knocks on DOROTHY's door, then goes off. There is a knock on the outside door. The knock is heard again. The door is opened, and JOHN enters, dressed for dinner.)

JOHN: Hello? The natives have fled in dismay.

(HE looks about, undecided as what to do. CARL enters, holding an envelope.)

JOHN: Oh, there you are. Where is everyone?

CARL: I'm sure they're about somewhere. There's plenty of time. We're eating downstairs.

JOHN: Are they expecting me?

LABOR OF LOVE

CARL: It's all arranged.

JOHN: Dottie had no objection?

CARL: On the contrary.

JOHN: What a stroke of luck, my running into you. I shall read your column faithfully from here on in. What paper is it in?

CARL: In Washington, The Post. In New York, The Wall Street Journal, and in Boston, The Tribune. I'm syndicated.

JOHN: It's a crazy world, isn't it? Who ever dreamed I'd be working for Robert Vickers? He despises me, you know. At least he did a year or so ago. Actually I feel sorry for the old man. His own daughter joining the enemy camp. He invited me to dinner, you know. That was quite a revelation. That huge, elegant table and just the three of us; the old man, the spinster, and the alcoholic. I don't think two words were spoken during the entire meal. Afterwards we were alone. He spoke then, and it broke my heart. Junior's a bum, you know. He pretends to be an artist, but he couldn't paint the side of a barn. He wears a beard. That's his claim to fame. The old man sends him a check every month, just to be rid of him. The old lady died six years ago. Cancer. I'm talking too much.

CARL: Not at all.

JOHN: This job means a great deal to me. If I'm repeating myself, just stop me. It's not just the job so much, it's just the fact that old man Vickers had that much faith in me. I'd hate to let him down.

CARL: And yourself.

LABOR OF LOVE

JOHN: Myself? This empty shell? God, I envy you. What a wonderful thing it must be to know where you're going, and to actually get there. And I think it's great Dottie marrying Oscar Zeller. That took a lot of courage. Are you sure she didn't mind my coming along?

CARL: She was the one that suggested it.

JOHN: She's way ahead of me, you know. She always has been. She could drink harder and ride faster, but she knew when to stop. That was the difference between us, you see. It's not easy to watch someone crawl on all fours, when you're sober yourself. They just look like what they are, disgusting. That was her favorite word.

CARL: You don't mind if I have a drink, do you?

JOHN: No, of course not.

CARL: Would you care for some ginger ale?

JOHN: No, thank you. Sometimes I switch to Coke or Seven Up. No, no. Not now. I think I'm starting to get the shakes. It doesn't last very long.

CARL: Can I get you anything?

JOHN: No, no. Just pretend that I'm a normal human being. That's the game I play with myself. They're gone, for the present. I guess I'm just scared.

CARL: Of what?

JOHN: Of spending an evening with Dottie, and trying to make an impression on her husband. Actually, it's rather humiliating, asking

LABOR OF LOVE

a favor of the husband of your ex-fiancee. It's an awful thing to have lost faith in oneself. Has it ever happened to you?

CARL: *(After a moment)* You're pretty much of a mess, aren't you? Not only are you a weakling and a hypocrite, you're a bigot as well. You despise Oscar Zeller because he's a Jew. You said as much this afternoon, but you stopped short because you realized that I was Jew as well.

JOHN: I've never been fond of the Jews as a race, but I happen to know some rather fine ones.

CARL: The exception to the rule.

JOHN: I never said that.

CARL: Why not? If that's what you think?

JOHN: How did this come up?

CARL: I brought it up. I've been gagging on it ever since we met.

JOHN: Then you're the hypocrite, not me. You pretended to be my friend...

CARL: I still am. I'm just a stickler for the truth.

JOHN: I'm really not anti-Semitic.

CARL: You just despise the Jews. Are you sure I can't get you anything?

JOHN: A gun, perhaps, or a dash of arsenic.

LABOR OF LOVE

CARL: You keep eyeing that Scotch as if it were a woman.

JOHN: You do understand.

CARL: Human frailty is my special field of research.

JOHN: Have you come up with any remedies?

CARL: To quote Oscar Wilde, "The only way to defeat temptation is to give into it." Or something to that effect.

JOHN: Would you try to stop me if I were to take a drink.

CARL: I'm a reformer, only as far as labor is concerned.

JOHN: It's been seven months, and I've never laid off that long. Well, old man Vickers is in Boston, and Boston's a long way off. If I should get polluted, would you see that I got back to my hotel?

CARL: Let's trust that you don't.

JOHN: Thank you, Carl. You're a good man.

CARL: Even if I am a Jew.

JOHN: *(HE pours a drink.)* This is a fine time for the shakes. *(HE pours a drink and downs it.)* This is damn good Scotch. Just one more. *(HE pours a second drink and downs it.)* I feel better already. I'll just pour a third, just to hold. A gentleman looks lost without a glass of Scotch in his hand. *(HE pours a third.)* You may not believe it, but I can be devilishly charming when the occasion calls for it. That's why old man Vickers sent me here. He told me so himself. *(HE drinks.)* I mean, after all, what do I know about the auto industry? Now how did this glass get emptied? Have I

LABOR OF LOVE

been a naughty boy? That's all for tonight. Mustn't make a beast of myself. *(HE puts the glass down.)* You're disappointed in me. I can see that familiar look of piteous condescension.

CARL: If you want to make it another night.

JOHN: No, no. Tonight's the night. The culmination of my career in debauchery... I mean diplomacy. I've gotta take a leak.

CARL: The bathroom's right through there. Knock first.

JOHN: Anchor's away. *(HE goes off downstage left.)*

CARL: Don't drown yourself.

   (OSCAR enters.)

OSCAR: Who are you talking to?

CARL: Young Sebastian. He's slightly under the weather at the moment.

OSCAR: I must say, Carl, it was most indelicate of you to bring him up here.

CARL: He latched on to me. What could I do?

OSCAR: What does he want?

CARL: Your guess is as good as mine.

OSCAR: He strikes me as being a very sneaky young man. Does he need any money?

LABOR OF LOVE

CARL: I doubt it.

OSCAR: He's a lush, I know that. And, from what I gather, he's a rather pitiful case. Esther seems quite taken with him.

CARL: Nonsense. She doesn't even know him.

OSCAR: By the time she does, it may be too late. How did I ever get the reputation for being a tactful man? Five minutes alone with my wife and daughter and I've offended both of them. It's that damn strike in Detroit, and what's happening over there in Europe. What a man he is, Franklin D.! I can manage to keep a poker face when everything falls to pieces, but I'll be damned if I can manage a smile, and a real one at that. Ten years is a long time to live alone. You sort of get used to it, and it's not easy to make room for someone else. Someone half your age. Though Dottie's mature where it counts.

CARL: And immature, where it's attractive.

OSCAR: I don't know why I'm coming to you for advice; you, a confirmed bachelor.

CARL: I'm the perfect choice. I have an objective point of view.

OSCAR: Women are fantastic creatures, Carl. They're braver than we are, gentler, prettier and, in many ways, more direct. But with Goldie it was different. We were always side by side, comrades in arms. And we were of an age. With Dottie, the gulf between us is frightening.

CARL: And the love more intense.

OSCAR: That's the paradox. At my age, when the body calls for

LABOR OF LOVE

temperance and the mind for tranquility. How drunk is he, young Lochinvar? That's all I need, a drunken ex-lover. Is he still in love with her?

CARL: Quite possibly. Now, Oscar, how was I to know? And besides, your wife was the one that invited him. Not that that means anything.

OSCAR: Do me a favor. See what Dottie and Esther are up to. And we should call downstairs for a table.

CARL: I've taken care of that. I said we'd be down in half an hour. That was fifteen minutes ago.

OSCAR: Try to smoothe things over.

CARL: I'll do my best.

> (CARL knocks on the door then goes off. OSCAR pours himself a drink. JOHN enters, his hair parted in the middle.)

JOHN: Ah, ah, ah! Temperance!

OSCAR: What have you done to your hair?

JOHN: It gives me an appearance of sobriety, don't you think?

OSCAR: You look ridiculous.

JOHN: Thank God. I thought you were going to say "disgusting." That was Dottie's favorite word.

OSCAR: Still at it, I see.

LABOR OF LOVE

JOHN: Ah, I see that your wife has been carrying tales. Well, I, for one, happen to be a gentleman, sir.

OSCAR: I think tonight would be a good time to show it.

JOHN: *(Eying the liquor.)* You're not much of a host.

OSCAR: I think you've had enough to drink.

JOHN: You're quite right. When does the party start?

OSCAR: Obviously, it's started already?

JOHN: I can see why Dottie married you. She had the same superior attitude, when she was sober, that is.

OSCAR: Dottie's come a long way since you've known each other.

JOHN: That much is obvious.

OSCAR: What do you mean by that?

JOHN: If the shoe fits...

OSCAR: For Dottie's sake, I hope you're not going to make a scene. What's past is past.

JOHN: Now that was a witty observation. Like "A stitch in time saves nine.," or "A rolling stone gathers no moss." Of course, in that case, one assumes that gathering moss is an occupation worthy of a stone.

OSCAR: I think you'd better go home and sleep it off.

LABOR OF LOVE

JOHN: You're trying to get rid of me. Could it be that you're afraid? Let her choose between us.

OSCAR: Dottie made her choice seven months ago.

JOHN: That was seven months ago, while I was in California, which was rather sneaky, don't you think? Let's stand side by side, and then let her choose. Let her choose between a dull, pompous, fathead and Bacchus, king of revelry. You're a fat old Jew! I'm sorry. Bad form, bad form. I shouldn't have said that. Please. Pour me a drink. Just one. Please. Unless you want to see me expire before your very eyes.

(OSCAR pours him a drink.)

JOHN: Thank you. I'm all mixed up. I mean about Dottie and you and everything. I'm sure you're very good for her. Have you ever been in an alcoholic ward? Take my advice. Stay away. And, for God sakes, don't ever get the DTs. Dottie's a wonderful girl. It was all my fault, every bit of it. And her father didn't help matters any. As a matter of fact, he was enough to drive anyone to drink. But she knew when to stop.

OSCAR: Why don't you go home and sleep it off.

JOHN: Let me stay. Please. It's Saturday night. If I don't drink here, I'll go to a bar. I've never been secretive about anything.

OSCAR: That's very admirable, I'm sure.

JOHN: Don't be so goddamned superior. Rosenberg...I beg your pardon, Roosevelt won't be in office forever, you know. As a matter of fact, you may be coming to me for a favor someday. You goddamned Jews are doing well now, but don't push your luck.

LABOR OF LOVE

OSCAR: Get out of here! I said, get out. Or must I call for the house detective to throw you out?

JOHN: Try it yourself, Izzy.

(The door is opened and DOROTHY enters, followed by ESTHER and CARL.)

OSCAR: Carl, get your friend out of here.

JOHN: Don't bother. I can find my own way, Mr. Zeller. I just hope, for the sake of this country, that you're better at you're job than you are as a host. I bid you, good night. *(HE goes off.)*

DOROTHY: Really, Oscar!

OSCAR: Dottie, please. You don't know what went on here just now.

DOROTHY: I think I know John pretty well by now. I don't care what pressure you're under, one can still be civil.

OSCAR: You're absolutely right!

ESTHER: Now, Papa, don't be angry, please.

OSCAR: I'm not the one that's angry. It's your step-mother.

CARL: We're all of us hungry, that's the trouble.

(The telephone rings.)

OSCAR: That's for me. Excuse me. *(HE goes off.)*

LABOR OF LOVE

DOROTHY: He's impossible. Was I to blame? I mean, really?

CARL: I wasn't here.

DOROTHY: I'm asking Esther.

ESTHER: He's used to giving orders. And sometimes a simple statement sounds like an order. My mother spoiled him, you see.

DOROTHY: She must have been quite a woman. It's not easy taking her place. I'm sorry this had to happen, your first day here. I've got to have something to eat. I am absolutely starved.

CARL: You two go on ahead. I'll wait for Oscar. There's a table being held for us.

DOROTHY: Try to calm him down, because I should hate to make a scene in the dining room. Let's go. I'm used to sitting down to dinner as a family. But since I married your father...

(DOROTHY and ESTHER go off. CARL pours himself a drink. OSCAR reenters.)

OSCAR: They've gone?

CARL: You ought to be ashamed of yourself.

OSCAR: Please, don't you start, too. He called me a fat, old Jew. Its not the Jew so much. Or even the fat. But old. That hit home. I'm almost twice her age.

CARL: Dottie is old enough to know her own mind.

LABOR OF LOVE

OSCAR: She regrets the marriage, I know. And I can't say that I blame her. Why has he come here? What does he want?

CARL: He says he's here on business.

OSCAR: What sort of business would anyone trust him with?

CARL: He says he represents the Vickers Corporation.

OSCAR: That's ridiculous. The old man has more sense than that. And besides, Vickers knows he hasn't got a chance with that attitude of his toward the unions. Of course, it's quite possible that Vickers did send him here to try and take her away from me. Well, if that's what she wants, she's welcome to him. Let's join the ladies?

CARL: You go on ahead. I have a call to make.

OSCAR: Thank you.

CARL: For what?

OSCAR: For being a friend. *(HE goes off.)*

CARL: *(HE picks up the phone.)* This is Mr. Newman, Honey. Would you get me The Statler, please. Hello? Has Mr. Sebastian come in yet? I see. When he does, would you have him get in touch with me? Carl Newman. Newman. He knows where I am.

(The lights come down as HE hangs up.)

ACT TWO

(Noon, the following day. ESTHER enters upstage right, as OSCAR enters through center doors.)

OSCAR: Did you sleep well?

ESTHER: Not really, no.

OSCAR: Is Dottie up yet?

ESTHER: She's been up for quite some time. We had a long talk.

OSCAR: You approve of her.

ESTHER: She's not like Mama, you know. And you're not the easiest man to live with.

OSCAR: I know. I'm a silly old man. Thank heaven for Carl. Whenever I find myself losing touch, he sits on me. So my little baby was in love, or was it just an infatuation?

ESTHER: It was the real thing.

OSCAR: So that was why you wouldn't come home. What changed your mind?

ESTHER: He was killed. He was a pilot in the R.A.F..

OSCAR: I'm so sorry. You never said a thing in your letters.

ESTHER: I was all set to write you about it, and that was the day he was shot down. He was a beautiful man, Papa. Twenty four years old. So gentle, so kind. And all I have left is a snapshot and some silly little trinkets.

LABOR OF LOVE

OSCAR: You were lovers?

ESTHER: We were planning on getting married. You're not shocked, are you?

OSCAR: Liebchen, you may be my daughter, but I am an adult.

ESTHER: The one thing I do regret, I don't have his child.

OSCAR: I understand. But don't do like I did. Don't cling to the dead.

ESTHER: I know, I know. When you wrote me that you were getting married, I was so happy for you.

OSCAR: You don't think I was foolish to marry a girl so young?

ESTHER: Papa, I've been waiting all my life for you to do just one foolish thing.

OSCAR: Well, I've done it.

ESTHER: Yes, you have. But it's not what you think.

OSCAR: I know, I know. I lost my temper.

ESTHER: She's just as insecure as you are, Papa. Maybe even more so.

OSCAR: So what am I supposed to do, apologize?

ESTHER: Would that be so terrible? "To know your cause is just." Isn't that enough?

LABOR OF LOVE

OSCAR: Is she in there now?

ESTHER: I'll call her out.

OSCAR: That isn't necessary

ESTHER: We're going for a walk anyway.

> *(SHE knocks on the door. The door is opened and DOROTHY appears.)*

ESTHER: Papa wants to talk to you. I'll go and change. *(SHE goes off.)*

OSCAR: I'm supposed to apologize.

DOROTHY: You don't have to.

OSCAR: I don't have to eat but, somehow, I feel much better when I do.

DOROTHY: You are a paradox, Oscar Zeller.

OSCAR: And you are not the simplest creature on earth.

DOROTHY: I do wish you would take it easy.

OSCAR: Look, I've never taken it easy in my life, and I never will. The few vacations I took I nearly went out of my mind. You saw how restless I was on our honeymoon.

DOROTHY: Yes, my dear. Oscar, sweet, you can't change the world single-handed.

LABOR OF LOVE

OSCAR: As a matter of fact, I have, to some extent. And you must admit, that if I was ever in a position to change the course of history, it's right now, at this very moment.

DOROTHY: You make me feel so useless.

OSCAR: Come here. What do you want most out of life?

DOROTHY: To make you happy.

OSCAR: And what do you think makes me happy? To come home and find that your day has been full, and that your life is rich.

DOROTHY: I feel that I should be at your side, the way Goldie was.

OSCAR: You are not Goldie. I want you to be yourself.

DOROTHY: And what, exactly, am I?

OSCAR: You're a woman, and that's a job in itself.

DOROTHY: And you're always making fun of me. You think I'm weak and spineless. Well, I am weak and decadent, and I have no cause, like you have.

OSCAR: You have me and mine.

DOROTHY: You do need me, don't you?

OSCAR: I can't tell you how much.

DOROTHY: Every once in a while, you might try. Just a look, a word.

LABOR OF LOVE

OSCAR: I'll remember that.

DOROTHY: You're so solemn. Like an owl. A wise old owl. That's better. You have the sweetest smile. You ought to use it more often.

OSCAR: I'll keep that in mind, and as far as Lochinvar is concerned...young Sebastian...you can have him here any time you like.

DOROTHY: The only thing is he may have some news from home. Daddy hasn't been well. And I suppose you're right in regard to Esther. He's not the sort of man for her. She's really very sweet.

OSCAR: I thought we were close, and now I find out she was almost married, and I knew nothing about it.

DOROTHY: What happened?

OSCAR: He was killed, in the war.

DOROTHY: Oh, poor thing. And here we are squabbling about absolutely nothing. Where have you been all morning?

OSCAR: I had some appointments at the office.

DOROTHY: One of these days I'm going to kidnap you, and whisk you away to some desert island, where there'll be nothing but me and some coconuts. They're very nourishing, you know.

(CARL enters downstage left.)

CARL: Domestic bliss. What a wonderful picture this would make for the front-piece of my book.

LABOR OF LOVE

DOROTHY: Am I going to be in that book of yours?

CARL: I've got to inject some glamor into that dreary tale of strikes and politics.

DOROTHY: Will you be long?

OSCAR: Half an hour. That's all he gets. It's ridiculous. Writing a biography of a man while he's still in his infancy.

DOROTHY: Do you have John's phone number?

CARL: He's at the Statler.

DOROTHY: Let me know when you're finished. *(SHE goes off.)*

CARL: You're very lucky.

OSCAR: I thought you didn't approve of my marriage.

CARL: Whatever gave you that idea? Did you read the chapter?

OSCAR: Where did you get this information?

CARL: Now you know I can't tell you that.

OSCAR: Even if your facts were accurate, we couldn't possibly print it.

CARL: Are you afraid of the truth?

OSCAR. That chapter is not to be used. I don't underhand. Up until now, you painted such a glowing picture of me I thought I was reading the life of a saint. And now suddenly I'm a murderer? We

LABOR OF LOVE

had thugs in the union, yes, but they were union members. I didn't go out and hire them.

CARL: Who did?

OSCAR: No one. They were there.

CARL: You had absolutely no idea these men worked for Camilio.

OSCAR: I did not.

CARL: You're a liar.

OSCAR: What are you trying to prove?

CARL: I'm not trying to prove anything. I'm just trying to tell the truth.

OSCAR: That is not the truth. And even if it were, what's to be gained by printing that?

CARL: Labor is infected with crooks, gangsters, hoodlums...

OSCAR: Not the Amalgamated. I'm asking you, as a friend, destroy that chapter.

CARL: Ah, but you see, I'm not writing this book as your friend.

OSCAR: This is something new.

CARL: If you had the courage...

OSCAR: What am I, a movie star? For a man in my position a scandal like this would be fatal. You really hate me, don't you?

LABOR OF LOVE

CARL: Oh the contrary. I used to worship you, Oscar. You and my father. Why do you think I write that stupid column of mine three times a week? Because I felt I wasn't worthy to follow in your footsteps, yours and his.

OSCAR: I had nothing to do with your father's death.

CARL: Not directly, perhaps.

OSCAR: Carl, we are on the brink of war. Is this a time for retribution, for pettiness?

CARL: Pettiness?

OSCAR: If I were to follow your logic, I would seek revenge on every capitalist in this country, as well as the police.

CARL: Goldie's death was entirely different. Goldie's death was an accident.

OSCAR: Because she wasn't your wife?

CARL: I was very fond of Goldie.

OSCAR: You were in love with her, and you want to destroy me.

CARL: Oh, please.

OSCAR: Your father would have done the same, if he'd been in my position.

CARL: Done what, Oscar? Done what? Hire murderers to butcher for him?

LABOR OF LOVE

OSCAR: Please. Not so loud. I am not ashamed of anything I have ever done. And I thought you were my friend.

CARL: I am your friend, Oscar, your best friend. And shall I tell you why? Because I love the movement more.

OSCAR: Are you a Communist?

CARL: You know me better than that. And please don't call me names.

OSCAR: I have great respect for Communism. There is much to be learned from every economic theory.

CARL: Is that where you learned your ruthlessness?

OSCAR: Don't talk to me about ruthlessness. I've seen you go after a story. You leave no stone unturned.

CARL: And you'd be surprised what crawls out from under. I'm sorry. I didn't mean that.

OSCAR: No, no. Please. Let's be honest. I've committed a crime, and I'm to atone for it. Is that it? All right. Just for the sake of argument; supposing what you wrote in that chapter was factual, and it appeared in print? What would you have accomplished?

CARL: What I set out to do, tell the story of your life. As you yourself said, I'm not writing the story of a saint. Let's not make this book a Hollywood screenplay.

OSCAR: You're a fanatic.

LABOR OF LOVE

CARL We're both fanatics, you and I. If we weren't I'd still be rolling cigars, and you'd be still cutting dresses.

OSCAR: I'm sorry, Carl, but I shall have to withdraw my approval of this project of yours. If you print that chapter, I shall sue you within an inch of your life. Think it over. And if you change your mind, we'll talk some more. *(HE starts off.)*

CARL: Just moment.

OSCAR: Yes?

CARL: The story of how you defied Camilio and ousted him from the union...is that accurate?

OSCAR: Both accurate...and graphic.

CARL: Suppose I tone it down?

OSCAR: No. Either we stick to our original agreement, or I withdraw my approval, and that book will never see the light of day.

CARL: Of course, we do have another alternative.

OSCAR: And what might that be?

CARL: We could change the tone of the biography, make it more personal.

OSCAR: My personal life is not very interesting.

CARL: That isn't true. Your early life in Russia. Your work in the movement over there, your courtship of Goldie. It's all very

LABOR OF LOVE

colorful. And now, after all these years, your second marriage to a girl half your age, especially a girl like Dottie.

OSCAR: What do you mean? A girl like Dottie?

CARL: The difference in your backgrounds, the sort of life she's led. That would make a story in itself.

OSCAR: What do you know about Dottie?

CARL: I know everything. I doubt if you can say the same.

OSCAR: Are you trying to blackmail me?

CARL: Oscar, please. Would I do anything as crude as that?

OSCAR: Apparently you've given this alternative a great deal of thought, and effort.

CARL: I'm interested in people.

OSCAR: Yes, I know all about that locked file of yours. So Dottie and I are in there, too.

CARL: You're in illustrious company. I assure you. Did she tell you about a certain New Years party, nine years ago? She was the belle of the ball. Did she ever mention Stella Martin?

OSCAR: Who is Stella Martin?

CARL: A notorious lesbian. And the night she smoked crack?

OSCAR: Dottie had a great emotional problem when she was young, and she's worked it out. And as to these incidents you're

LABOR OF LOVE

referring to... She offered to tell me about them. I didn't want to hear them. All I'm concerned with is the present, and the future.

CARL: Ah, but the past, the present and the future are one.

OSCAR: Where is this all leading to?

CARL: How much faith have you in your wife? Would you be willing to stake your career on her character?

OSCAR: I'm not a gambler, Carl. And I find this talk offensive.

CARL: I say your wife is now what she has always been. If I'm wrong, I'll destroy those three pages. If I'm not, they go to press.

OSCAR: I would never even entertain such a bargain. The character of my wife is something private.

CARL: But you're sure of her, aren't you? Actually I'm giving you the best of the bargain. Because if you take me to court, it will hit the papers and it will all come out, whether you like it or not.

OSCAR: All right.

CARL: I want this in writing. The wording, of course, subject to your approval.

OSCAR: Let's go into my study.

> (OSCAR and CARL go off, closing the door behind them. ESTHER enters. SHE starts for the study, when there's a knock on the outside door. ESTHER opens the door and JOHN is discovered.)

LABOR OF LOVE

ESTHER: Well, hello.

JOHN: Is Mr. Newman in?

ESTHER: I think so. Would you like to come in?

JOHN: I don't know whether I should or not. Is your father in?

ESTHER: He's not here at the moment.

JOHN: Oh, well. What have I got to lose?

ESTHER: Can I get you a drink?

JOHN: Ah, no, Honey, no.

ESTHER: You had too much last night. Well, you know what they say. Something about the "hair of the dog..."

JOHN: I'm sure you mean well, but I belong to A. A..

ESTHER: Oh, I'm sorry. I didn't know.

JOHN: That's quite all right. Mr. Newman said he wanted to see me. I suppose I should have called first, but the message said that he'd be in.

ESTHER: He might be in with my father. *(SHE approaches the door to knock.)*

JOHN: No, please. Will they be long, do you think?

ESTHER: It's hard to tell.

LABOR OF LOVE

JOHN: Did your father say anything about what happened last night?

ESTHER: He said that you got high, and said some rather offensive things. What did you say?

JOHN: I'm not quite sure. But I've got a vague suspicion that I owe him an apology.

ESTHER: If it affects you that way, why do you drink?

JOHN: It's a habit, a refuge.

ESTHER: Are you still in love with Dottie? Is that why you drink?

JOHN: No, no. I drank long before that.

ESTHER: I shouldn't be asking you these personal questions.

JOHN: That's quite all right. I'm used to it. That's what we do at those meetings. I can go on for hours about how no one ever loved me as a child. How each succeeding step-parent was ghastlier than the one before. How I had nothing but money, and how I could never think of anything I wanted to buy. I can see that you're a very serious young lady.

ESTHER: Is that too awful?

JOHN: I think it's rather charming. Your father doesn't approve of me, you know.

ESTHER: I know. However I do have a mind of my own. Have you ever been to Washington before?

LABOR OF LOVE

JOHN: Once or twice, briefly.

ESTHER: It's my favorite city, except for Paris. I can show you the sights, if you're willing to put up with my sober disposition.

JOHN: That's very sweet of you

ESTHER: But you're much too busy.

JOHN: Oh, no. It isn't that. It's just that I've offended your father already, and he might not approve. Let me give you a ring? What time would be best for you?

ESTHER: I have nothing planned for the next three weeks. You're anxious to see Carl. I'll get him for you.

JOHN: Thank you.

> *(ESTHER knocks at the door and goes off. JOHN paces about. DOROTHY enters.)*

DOROTHY: Oh, John. I wasn't expecting you.

JOHN: You know me. Always the unexpected. You're looking great.

DOROTHY: Have you come to apologize?

JOHN: Mr. Newman left a message for me to get in touch with him.

DOROTHY: You seem to have hit it off with Carl.

LABOR OF LOVE

JOHN: I sense a kindred spirit. So, here we are, years later and miles apart.

DOROTHY: Weren't we always miles apart?

JOHN: Did you hear about poor Fred Culpepper? He killed himself.

DOROTHY: Oh, no! When was this?

JOHN: A few weeks ago. The train stopped with a jerk, and Fred got off. His favorite joke.

DOROTHY: Poor Fred. I saw him just before my marriage, and he seemed genuinely happy for me.

(CARL enters.)

CARL: I'm sorry. I didn't mean to intrude.

DOROTHY: John's here to see you.

CARL: How's your head this afternoon?

JOHN: Actually I was rather good after I left here.

CARL: And now we've got to find a way to restore you into the good graces of Mr. Zeller.

JOHN: That will take some doing, I'm afraid.

DOROTHY: Why is it so necessary for you to be on good terms with Oscar?

LABOR OF LOVE

JOHN: I'm here on business with your husband. I've been working for your father for several months now.

DOROTHY: How did that come about?

JOHN: Your guess is as good as mine.

DOROTHY: How is he?

JOHN: Not too well.

DOROTHY: Does he talk about me at all?

JOHN: Not really. But he thinks about you, I know that. And he's given up on Junior. So I guess I've been elected to take your place.

DOROTHY: I always felt that you two could get along, if he ever gave you a chance.

JOHN: Well, he has now, and I've let him down.

DOROTHY: You should have come to me. What exactly do you want?

JOHN: An appointment with your husband. That's all. Just an appointment. The old man's willing to make room for the union. And he can switch production, just like that. Did I say something wrong?

DOROTHY: No, no. It's just that I've never seen you like this, so businesslike. You should have come to me first. *(To CARL)* What's he doing now?

CARL: He's going over his speech for tonight's dinner.

LABOR OF LOVE

DOROTHY: Good. He'll need an audience. I'll get in touch with you tonight. Wish me luck. *(SHE taps lightly on the door and goes off.)*

CARL: She's quite a girl.

JOHN: Yes, she is, only I was too dumb to see it.

CARL: Well, you have nothing to worry about now.

JOHN: Do you really think he'll see me?

CARL: Oscar will do anything to prevent Dottie from leaving him.

JOHN: You think she regrets the marriage?

CARL: What do you think?

JOHN: She seemed glad to see me. Are they happy, do you think?

CARL: With Oscar, it's hard to tell. He's always wrapped up in his work.

JOHN: Which couldn't possibly interest Dottie.

CARL: And, as far as Dottie is concerned, you know her better than I do.

JOHN: She hasn't changed. I could see that same look in her eye. I think she married Zeller just to spite the old man. That's the only reason that makes any sense. I can't thank you enough, Mr. Newman. If I can help you in any way with your biography, I mean in regard to Dottie.

LABOR OF LOVE

CARL: There's plenty of time. I'll make an appointment for you through my secretary.

JOHN: Can I buy you a drink?

CARL: Not right now.

JOHN: Do you think I ought to wait around?

CARL: She said she'd call you.

JOHN: That's right, she did. *(HE starts toward the door and stops.)* And say Carl...

CARL: Yes? What is it?

JOHN: I feel awful about the things I said. I mean about the Jews. I mean I don't hate the Jews. It's just that they're rather pushy. I mean, speaking generally. Take you for instance, and Mr. Zeller. You're not like that at all. And his daughter's quite charming. As a matter of fact, I have several Jewish friends.

CARL: We'll soon have you converted.

JOHN: And I think it's a shame what's happening to the Jews over in Europe right now. I just want you to know that, that's all.

CARL: We'll be in touch.

JOHN: Right. Thanks again.

> *(JOHN shakes CARL's hand. CARL sees him out as OSCAR enters.)*

LABOR OF LOVE

OSCAR: Who was that, that just left.

CARL: John Sebastian the third, reformed alcoholic, and lover of the Jews.

OSCAR: Please, put this chapter away. I don't want these pages laying around.

CARL: Surely you're not afraid to let your family know the truth.

OSCAR: Put them away.

(DOROTHY enters.)

DOROTHY: I insist on reading that chapter.

CARL: It's up to Oscar.

OSCAR: What was John Sebastian doing here?

CARL: Now, now. Just because you don't get along with him, doesn't mean that others can't.

DOROTHY: Stop changing the subject.

OSCAR: Dottie, please. I've told you once and for all, I don't want you to read this chapter.

(ESTHER enters.)

DOROTHY: What could there possibly be in those pages that you wouldn't want me to see? I mean, after all, this book is going to be sold across the country...we hope.

LABOR OF LOVE

OSCAR: After it's been edited. There are inaccuracies that I want corrected.

DOROTHY: Just tell me what they are, and I'll ignore them.

ESTHER: Oh, Papa, don't be such a stuffed shirt. I've never known you to be vain, and you're certainly not ashamed of what you've done.

OSCAR: If you must know, our friend here, and I use the term loosely, insists that I had dealings with Victor Camilio.

DOROTHY: That's ridiculous.

OSCAR: Of course, you must understand, the war between Labor and Capital is a very real one, and the use of gangsters is not uncommon. As a matter of fact, there have been unions that hired gunmen to fight the Communists who were threatening to take over. We never did that. We fought the Reds in our own quiet way, and we got rid of them, as a threat, I mean. What I mean to say is, Carl's accusation is not unbelievable.

DOROTHY: Is it true?

CARL: She's asking you a question, Oscar.

OSCAR: That is not the point. I have work to do, vital work, and with an allegation like this, I would be asked to step down. The president would have no choice.

DOROTHY: What exactly do you hope to gain by printing this slander?

OSCAR: Dottie, please. This is a matter between Carl and myself.

LABOR OF LOVE

ESTHER: If it's a lie, you have nothing to worry about.

DOROTHY: Of course, it's a lie. I'm ashamed of you, Carl. I thought you were a friend of ours.

CARL: Friendship excuses nothing.

DOROTHY: In other words, in printing these lies, you feel you're performing a public service.

CARL: Something like that. And they aren't lies.

DOROTHY: You have proof, I suppose.

CARL: As a matter of fact, I do.

OSCAR: There's no point in arguing with him, Dottie. I'm sure Carl will come to his senses. Besides, we have an understanding.

DOROTHY: I see. Go change your clothes, dear.

OSCAR: I won't be long. *(HE goes off.)*

DOROTHY: What sort of an understanding?

CARL: It's private.

DOROTHY: Then you won't print that chapter.

CARL: On the contrary, it will go to press as is, with his approval.

DOROTHY: You are an enigma. On the one hand you pretend to...almost worship Oscar..and here you are setting out to destroy him.

LABOR OF LOVE

CARL: Nothing can destroy Oscar Zeller

DOROTHY: What is this proof?

CARL: That's my affair.

DOROTHY: I won't pretend to understand your motives, Carl.

CARL: With the sort of life you've led, and the background you have, I doubt if you would understand.

DOROTHY: You really are a nasty person. It's a wonder, that in all these years, Oscar hasn't seen through you.

CARL: Perhaps he has, and perhaps I've been of use to him, up until now.

DOROTHY: You think everyone is as ruthless as you are?

CARL: No, my dear. My father was not, and he was beaten to death. Your husband thinks I hold a personal grudge against him, but he's wrong.

DOROTHY: You hold a grudge against the world. Is that it? I'm warning you, Carl. Oscar's a gentle person, and he'll fight fair. But when it comes to a fight, I don't concern myself with the rules. For one thing, Barbara Camelot is a friend of mine. We went to school together.

CARL: Richard Camelot is in business to sell books, not to do favors for his daughter. But even if he should be that foolish, there are lots of other publishers.

DOROTHY: Oscar has many friends as well, many powerful

LABOR OF LOVE

friends, and between the two of us, your book will never see the light of day. Think it over, my dear.

CARL: You are your father's daughter, after all.

DOROTHY: And you are a son-of-a-bitch. *(To ESTHER)* I'm sorry, my dear. Excuse me. *(SHE goes off, slamming the door behind her.)*

CARL: So, there we are. If I had any misgivings about airing all of this, it was because of you. Whom do you despise more, your father or me?

ESTHER: I don't despise either one of you. In a world as complicated as ours, it's hard to know the right thing to do. There are many people fighting Hitler now who were his sponsors once. They had their reasons then, and they have their reasons now.

CARL: It isn't always easy to look in the mirror and like what you see. I've done things that have made me sick to my stomach. But there are times when one has to wade through shit. I know your father's worth better than anyone, but the cause of labor is bigger than one man's career. There were other men as well, and everyone of them had to start at the bottom, because that's where the Labor movement came from, the sweatshops and the cellars and the attics. I have a college degree, and how do you think I got it? I worked in the steel mills and I went to school at night. It took me seven years. I dipped my pen in my sweat and my blood, and that's what I wrote my columns with. Your father's success came easily, compared to mine, and without your mother behind him, he would still be cutting dresses. She would have made a great man of anyone. Oh, yes, I think your father's a great man, and if you hate me for what I'm doing, I will understand.

LABOR OF LOVE

ESTHER: Oh, Carl, I've come to the point where I'm incapable of hating anyone. I lost someone very dear to me in the war, and I can't even hate the Germans. There are Germans being killed every day. I'm ashamed to admit it, but I keep asking myself, "Is it really important whether the human race survives or not?"

CARL: You mustn't talk like that. You're on the threshold of life, and he's neglected you shamefully. If I'd been lucky enough to have a daughter like you...

ESTHER: It's never too late. You're still a young man.

CARL: In the mind, maybe.

ESTHER: Papa's older than you, and look at him.

CARL: Exactly.

ESTHER: Don't you think they're happy?

(CARL shrugs.)

ESTHER: Sometimes I look at the families I know, and I feel sorry for them. None of them have any privacy. And then I look at the spinsters I know, and family life doesn't look that bad.

CARL: Don't you ever think about spinsterhood.

ESTHER: You seem to enjoy your bachelorhood.

CARL: It's different for a man.

ESTHER: You were in love with Mama, weren't you?

LABOR OF LOVE

CARL: I suppose I could have been, if I'd let myself. And besides, she never cared for me in that way.

ESTHER: I've always been fond of you.

CARL: That's because I always brought you toys, and took you for walks.

ESTHER: You're a fine man, and whatever you've done, you've done because you thought it was right.

CARL: "If the cause is just." Everyone believes in what they do, even a murderer. Would you want me to suppress that chapter? I'm asking you.

ESTHER: I want you to do what you have to do. But just make sure you have the proof.

CARL: You're the spitting image of your mother.

(DOROTHY and OSCAR enter.)

CARL: Excuse me.

DOROTHY: With pleasure.

(CARL goes off.)

OSCAR: There's no point in being uncivil. Are we ready for our walk?

ESTHER: I don't feel up to it. Besides I've got some letters I've got to get off.

LABOR OF LOVE

DOROTHY: I don't know how you can bear to be in the same room with that man.

OSCAR: Now, Dottie. He is her godfather.

ESTHER: I'm fond of Carl. I always have been.

DOROTHY: You're not actually taking his side, are you?

ESTHER: I'm not taking anyone's side.

DOROTHY: That amounts to the same thing.

OSCAR: Dottie, please. Let's not make an issue of it.

DOROTHY: Turning against your own father.

ESTHER: Oh?

DOROTHY: In my case it's different. My father's a martinet, a dictator.

OSCAR: It's quite possible that Esther has the same opinion of me. You did, yesterday afternoon.

DOROTHY: This is something entirely different. That man's an opportunist. He's made use of your father for all this time, and now it suits his purpose to destroy him.

OSCAR: Are you condemning me for what I've been accused of doing?

ESTHER: No, of course not.

LABOR OF LOVE

OSCAR: But you think it's true.

ESTHER: Yes, I do. And I'd respect you more if you had the courage to admit it. To us, at any rate.

OSCAR: You make a bargain with the devil, and it will haunt you for the rest of your life.

DOROTHY: You wouldn't be human, if you hadn't made one mistake.

OSCAR: I didn't call them in. One of the locals did. I didn't hear about it, till afterwards. They were taking an awful beating. The police, the government, they just stood by, watched and collected the graft. Then another local called them in. This was shortly after your mother was killed. She was picketing peacefully. The police, on horseback, tried to break it up. She was ridden down by one of New York's finest. I was being urged on all sides. "We must defend ourselves," they hollered. But I'd seen enough of violence in Russia, violence and tyranny. But finally, against my better judgement, I gave in. I met with Camilio. There was nothing signed, but there were witnesses, on both sides. If I had it to do over again, I would have listened to my conscience.

DOROTHY: You don't have to explain to us.

OSCAR: But I do, above all to you. The both of you. In my darkest hour, I've always been sustained by the love of those that were close to me.

ESTHER: You were lucky. Not everyone has been blessed like that.

OSCAR: I haven't been much of a father, I know. Your mother and

LABOR OF LOVE

I should never have had a child. Not that we didn't want you. It's just that we couldn't make the time for you.

DOROTHY: But you did rid your union of those gangsters, didn't you?

OSCAR. Yes, I did. And, in all fairness to Carl, he's told the entire story from beginning to end. I'm not condemning him. He is and he's always been as devoted to the Labor movement as I've been. And in a way, the movement means more to him than it does to me, since he has nothing else.

DOROTHY: *(To ESTHER)* Perhaps, if you had a talk with him.

ESTHER: I have.

DOROTHY: Oh? And?

ESTHER: I told him to follow his own consience.

DOROTHY: That was hateful of you.

ESTHER: I'm sorry. And I'm not being spiteful, I assure you I'm not. I'm sure you didn't marry my father in order to upset yours. And when I told John Sebastian this afternoon, that I would be glad to see him, it was only because I think I would enjoy his company.

DOROTHY: If there's anything you want to know about John Sebastian, just come o me.

ESTHER: Do you object to my seeing him?

LABOR OF LOVE

DOROTHY: No, of course not. It's just that I don't think it's going to lead anywhere.

ESTHER: When Daddy objected to my seeing him, why did you put up such an argument.

DOROTHY: I just didn't approve of the tone he used. That was all.

ESTHER: Well, I can assure you, I've been making my own decisions for as along as I can remember. And now that I've over twenty-one, my family's relieved of even the legal responsibility. Enjoy your walk. *(SHE goes off.)*

OSCAR: Let her go, Dottie, please.

DOROTHY: I'll have a talk with John. How could you be so deceived in that man. The minute I met him I felt instinctively that there was something sneaky about him.

OSCAR: Let's wait and see. It helps to know that you're in my corner. I've always found that a woman aroused is worth twenty men.

DOROTHY: You're making fun of me again.

OSCAR: Indeed I'm not. The first strike I was ever involved in, do you know who started it?

DOROTHY: Who?

OSCAR: Goldie.

DOROTHY: She must have been quite a woman. Shall we go?

LABOR OF LOVE

OSCAR: I'd just as soon sit here for a while, if you don't mind.

(THEY sit.)

DOROTHY: You know, my dear, you don't know how lucky you are having such a wonderful purpose. Some people go through life with no direction whatsoever. Like I did, and John. But I've been lucky. Meeting you has given me a new lease on life. Poor John is still struggling to find one. Do you know why he's here in Washington?

OSCAR: I don't know, and I don't care.

DOROTHY: That's not like you. I've said that I would speak to him about Esther.

OSCAR: And I said that wasn't necessary Unless you need some excuse to see him.

DOROTHY: You're not jealous?

OSCAR: Have I reason to be? We've quarreled continually since his name came up. Why is he here? Who sent for him?

DOROTHY: He's here on business. He's trying to make a new life for himself.

OSCAR: With whose help?

DOROTHY: With mine, for one. I volunteered to help him.

OSCAR: I see.

LABOR OF LOVE

DOROTHY: It's ridiculous for you to be jealous of John. It's as silly as for me to be jealous of Goldie.

OSCAR: Goldie is dead.

DOROTHY: And so is John, as far as I'm concerned. And for that matter, Goldie is far from dead.

OSCAR: You can't ask Goldie to dinner. And Goldie can't call you names, or try to seduce your daughter.

DOROTHY: Oh, Oscar, don't be such a fool.

OSCAR: Then why don't you want Esther to see him?

DOROTHY: Because I'm saving him for myself.

OSCAR: I'm beginning to think that you are.

DOROTHY: What sort of names did he call you?

OSCAR: If you must know, he called me "a fat old Jew." I'm glad you find that amusing.

DOROTHY: John is not himself when he's drunk.

OSCAR: On the contrary. I think that's exactly when he's himself.

DOROTHY: You can't take it seriously.

OSCAR: Oh, but I do. I take it very seriously. When I came here to America I thought this was the land of the free, the land of brotherly love. I guess a dirty Jew is a dirty Jew no matter where

LABOR OF LOVE

you go. But the Germans are working on it. They'll solve the problem for you. You don't know what it's like to be a Jew. I can't blame you for that. But how can you be so insensitive?

DOROTHY: Oscar, John is nobody. He can afford his faults. But, at the moment, you are one of the most important men in this country, and you've got to rise above your personal feelings. My father has a genuine business offer to make.

OSCAR: I've had dealings with your father. He's a despot, a pirate. a money grabbing thief.

DOROTHY: You haven't even heard his offer.

OSCAR: And that's why Mr. Sebastian is here?

DOROTHY: Why do you think he's here?

OSCAR: To make an offer of his own.

DOROTHY: I just can't talk to you when you're like this.

OSCAR: Go talk to your fiancee then.

DOROTHY: Is that what you want?

OSCAR: Isn't that what you want?

DOROTHY: If you don't know by now, then our marriage has been built on pretty rocky ground. I need some air. Are you coming or not?

OSCAR: Go to your lover. I won't stand in your way. Go on, go on. Don't let me stop you.

LABOR OF LOVE

DOROTHY: Okay.

OSCAR: Will you be back in time for the dinner this evening?

DOROTHY: Is that what you're concerned about? What people will say?

OSCAR: I can always make some excuse.

DOROTHY: Well, you'd better start thinking of a good one. Are you coming or aren't you?

OSCAR: I've got to go over my speech.

DOROTHY: You just went over it.

OSCAR: Again. May I ask where you're going?

DOROTHY: I'm going to John's room, and we'll both get loaded, and, who knows, I may just spend the night there.

OSCAR: In that case, you needn't bother coming back.

DOROTHY: Oh, go to hell!

> (SHE goes off, slamming the door behind her. After a moment, CARL enters.)

CARL: I thought you were going for a walk.

OSCAR: The plans have changed.

CARL: Had a quarrel?

LABOR OF LOVE

OSCAR: Not really.

CARL: Good. *(HE starts off.)*

OSCAR: Carl. Just a minute.

CARL: Yes? What is it?

OSCAR: That little agreement we made.

CARL: What about it?

OSCAR: I'm sorry, but I can't go along with it.

CARL: What a pity! And here I've got your signature.

(CARL goes off. OSCAR sinks into a chair as the lights come down.)

ACT THREE

(Several hours later. ESTHER is discovered reading. CARL enters from the outside.)

CARL: What are you reading?

ESTHER: Your book. I hope you don't mind. It was lying on your desk.

CARL: What do you think of it?

ESTHER: It's quite well written. What made you become a columnist?

CARL: The book is about your father.

ESTHER: Like most biographies, it reveals as much about the writer, as it does the subject.

CARL: And what do you see, oh wise one?

ESTHER: Why can't you talk simply and openly about yourself? Why must there always be some cynical comment?

CARL: You're a regular intellectual. Just like your mother.

ESTHER: Were you in love with my mother?

CARL: I have never been in love. That is to say, I've never allowed myself to fall in love. And please, I am not a homosexual.

ESTHER: What are your feelings toward my father?

CARL: I have great respect for him.

LABOR OF LOVE

ESTHER: And for yourself?

CARL: You want me to withdraw that chapter.

ESTHER: Why is it so important to you what I think?

CARL: You're one of the few people in this world that means something to me. You want to know the difference between me and your father? Parenthood. It's the one human relationship that I respect. I honored my parents when they were alive, and if I had children, they would never have wanted for anything.

ESTHER: Then why haven't you had any children of your own?

CARL: In order to have a child, one has to have a wife. I am not that unique, and I am not an unhappy man. I have a social life, and my work is all.

ESTHER: Suppose you're faced with a libel suit?

CARL: It'll never come to that.

ESTHER: You have witnesses.

CARL: I do.

ESTHER: Respectable ones? Ones whose testimony would hold up in court. No union member will testify against Oscar Zeller. You know that, don't you?

CARL: And documents as well.

ESTHER: With signatures. Papa's, of course, and Camilio's.

LABOR OF LOVE

CARL: Don't you worry about your father.

ESTHER: Myrna called before. She's not feeling well. She's pregnant, you know.

CARL: She won't let me forget it.

ESTHER: You'll need someone to take her place.

CARL: That's true.

ESTHER: I'd like to apply for the job.

CARL: What are your qualifications?

ESTHER: As far as labor is concerned, I'm a fund of knowledge. I'm quite intelligent. My legs aren't bad, and I can type.

CARL: Can you take short-hand?

ESTHER: By time the job is vacant, I'll be an expert.

CARL: I shall give your application my most serious consideration.

    (OSCAR enters.)

OSCAR: I beg your pardon. I thought I heard Dottie's voice.

CARL: Esther would like to work for me. Would you have any objection?

OSCAR: And if I did?

CARL: I wouldn't want her to take the job without your approval.

LABOR OF LOVE

OSCAR: Since when have you been so concerned about my approval?

CARL: I've always sought your approval, Oscar. You know that. And I'm sure Esther feels the same.

OSCAR: Then you're more certain of her than I am.

CARL: I think I'll take a quick shower. Excuse me. *(HE goes off.)*

ESTHER: Have you and Dottie had a quarrel?

OSCAR: No, no. She had some last minute errands to take care of. So, you've gone over to the enemy camp.

ESTHER: Then you object to my working with him.

OSCAR: Why not me? I could make a place for you.

ESTHER: Myrna's pregnant. It would only be until she comes back.

OSCAR: Which might be never.

ESTHER: He needs me, Papa.

OSCAR: It's no consequence to you that he's set out to ruin your father.

ESTHER: It's all a bluff. Did you sign anything with Camilio?

OSCAR: No. But there were witnesses.

LABOR OF LOVE

ESTHER: Do you really think that a union member would testify against you?

OSCAR: There were others.

ESTHER: Gangsters? And you think their word would carry any weight?

OSCAR: *(After a moment)* But I did sign something. Something rather foolish. How in the world did I get to be where I am, a man so stupid, so blind? What will you do this evening? Would you care to come with me tonight?

ESTHER: That's an official dinner.

OSCAR: Dottie may not be up to it. Why don't you get dressed, just in case? Have you anything to wear?

ESTHER: I have something that might just pass. Let's hope that Dottie's okay. You're a very lucky man. *(SHE kisses him and goes off.)*

OSCAR: I used to think so.

> *(HE goes to the phone, hesitates, picks it up, changes his mind, puts it down and goes off. A moment later DOROTHY enters, starts for her room, changes her mind and sits. There's a knock at the door. DOROTHY opens the door and JOHN enters)*

JOHN: I just missed you on the elevator.

DOROTHY: I said I would call you, John.

LABOR OF LOVE

JOHN: I have some rather upsetting news.

DOROTHY: He's dead.

JOHN: He died this morning. Ruth was with him. I came to mean a great deal to him. And it's a funny thing. It's the closest I came to having a father.

DOROTHY: Does Junior know?

JOHN: Not yet, I don't think.

DOROTHY: I can't believe he's dead. I've been fighting so long to be free of him, and now I wonder...was it him I wanted to be free of.

JOHN: It may be hard for you to believe, but your father had faith in me, and I didn't want to let him down. It wasn't easy to take a good look at myself, but I did.

DOROTHY: I know what you mean.

JOHN: Do you, Dottie? Oh, Honey... What a fool I've been. This is not the time, I know. But I can wait.

DOROTHY: John, I...

JOHN: You're not still kidding yourself?

DOROTHY: I think you'd better go.

JOHN: Are you going to try to convince me that you're happy?

DOROTHY: I don't have to convince you of anything.

LABOR OF LOVE

JOHN: You're not really in love with that man?

DOROTHY: Would you believe me if I said that to me Oscar Zeller is Prince Charming, Lochinvar and Lord Byron all rolled into one?

JOHN: Hardly Lord Byron.

DOROTHY: Poor John. You still have a lot to learn.

JOHN: Oh, come off it, Dottie. This is Johnny boy you're talking to. I've seen you naked.

DOROTHY: *(SHE slaps him.)* I'm sorry. I shouldn't have done that.

JOHN: Forget it. It's just like old times. We made some beautiful music together. Didn't we, Baby? We're pagans, you and I. And besides, your father would have wanted this.

DOROTHY: I don't want to hurt you, John. And I know it may be hard for you to believe, but Oscar Zeller is the most beautiful man I've ever known.

JOHN: I think you really mean that. And the fact that he's a Jew...? I'm sorry.

DOROTHY: No, no. That's quite all right. I'm beginning to understand a lot of things.

JOHN: It's just that... You see, I was led to believe that you still cared.

DOROTHY: You've been talking to Carl.

LABOR OF LOVE

JOHN: Well, yes. And I guess I am still in love with you. I don't understand it. I mean you're being in love with a man like that...but maybe I will some day. And I am learning to face up to things. I really am.

DOROTHY: I'm sure you are. And I'm sure Daddy wouldn't have put so much trust in you, if he didn't see something there. I suppose I should fly up for the funeral, even if he wouldn't have wanted me there.

> (OSCAR *appears in the doorway, in his shirtsleeves, a bow tie in his hand.*)

JOHN: I'm flying up tomorrow afternoon. We could go up together.

DOROTHY: I don't want to make any plans until I've spoken with Oscar.

JOHN: But you will come up.

DOROTHY: I'll be there. Oh, God I'm not up to that dinner tonight.

OSCAR: There's no need for you to go. There's no need for you to put up with anything you have no taste for.

DOROTHY: Oscar, please.

JOHN: You don't understand.

DOROTHY: John, please. Let me handle this. Please go. I'll call you later.

LABOR OF LOVE

OSCAR: I'd like him to stay.

DOROTHY: If you prefer.

OSCAR: I do. I have my weaknesses, just like any man. The fact of the matter is I've always been sensitive about being a Jew. But it's wrong to return prejudice with prejudice, and let it get in the way of my job. I understand you're here as a representative of the Vickers Motor Company. Up until now Mr. Vickers has been unreasonable in regard to unions, and in regard to his workers. I work for the government now, and it's quite possible that Mr. Vickers has had a change of heart. If you'll be in my office tomorrow at nine o'clock, I'll see you, and whomever you wish to bring along.

JOHN: Thank you.

OSCAR: Now in regard to personal matters.

JOHN: Really, there's no need...

OSCAR: Ah, but there is, and I think Dottie will agree with me. When I met Dottie I was an enemy of her father's. At least, that was the way I appeared to her, and certainly to her father. Seeing me was a pleasurable act of treason. She allowed me to fall in love her, and fooled herself into thinking that she was in love with me. Don't misunderstand me. I don't think our marriage was a mistake. As a matter of fact, it's done a great deal for both of us. But now I think it's time to renegotiate. I'm more in love with Dottie than I ever was. But during these past seven months Dottie has come face to face with many facts, some shocking perhaps. And it would be wrong of me to hold her to an outmoded agreement.

LABOR OF LOVE

DOROTHY: That's very noble of you.

JOHN: Mr. Zeller, Dottie has just finished telling me how much she's in love with you. I came here to Washington with the most honorable intentions. As a matter of fact, I hadn't intended to see Dottie until I'd gotten through to you. But then I ran into Mr. Newman yesterday afternoon, and before I knew it, I found myself here in your suite. I'm sure he meant well. I'm sure he couldn't have known the effect it might have on the three of us. He even bawled me out about my drinking, and about my attitude toward the Jews. I'm sure he couldn't have known how sensitive you were on the subject, and how stupidly I would behave.

(CARL enters.)

CARL: Oh, I beg your pardon. Don't let me interrupt. I was just passing through.

OSCAR: Just a moment, Carl. As a matter of fact, we were just talking about you.

CARL: How flattering, I hope.

OSCAR: John, here, has been telling us how you took him on as a sort of protege.

CARL: I'd hardly consider Mr. Sebastian my protege. What exactly have you told my friends, here.

DOROTHY: Your friends?!

CARL: He's obviously neglected to inform you of our little agreement. Shall I tell them or shall you?

LABOR OF LOVE

JOHN: I agreed to tell Mr. Newman what I knew about Dottie. He wanted information for your biography that he was writing. I can assure you, nothing I would have said would have reflected badly on Dottie.

CARL: I see. So, you intended to fill me full of lies.

JOHN: I intended to give you the facts. I assumed, of course, you were writing a respectable book.

CARL: You're both a liar and a cheat.

JOHN: Now let's not start calling each other names. I thought you were my friend.

CARL: Your friend? I hardly know you, sir. And from what I do know, I'm not the least bit interested in furthering our acquaintance.

OSCAR: You are unscrupulous.

CARL: Come, come. We're getting on dangerous ground.

DOTTIE: I think you'd better leave, John.

OSCAR: Let him stay. There's nothing that Carl can say that Mr. Sebastian couldn't hear.

JOHN: I think I'd better go. Whether you meant well or not, Mr. Newman, it's all worked out for the best. So thank you. I'll see you tomorrow at nine, sir. And would you please give my best to your daughter. I was supposed to call her, but since I'll be leaving tomorrow evening, I may not get the opportunity. Good-bye. *(HE goes off.)*

LABOR OF LOVE

CARL: A very deceitful young man. I wouldn't bother seeing him.

DOROTHY: And yet you encouraged him to seek my help.

CARL: That was his idea, not mine.

OSCAR: Let me handle this. Anyone who might be unacquainted with your work, would say, "There goes the devil." But I know your heart. It pumps printer's ink, and appears three times a week for everyone to see. I know, I know. The movement is everything. And that's the difference between us. To me, one human life is worth more than any ten unions, because that one mind is capable of creating the universe.

CARL: Don't speechify to me, Mr. Zeller. You'll use anything to further your career, even your wife's reputation. Does she know that, or is that a secret too? You pretentious ass. A human being! What, my dear Oscar, is a human being? That glorious president of yours? He needs you now. But the moment you've served your usefulness, he'll drop you so fast, it will make your head swim.

DOROTHY: It's getting late. I've got to get dressed.

OSCAR: There's no need to go, if you don't feel up to it.

DOROTHY: I'll be fine. *(SHE goes off.)*

CARL: Having trouble with your tie?

OSCAR: That's all right. Dottie will do it for me.

CARL: If she stays around long enough.

LABOR OF LOVE

OSCAR: You were always jealous of me, weren't you? But if you had really wanted to be an organizer, you could have been one.

CARL: I am what I've always wanted to be.

OSCAR: And what might that be?

CARL: Your conscience, Mr. Labor.

OSCAR: A more ruthless conscience I've never known.

CARL: You were my teacher, Mr. Zeller. The wheels of success, you showed me how they turn, with your overpowering arrogance, your charming immigrant's humility; the affable shrug, the angelic smile. And it was all for the love of man. Well, I'll tell you something, Mr. Zeller, my father was worth ten of you, ten thousand. My father was a saint, and he was beaten to death by the thugs that took over. And as for the worker, the common man, the first day my father took me into the union meeting hall, and I saw a strong man sob because he had no job; because he had no money to feed his family...God help me, I wept. And when I saw my father die, day by day, inch by inch, I drowned my pillow in tears.

OSCAR: There are gangsters in labor and I think they should be removed. If you will come to me with proof, I will see to it that you get action. You can publish anything you like, but you'd better have the evidence to back it up.

>(DOROTHY *enters wearing an evening gown, and holding a wrap.*)

DOROTHY: I'm ready, almost. Would you zip me up?

LABOR OF LOVE

OSCAR: *(HE zips her up.)* I'd better tell Esther that you're going. I wasn't sure, and she's getting ready to take your place.

DOROTHY: Let me fix your tie first.

CARL: Apparently you've got your signals crossed. Better straighten them out before you get to the dinner. I'll speak to Esther. *(HE knocks at the door, and goes off.)*

DOROTHY: Did Goldie always do this for you?

OSCAR: When she was there.

DOROTHY: You mean when she was alive.

OSCAR: That's not what I said.

DOROTHY: There you are.

OSCAR: You have very clever hands.

DOROTHY: Thank you, sir.

OSCAR: I was unfaithful to Goldie, you know.

DOROTHY: Why are you telling me this?

OSCAR: I want you to know the truth.

DOROTHY: Was she unfaithful to you?

OSCAR: With another man? Not as far as I know. I'm not like Carl, you see. I need someone, and she was never there when I needed her. I won't try to stop you. You've got your whole life ahead of you. But before you take that plane tomorrow, I want you to know that you are the whole world to me.

DOROTHY: That reference to my reputation. What did Carl mean by that?

OSCAR: The cards were stacked against me, or so I thought, and we made a little bargain. He brought up the past, and said you hadn't changed. I signed an agreement giving him permission to print the book, as he saw fit, if, and if, and if. It would never hold up in court. And besides, the chapter will appear as I wish it to appear.

DOROTHY: Why?

OSCAR: Because he has no proof. If he had, he wouldn't have had to go through all that rigmarole. Please be kind. I was willing to stake my career on your love.

DOROTHY: What I can't understand is how you haven't seen through him in all these years.

OSCAR: What makes you think that I haven't?

DOROTHY: But you treat him as a friend.

OSCAR: He is my friend. We're fond of one another. He's been of great use and besides, I want him close, where I can keep an eye on him.

DOROTHY: Sometimes you frighten me. But I won't be afraid anymore.

OSCAR: And that plane tomorrow?

LABOR OF LOVE

DOROTHY: I did not spend the afternoon with John. He came into the room just a few minutes before you, to tell me that my father died this morning.

OSCAR: I'm so sorry. What a fool I am! If you're not up to the dinner...

DOROTHY: I'd rather go.

OSCAR: Your father was a remarkable man, part of an era we may never see again. The individualist, full of fight and daring.

DOROTHY: I'll get your coat.

> (*DOROTHY goes off. ESTHER enters in an evening gown, followed by CARL.*)

OSCAR: You look very nice.

ESTHER: You chose the right word. Polite and discreet.

CARL: Has Dottie changed her mind?

> (*DOROTHY re-enters with OSCAR's evening jacket and top-coat.*)

DOROTHY: Apparently.

> (*DOROTHY puts down the top-coat and helps OSCAR into the jacket, and looks him over.*)

DOROTHY: Don't we look elegant.

LABOR OF LOVE

OSCAR: One half of us does. *(To CARL)* What's on your agenda for tonight?

CARL: A game of poker, I guess. What about you, Miss Zeller. All dressed up and no place to go.

ESTHER: I'd love to play a game of chess.

CARL: Where's the set?

ESTHER: What about your poker game?

CARL: That doesn't start until midnight.

OSCAR: The set's in my study, on the bookcase, behind my desk.

CARL: I'll be right back. *(HE goes off.)*

OSCAR: I have a message from Mr. Sebastian. He said to give you his best. He's leaving town tomorrow and may not have a chance to get in touch with you.

ESTHER: Thank you. That's quite all right, Papa.

DOROTHY: I'm beginning to think that it's as difficult to be a parent, as it is to be a child. Maybe evem more so.

(CARL re-enters with the chess set.)

CARL: Here we are.

DOROTHY: It's late. We'd better get going.

ESTHER: You look lovely.

LABOR OF LOVE

DOROTHY: Thank you, dear. But then, why shouldn't I? I've never been happier. Good night, Carl.

(DOROTHY goes out the door, which OSCAR is holding open for her.)

CARL: Oh, Oscar.

OSCAR: Yes?

CARL: That little agreement this afternoon. I was only joking.

OSCAR: Of course, you were. God bless. *(HE goes off.)*

ESTHER: *(Holding out her fists each containing a chess piece.)* Choose. You're black. I'm white.

CARL: It's amazing what the prospects of a speech does to your father's ego.

ESTHER: What about that job?

CARL: It's yours, you sly little thing.

ESTHER: It's your move.

CARL: Sorry. Your father thinks I'm the devil.

ESTHER: So do I. But if the devil puts up such a fight, he must really care. You said a while ago that you had an agreement signed by Papa and Camilio.

CARL: Did I?

LABOR OF LOVE

ESTHER: Yes, you did.

CARL: What of it?

ESTHER: That agreement does not exist.

CARL: Then your father has nothing to worry about. It's your move.

ESTHER: Sorry. What were you thinking about?

CARL: The future. *(HE moves.)* It's your move.

ESTHER: What? Oh, yes.

(The lights come down as THEY continue to play.)

THE ESTABLISHMENT

CAST OF CHARACTERS

Cleo Johnson

Dick Johnson

Ben Grady

Ralph Erickson

Bill Donovan

SCENE
An American Metropolis.

TIME
The nineteen sixties.

SCENE ONE

PROSTITUTION

(The living room of a small apartment, furnished sparsely and cheaply, with no particular taste. It is early evening. A radio is playing softly. RALPH ERICKSON enters from the bedroom in a T-shirt and dark trousers. HE stands in front of the mirror, combs his hair neatly and examines himself. HE picks up a bottle of cologne and dabs some on his face and under his arms. The doorbell rings. HE opens the door and CLEO JOHNSON is discovered.)

CLEO: Ralph Erickson?

ERICKSON: You got it.

CLEO: I'm Fanny.

ERICKSON: Come right in.

(CLEO enters as ERICKSON closes the door.)

CLEO: Where's the bedroom?

ERICKSON: What's the rush? Sit down. Take it easy.

(CLEO examines the room.)

ERICKSON: Haven't I seen you somewhere?

(CLEO shrugs.)

ERICKSON: What's that supposed to mean?

CLEO: You wanna just sit and talk?

THE ESTABLISHMENT

ERICKSON: To begin with. Is there anything wrong with that?

CLEO: It's your call, mister.

ERICKSON: Would you care for a drink?

CLEO: What have you got?

ERICKSON: Scotch or beer.

CLEO: Scotch, on the rocks.

ERICKSON: Have a seat.

> (*ERICKSON goes off to the kitchen. CLEO sits, takes off her earrings and places them in her bag. ERICKSON reenters with two drinks and hands her one.*)

CLEO: Thanks.

ERICKSON: Skoal.

CLEO: Skoal.

> (*THEY drink.*)

CLEO: *(Points to photograph.)* Those your parents?

ERICKSON: Yeah.

CLEO: *(After a moment)* You got until ten, you know.

ERICKSON: Yes, I know.

THE ESTABLISHMENT

CLEO: They look like nice people...your parents.

ERICKSON: Thank you. Your parents still alive?

CLEO: Oh, yes.

ERICKSON: Where are you from?

CLEO: Michigan.

ERICKSON: How's the drink?

CLEO: It's okay.

ERICKSON: You like your job? Or should I say profession?

CLEO: It's a job. You like yours?

ERICKSON: It's okay.

CLEO: Or should I say profession?

ERICKSON: I'm just trying to be friendly, to get to know each other.

CLEO: That's what I'm here for, to be friendly. What do you wanna know? I'm married. I got two kids. My husband's in the "poke," and my name isn't Fanny.

ERICKSON: Okay, okay. You sure got a chip on your shoulder.

CLEO: And you keep knocking it off.

ERICKSON: You're not in a very friendly mood.

THE ESTABLISHMENT

CLEO: I got problems.

ERICKSON: What kind of problems?

CLEO: What difference does it make?

ERICKSON: I was just asking.

CLEO: Family problems.

ERICKSON: Your kids?

CLEO: No.

ERICKSON: You got two kids? You sure don't look it.

CLEO: Thank you.

ERICKSON: How old are they?

CLEO: The girl's thirteen. The boy is six.

ERICKSON: You musta been married pretty young. High school romance?

CLEO: Sort of.

ERICKSON: What do you mean, sort of.

CLEO: What difference does it make? We dropped out.

ERICKSON: Yeah, that happens.

THE ESTABLISHMENT

CLEO: Why don't we talk about you?

ERICKSON: What do you wanna know?

CLEO: Where are your parents from?

ERICKSON: They're here, in the city. You're kinda...what's the word?

CLEO: Cynical?

ERICKSON: Yeah, cynical. You always been cynical?

CLEO: No. I grew into it. *(After HE eyes her breasts.)* It's all real. You won't be disappointed. *(SHE rises.)*

ERICKSON: Where you goin'?

CLEO: The way you looked at me...I thought you were ready.

ERICKSON: I'll let you know when I'm ready.

CLEO: Okay, okay. *(SHE sits.)* I'm just trying to be accommodating.

ERICKSON: How much you get a night?

CLEO: Tonight's on the house.

ERICKSON: That's not what I asked you.

CLEO: We're not supposed to discuss money.

ERICKSON: I was just curious.

THE ESTABLISHMENT

CLEO: I gather you're somebody important. I'm not supposed to ask, but if you are important you sure don't live like it. I'm not putting you down or anything. *(SHE finishes her drink.)* How about another shot? Do you mind if I use your phone?

ERICKSON: Help yourself.

> *(ERICKSON takes her glass and his own and goes off to the kitchen. CLEO picks up the phone and dials.)*

CLEO: Are the kids okay? How are they behaving? Well, ten o'clock's their bed time, no matter what. Who? That's the lawyer. Did he leave his number? I'll call him in the morning. What did she want? Okay, okay. I'll call her. I should be home by ten thirty or so. Gotta go.

> *(CLEO hangs up as ERICKSON reenters with the drinks. HE hands her hers.)*

CLEO: Thanks.

ERICKSON: Good news or bad? I heard you mention a lawyer.

CLEO: Do you always listen in on people's conversations?

ERICKSON: You weren't exactly whispering. You must be a good mother.

CLEO: I'm good at everything.

ERICKSON: So I've been told. How long's your old man in for?

CLEO: Why?

THE ESTABLISHMENT

ERICKSON: I'm just curious.

CLEO: It's none of your business.

ERICKSON: Suppose I send in a bad report?

CLEO: It's been done before.

ERICKSON: What happened?

CLEO: Nothing.

ERICKSON: How come?

CLEO: I said the guy was a creep.

ERICKSON: And they took your word for it?

CLEO: That's right.

ERICKSON: You must be a valuable property.

CLEO: I earn my money. How come a guy like you has to pay for it?

ERICKSON: I don't. Remember? You came highly recommended.

CLEO: You must have some pull.

ERICKSON: What have you got on your mind?

CLEO: What?

ERICKSON: You said you had problems.

THE ESTABLISHMENT

CLEO: If you must know, it's my sister. She's in trouble.

ERICKSON: What sort of trouble?

CLEO: She was arrested.

ERICKSON: For what?

CLEO: For selling crack, and for resisting arrest. And she wasn't resisting arrest. That fucking cop wanted her to put out, and when she wouldn't he beat her up, and then he said that she was trying to resist arrest. And he really messed her up, that fucking cop.

ERICKSON: She's got a lawyer, hasn't she?

CLEO: Sometimes the lawyers are as bad as the cops. She's a sweet kid, my sister. She's a dancer. Real pretty. She used to be, until she got hooked. She's still not bad to look at.

ERICKSON: Where does she dance?

CLEO: In a club sometimes. Sometimes at private parties. She's got an agent, not that he does her any good. She always used to dream about being a movie star, like Lena Horne.

ERICKSON: She ever been in a movie?

CLEO: She's done some extra work, that's all. Maybe if she had someone to speak up for her, they might go easy on her.

ERICKSON: Is this the first time she's been pulled in?

CLEO: Yeah.

THE ESTABLISHMENT

ERICKSON: They'll probably go easy on her.

CLEO: How do you know?

ERICKSON: I don't know. I'm just guessing.

CLEO: Don't you have a girl? Someone steady?

ERICKSON: No.

CLEO: How old are you?

ERICKSON: What difference does it make?

CLEO: To me, none.

ERICKSON: I'll get around to it.

CLEO: What?

ERICKSON: Never mind what.

CLEO: Are we gonna spend your time talking?

ERICKSON: Don't worry about it.

CLEO: It's fine with me.

ERICKSON: I think it's much nicer if we're kinda friendly like. I just don't wanna fuck, honey. I wanna FUCK.

CLEO: You're kinna scary, you know?

THE ESTABLISHMENT

ERICKSON: I can assure you, I am a perfect gentleman. But some women just lay there, like a piece of meat. Come here.

(SHE rises and walks over to him. HE rises, takes her in his arms and kisses her. HE looks into her eyes and kisses her again, passionately. SHE responds very professionally.)

ERICKSON: Come on. Let's go.

(HE takes her by the hand and leads her off. The lights slowly dim. The orchestra on the radio plays "Cocktails For Two.)

RADIO ANNOUNCER: Chez Moi. A little French bistro on East Twenty-Third Street just east of Second Avenue. You walk down three short steps and, voila, you are in Paree. Coq au vin like you never tasted before. Steak a la Brochette. Little pieces of tender meat served in a sauce divine. The onion soup, incidentally, is out of this world. I usually don't go in for desserts but I thought I'd try the creme brulee highly recommended by the charming Madame Fedora, the owner. And that's really her name. Honest to God, my toes actually curled at the very first taste. I suggest the fixed price dinner. It's a steal.

(The orchestra has switched to Noel Coward's "Someday I'll Find You." The lights come up and CLEO reenters straightening her dress. SHE opens her purse and applies some lipstick. ERICKSON reenters.)

ERICKSON: My compliments to the chef.

CLEO: What?

THE ESTABLISHMENT

ERICKSON: I'm just trying to pay you a compliment.

CLEO: Thanks.

ERICKSON: You ever been fucked like that? Come on.

CLEO: You're a tiger, Honey.

ERICKSON: How much do you charge?

CLEO: You couldn't afford me.

ERICKSON: How much do you charge?

CLEO: I'm not supposed to discuss price. You take it up with the boss.

ERICKSON: Okay, okay. How about some coffee? I still got forty five minutes.

CLEO: Sure. Why not? You don't mind if I make another call, do you?

ERICKSON: Help yourself.

> *(HE goes into the kitchen. CLEO picks up the phone and dials.)*

ERICKSON: *(Offstage)* How do you take your coffee?

CLEO: Black. Two sugars. *(On the phone)* Hello? Ethel? Mae said you called. Why didn't you tell me you were going? I would have liked to send him some things. How is he? I was up there two weeks ago. What's that supposed to mean? When? Oh, go fuck

THE ESTABLISHMENT

yourself. *(SHE slams the phone down.)* And that's the only way you'll get fucked.

(SHE rises and paces about. ERICKSON enters with two mugs of coffee, and hands her one.)

ERICKSON: What's that all about?

CLEO: My sister-in-law. She's a real bitch. Her husband ran out on her a couple of years ago. She was nasty before that. Now..she's impossible.

ERICKSON: Bad news?

(SHE sits and drinks her coffee.)

ERICKSON: You don't wanna talk about it.

CLEO: My old man may be coming out next week. He's up for parole.

ERICKSON: Does he know what you've been up to, your old man? *(After a moment)* Suppose he finds out? You love him?

(SHE looks at him and sniffs ironically.)

ERICKSON: What's that supposed to mean?

CLEO: I love my kids.

ERICKSON: And what about the old man?

CLEO: He's my husband. I'm his wife.

THE ESTABLISHMENT

ERICKSON: Does your sister-in-law know about this?

CLEO: If she does, I'm in real trouble.

ERICKSON: How'd you get hooked?

CLEO: Sometimes...

ERICKSON: Sometimes...what?

CLEO: Nothing.

ERICKSON: Is it that bad?

CLEO: You're born. You fuck. You die. The only thing worthwhile are the kids.

ERICKSON: You wanna talk about it? Sometimes it's easier to talk to a stranger. Not that I'm that strange.

CLEO: When you're young and you're starting out, everything looks so rosy. Not that I wasn't surrounded by trouble. The neighborhood we lived in... But my life was gonna be different. Dick and me, we were special. Our first year, it was really great. All lovey-dovey. I knew he belonged to a gang. Most of the kids did. What I didn't know were half the things the gang was up to. The first time it was six months for petty larceny. Now he's in for seven. Armed robbery. It's been three years, so far. He's a good man, he really is. He loves the kids, and he's pretty strict with them, which is kind of ironic, don't you think? I mean, when he found out that my sister was pushing dope, he wouldn't let her come around the house. He thought she'd contaminate them. That's my husband for you. And the kids love Mona. I took them to see

THE ESTABLISHMENT

her on the sly, and made the kids promise not to say anything. I don't know why I'm telling you all this.

ERICKSON: Because you want to.

CLEO: There's no one I can talk to, no one. My sister-in-law blames me. He really cares about me, my old man...and the kids. He wants us to have things. She says it's all my fault. But you can't tell a man what to do. I gave up trying. He doesn't want me to work. He's the man of the house. It's like the Middle Ages. His father was a no-good bum, and he wants to prove that he's a real man.

ERICKSON: You can't blame him for that.

CLEO: So now, I'm working all right.

ERICKSON: How'd you get started?

CLEO: A year or so ago I was at a party. I got drunk. When I came to, I found myself in bed with this guy.

ERICKSON: Mel Peters?

CLEO: Yeah. He tried to recruit me. When I refused he threatened to write to my old man. So, I got roped in.

ERICKSON: How are you gonna explain the money you're making?

CLEO: Mel fixed me up with this part time job with this fancy company. I don't do anything really. I just go in for a couple hours, but I'm on the books, so it all looks legit. What I'm worried about right now is my kid sister. She's a basket case really. She tried to

THE ESTABLISHMENT

kill herself once. If she has to spend time, I don't think she'd come out alive. I gotta powder my nose.

> *(CLEO goes off. ERICKSON picks up the coffee cups and starts off. HE changes his mind, sets down the cups and opens her purse. HE takes a couple of bills from his pocket and puts them into the purse. HE picks up a card and reads it, puts it back, picks up the cups and goes off to the kitchen. A moment later CLEO reenters, picks up her purse, opens it and takes out a comb. She sees the bills, takes them out and places them on the table. SHE combs her hair and replaces the comb as ERICKSON reenters.)*

CLEO: This is all paid for, you know.

ERICKSON: Yes, I know. Buy yourself some perfume.

CLEO: Are you trying to tell me something? I'm just kidding. *(SHE puts the bills back into the purse and closes it.)*

ERICKSON: Will I see you again?

CLEO: It's not up to me.

ERICKSON: I guess you don't put out for friends.

CLEO: I'm sorry.

ERICKSON: That's all right, Cleo. You know my name. Now I know yours.

CLEO: My sister's name is Mona. Mona Davis. She's in the "tombs" right now, in case you can do something for her.

THE ESTABLISHMENT

ERICKSON: Good luck, Cleo.

(HE extends his hand. SHE shakes it. HE holds onto her hand.)

ERICKSON: Don't I get a good-night kiss?

(SHE kisses him on the cheek and starts for the door. HE opens the door.)

ERICKSON: Take care.

CLEO: Talk to Mel Peters.

(CLEO goes off. HE closes the door, sighs and goes off to the bedroom as we hear the RADIO ANNOUNCER.)

RADIO ANNOUNCER: "An unforgettable love story," says the Times. "A movie that touches the heart," says the Daily News. "Rare, moving and unique" That's what they're saying about the new Swedish film that opened at the Cinema on Friday. "An Evening Romance" is a story of young love, both frank and beautiful. Frank as only the Swedish can be, and as beautiful as a sunset. Don't miss it.

(During the Announcer's speech. ERICKSON has entered wearing a police uniform which he continues to button. HE looks at himself in the mirror, salutes himself, turns off the radio and starts off as the lights come down.)

SCENE TWO

GAMBLING

(Late morning. Two months later. Blues music is heard softly in the distance. An unoccupied tenement room furnished with a bureau, a table and a couple of chairs. In the rear wall are a couple of windows. Outside one of the windows is a fire escape. The door is swung open and LIEUTENANT BILL DONOVAN enters, gun drawn. HE glances about.)

DONOVAN: It's okay. It's empty.

(LIEUTENANT RALPH ERICKSON enters, closing the door behind him. Both the men are in plain clothes.)

ERICKSON: Are you sure this is the room?

DONOVAN: It's number six on the second floor.

ERICKSON: *(HE walks about, inspecting drawers.)* It doesn't look like anybody's been here.

DONOVAN: It's not an office. It's just a pick up place. What's in that closet?

ERICKSON: *(HE opens the closet door.)* Nothing, except for a couple of hangars. Phew! What a smell! There must be a dead rat here somewhere. We're not gonna hole up in that closet, are we?

DONOVAN: No, no, no. We'll hang out on that fire escape.

ERICKSON: It looks kind of rickety.

DONOVAN: *(Looking out the window.)* It'll be fine.

THE ESTABLISHMENT

ERICKSON: How long is this gonna take?

DONOVAN: It's almost noon. That's when they're due.

(ERICKSON goes off to the other room. DONOVAN produces a walkie-talkie.)

DONOVAN: It's empty. We're gonna use the fire escape.

(DONOVAN disposes of the walkie-talkie. ERICKSON reenters.)

DONOVAN: What's in there?

ERICKSON: A table, a couple of chairs and a phone.

DONOVAN: Is it working?

ERICKSON: Yes, it's working...and I used my handkerchief.

DONOVAN: Well, we might as well take it easy. *(HE sits.)*

ERICKSON: You're not gonna smoke, are you?

DONOVAN: *(Sarcastically)* No, dear, I'm not gonna smoke.

ERICKSON: I'm sensitive to smoke. Can I help it? Who we expecting?

DONOVAN: There'll be someone here to pick up the money that's been collected.

ERICKSON: Well, I hope this isn't a wild goose chase, like last week.

THE ESTABLISHMENT

DONOVAN: They'll be here. We got a tip. Sit down. Relax.

ERICKSON: I am relaxed. I just hate sitting around and waiting.

DONOVAN: That's what life is, buddy, sitting around and waiting. How come we never hear you talking about women?

ERICKSON: What's that supposed to mean?

DONOVAN: You're not queer, are you?

ERICKSON: Do I look queer?

DONOVAN: Yeah, well they come in all shapes and sizes.

ERICKSON: Well, there are doers, and there are talkers?

DONOVAN: How old are you?

ERICKSON: Old enough to know better.

DONOVAN: Get yourself a wife. Saves all the wear and tear. And it's not the end of the world.

ERICKSON: So I've noticed.

DONOVAN: Look, just because you're married, it doesn't mean you're dead. And besides, what they don't know won't hurt 'em.

ERICKSON: I thought the idea of marriage is not to have to look around.

DONOVAN: Just a minute. *(HE picks up the walkie-talkie and*

THE ESTABLISHMENT

listens.) Right. *(HE replaces the walkie-talkie.)* A man and woman just entered the building. Come on. *(HE walks toward the window.)*

ERICKSON: It doesn't look to safe to me.

DONOVAN: Oh, come on!

(DONOVAN climbs out the window onto the fire escape.)

DONOVAN: Will you get out here!

(ERICKSON climbs onto the fire escape and the two men conceal themselves. The sound of footsteps is heard and the murmur of voices. The sounds fade. DONOVAN climbs back into the room, goes to the door and listens.)

DONOVAN: It's okay. I said, it's okay.

ERICKSON: Okay, okay. I heard you. *(HE climbs back into the room.)* I don't know why we have to bother with this penny ante stuff?

DONOVAN: Are you kidding? These men make a fortune on this numbers racket.

ERICKSON: My old man used to play the numbers all the time. He probably still does, for all I know. What do they get now...a couple of years?

DONOVAN: If it's a misdemeanor, the most they can get is a year. If we can catch 'em with more than five hundred plays or five thousand dollars it's a felony, and they can get one to four. Sit down, for God's sake.

THE ESTABLISHMENT

(THEY both sit.)

DONOVAN: Some of the men think you're queer.

ERICKSON: That's their privilege.

DONOVAN: Doesn't that make you uncomfortable?

ERICKSON: You think I'm queer?

DONOVAN: Not really, no.

ERICKSON: So what are you worried about?

DONOVAN: You're a...

ERICKSON: Queer duck.

DONOVAN: You do get laid once in a while?

ERICKSON: Yeah. You want the details?

DONOVAN: What's the matter with you? We're a team. I'm trying to be friendly. You pissed off with me about something?

ERICKSON: As a matter of fact, I am.

DONOVAN: Uh oh! What did I do?

ERICKSON: That young girl you messed up?

DONOVAN: What young girl? I never messed anyone up.

ERICKSON: Okay, okay.

THE ESTABLISHMENT

DONOVAN: You don't mean that little whore?

ERICKSON: I thought she was selling crack.

DONOVAN: She was a little whore. And I didn't mess her up. That was one of her "johns." You think I messed her up? That skinny little thing? And even if I did, which I didn't, what are you? Some sort of evangelist?

ERICKSON: Forget it.

DONOVAN: And that was almost a year ago. You didn't say anything to anyone about that, did you?

ERICKSON: If I did, you would have heard about it.

DONOVAN: I can't figure you out. What? Have you got a thing for whores?

ERICKSON: Well, at least you get what you pay for. And some of them are pretty classy.

DONOVAN: A guy like you, he doesn't have to pay for it.

ERICKSON: When you take a girl out, aren't you paying for it? And then maybe you don't even get your money's worth.

DONOVAN: So that's how you get your kicks?

ERICKSON: Sometimes.

DONOVAN: I haven't been with a whore in years. And the ones I did see weren't worth the money. Of course, I was just a kid then.

THE ESTABLISHMENT

ERICKSON: There was this one whore. She was really something.

DONOVAN: Hold it. *(HE takes out the walkie-talkie.)* Yeah? Right. *(HE replaces the walkie-talkie.)* Two men just entered the building.

> *(ERICKSON starts for the window. DONOVAN follows him off onto the fire escape. A moment later DONOVAN reenters, places the chairs in the position they were found, then goes off again. Footsteps are heard, then three knocks on the door, followed by two more. A moment later the door is opened and DICK JOHNSON enters.)*

DICK: Come on in, kid.

(DICK enters, followed by BEN GRADY.)

DICK: This won't take long. How have you been?

BEN: Okay, I guess.

DICK: What do you mean, I guess? You're keeping your nose clean, aren't you?

BEN: Oh, yes.

DICK: It's good to see you, kid. You've grown up.

BEN: A little.

DICK: You've finished high school, haven't you?

BEN: Oh, yes.

THE ESTABLISHMENT

DICK: That's great, kid. That's really great.

BEN: And I'm thinking of going to college.

DICK: I guess your mother's happy about that.

BEN: Mom's not happy about anything.

DICK: Have you heard anything from your old man?

BEN: No.

DICK: Well, now that I'm back, you come to me with any problems. What are you smiling at? I guess I'm not the greatest example. But I'm out now, and rarin' to go. So you're thinking of goin' to college. That's great. What are you gonna study?

BEN: I'm not sure yet. I'm interested in everything.

DICK: I remember you're always reading a book. How come you don't come around anymore? Cleo says she never sees you.

BEN: Well, I've got this job, and I've been busy with all sorts of things.

DICK: Has she offended you in anyway?

BEN: No, no.

DICK: I know your mother doesn't like her. She never has. But you used to be...real close. I mean, I feel more like a father than an uncle. And I guess I'm a pretty lucky guy, having a wife like Cleo. Some guys come out of the pen, and they don't have any family anymore. But I got a wife that's the best. The best wife, the best

THE ESTABLISHMENT

mother, the best everything. She was even good to that no good sister of hers.

BEN: I really liked Mona.

DICK: Well, there's a lesson to be learned. Don't you get hooked on anything.

BEN: Oh, no. Not me. That's one thing I'll never touch. What time are you supposed to meet this guy?

DICK: He's supposed to be here at noon. Sometimes he's a few minutes late.

BEN: So, what are you up to now?

DICK: Still looking for a job.

BEN: I thought you had one.

DICK: I did too, until the boss's nephew came along. A friend of mine said that there's going to be an opening in this company in a few weeks, and he put in a word for me, so I'm waiting on that. It would be a good job, too.

BEN: What kind of job?

DICK: Fixing TV sets. I took a course while I was...away.

BEN: That's great. That should pay well.

DICK: Yesireee, I'm making a new start. I got in with the wrong guys, but from now on in, I'm keeping my nose clean. 'Cause I

THE ESTABLISHMENT

don't know how lucky I am. Two beautiful kids and a wonderful wife.

BEN: Who's this guy you're meeting?

DICK: His name is Mack. I never met him before. I'm just helping this friend of mine out. He's in bed with the flu. He helps collecting for the numbers, you know.

BEN: He's running numbers?

DICK: No, no, no. He's not running numbers. He's just an errand boy.

BEN: But that's against the law.

DICK: No one pays any attention to this penny ante stuff. And it's just for today. What are you looking at me like that for? You look just like your mother. Nothing I ever did was right. She's two years older than me, and you'd think I was her son, instead of her brother.

BEN: Well, she loves you. And she worries about you. Does Cleo know you're doing this?

DICK: No, no. It's just for today. I didn't have anything else to do, and the guy was really strapped. And there's a few bucks in it for me. Everybody plays the numbers, kid. It's no big deal.

BEN: But you're on parole.

DICK: Okay, okay. Jesus Christ! Everybody's telling me what to do. Don't do that, and don't do that. Even Cleo gets on my nerves

THE ESTABLISHMENT

some time. I'm sick and tired of it. People pushing me around all the time.

BEN: Okay, okay. Take it easy.

DICK: And don't tell me to take it easy, you little snot. Ever since I can remember everybody's down on me. My old man, beating the shit out of me because I came home with a fin I found on the street, and he kept telling me that I stole it, that I was a thief and a liar. And he was the one, that fucking liar. I couldn't hear out of that ear for over a week. And that mother of yours, always looking at me like I did something wrong. I'm sorry, kid. But getting out of the pen, and starting all over again. It hasn't been easy.

BEN: Did you get into any fights when you were in there?

DICK: One or two. I do have a temper, you know. This one time, I was in the shower and this big buck tries to bugger me. I beat the shit out of him. He was in the hospital for a month.

BEN: What did they do to you?

DICK: Me, nothing. What could they do to me? The poor guy slipped on the soap. Boy, I tell you, some of these guys. They go into the clink like a bull and tiptoe out like a little lady.

BEN: I remember that time...when you thought that someone made a pass at Aunt Cleo...

DICK: Yeah, well...when you get pushed around like that, you gotta stand up for yourself. By the way, you know this place where Cleo works?

BEN: Not really, no.

THE ESTABLISHMENT

DICK: They've been treating her pretty good, haven't they?

BEN: So I gather.

DICK: Well, as soon as I start on my job, and money starts coming in, she's gonna give it up.

BEN: It's twenty after twelve, you know.

DICK: Yeah, he should be here by now.

BEN: I've got to be at my job by two.

DICK: I'd like to take you out to lunch, but I can't leave here, 'cause I've got all this money, and this list of numbers that they're waiting for. My friend said there was a phone here somewhere, in case I had any problems, but I don't see any phone.

(The telephone rings.)

DICK: There it is. It must be in the other room.

BEN: I guess you better answer it.

(DICK goes into the other room. The phone stops ringing. DICK reenters a moment later.)

DICK: Come on, kid. Let's get out of here. There's been some sort of slip up.

(DONOVAN enters, gun drawn, followed by ERICKSON.)

DONOVAN: Okay, buddy. Stay where you are. You, too, kid.

THE ESTABLISHMENT

DICK: Oh, Jesus!

DONOVAN: That's right, Buddy. You done a bad thing.

DICK: We ain't done nothing.

DONOVAN: *(To ERICKSON)* Put the cuffs on 'em, and frisk 'em. *(To DICK)* Just take it easy and you won't get hurt.

DICK: It's all a mistake.

> *(ERICKSON puts the cuffs on DICK and frisks him. HE produces a notebook and a thick wad of bills.)*

DONOVAN: Well, lookee here. Look what we've got.

DICK: I was just standing in for someone.

DONOVAN: Well, buddy, you took the wrong time to stand in, and you took the wrong place. *(To ERICKSON)* Frisk the kid, too.

DICK: He's not involved in any of this. He's my nephew. We just ran into each other on the street, and I was gonna take him to lunch.

DONOVAN: Well, you can take him to lunch at the city's expense.

DICK: Can't you let him go? He ain't got any sort of a record, and he didn't do anything. Please. Have a heart. Let the kid go.

> *(ERICKSON whispers something to DONOVAN, who shakes his head. DONOVAN takes out the walkie-talkie.)*

THE ESTABLISHMENT

DONOVAN: Okay. We got 'em. Come on upstairs and pick 'em up.

DICK: *(To BEN)* I'm sorry, kid.

ERICKSON: If the kid is clean, we'll let him go.

DICK: I'd appreciate that.

DONOVAN: You wanna tell us about that phone call?

DICK: I don't know anything. When I picked up the phone a voice said, "There's been a problem. Get the hell out of there."

DONOVAN: You don't know who it was?

DICK: No. I'm telling you, I've never been here before.

DONOVAN: You said you were standing in for someone.

DICK: That's right.

DONOVAN: Who?

DICK: Who?

DONOVAN: That's right, who?

DICK: I don't remember his name.

DONOVAN: Oh, really, Well, maybe in time you will. If not, we'll help you refresh your memory. Put the cuffs on the kid.

THE ESTABLISHMENT

(DONOVAN tosses cuffs to ERICKSON who handcuffs BEN. Footsteps are heard. DONOVAN opens the door.)

DONOVAN: *(Addressing the man in the hallway)* Here they are. *(HE turns to DICK.)* Okay, march. You, too, kid.

(DICK goes off, followed by BEN. DONOVAN inspects the notebook and the money.)

DONOVAN: That's quite a load here.

ERICKSON: How much time do you think he'll do?

DONOVAN: Why? You worried about him? Why don't we check those drawers again?

(ERICKSON checks the drawers.)

DONOVAN: Find anything?

ERICKSON: No.

(The blues are heard softly in the distance.)

DONOVAN: *(HE starts for the door.)* Damn!

ERICKSON: What's the matter?

DONOVAN: I almost forgot. My wife asked me to pick up some lottery tickets. She's always playing the lottery, and she even picks up tickets for her sister who lives in Jersey.

(DONOVAN has gone off, followed by ERICKSON as the lights come down.)

SCENE THREE

MURDER

Two years later. Three o'clock in the morning. The back room of a police station. Some chairs, a table and a telephone. The blues are heard before the lights come up. DONOVAN enters, followed by ERICKSON, holding a paper bag. THEY sit at the table. ERICKSON opens the bag and produces some pastry and two containers of coffee.

ERICKSON: Prune or cheese.

DONOVAN: I'll take the cheese. *(HE sips the coffee.)* This coffee's awful. Where'd it come from?

ERICKSON: The same place; the place on the corner.

DONOVAN: Tastes bitter.

ERICKSON: You're always complaining.

DONOVAN: Me? You're the one that does the bitching. You kept pushing for homicide, and now that we've got homicide, you're still bitching.

ERICKSON: I'm not bitching.

DONOVAN: You're never satisfied.

(ERICKSON sighs, then takes a bite of his prune danish, and THEY continues eating.)

ERICKSON: You really think the nephew did it?

DONOVAN: What do you think?

THE ESTABLISHMENT

ERICKSON: He's kind of scrawny.

DONOVAN: How much strength does it take to use a knife?

ERICKSON: I'd like to have another talk with those kids.

DONOVAN: They just heard a lot of screams.

ERICKSON: They knew who was in that room. They just don't wanna say.

DONOVAN: What bugs me is that there are no prints on the knife, and it was not premedicated.

ERICKSON: What makes you so sure of that?

DONOVAN: It was too messy. Too violent.

ERICKSON: Someone did have sense enough to wipe the knife clean.

DONOVAN: That's what puzzles me.

ERICKSON: You think someone other than the murderer cleaned the knife?

DONOVAN: I'd sure like to know where the husband is.

ERICKSON: Of course, there was a party, and drinking.

DONOVAN: From what I gather, the husband was in the can for a couple of years. That's what the party was for, I gather. A welcome home party. My theory is, he found out the wife was

THE ESTABLISHMENT

playing around while he was in the can. They had a fight. He lost his temper, and he stabbed her. What?

ERICKSON: Nothing.

DONOVAN: She sure was a nice looking woman. What'sa matter?

ERICKSON: Nothing. It just got to me, that's all.

DONOVAN: You sure have been acting strange. You didn't know the dame, did you?

ERICKSON: No. I didn't know her.

DONOVAN: You sure acted like you did.

ERICKSON: All right, so I acted like I did!

DONOVAN: Okay, okay. I don't know what's gotten into you.

ERICKSON: I suppose you enjoy all this.

DONOVAN: I think you're cracking up.

ERICKSON: It's just that you're so fucking callous.

DONOVAN: I am not callous. It's just that we've got a job to do, and we can't get all mushy. As a matter of fact, I feel really bad for those two kids.

ERICKSON: Okay, okay.

(THEY continue to eat.)

THE ESTABLISHMENT

DONOVAN: She kept a clean house, I will say that for her, and the kids looked as if they were well looked after. The neighbors had only nice things to say about her. One thing that struck me though.

ERICKSON: What was that?

DONOVAN: She often used a baby-sitter, which meant that she was out a lot; out on the town, maybe. And two bank accounts. Why would an ordinary housewife have two bank accounts? And what were the bank books doing on the floor? If it was a thief, he would have taken off with the bank books.

ERICKSON: Or she. I gather the sister-in-law wasn't too fond of the wife.

DONOVAN: She had an alibi. If the party was over, why did the nephew come back? And if he didn't do it, he was probably the one who wiped the knife clean. What do you think?

ERICKSON: I guess that makes sense.

DONOVAN: That nephew's a smart-ass.

ERICKSON: Well, you're not gonna get anywhere attacking him.

DONOVAN: You want me to offer him a cup of tea?

ERICKSON: That might not be a bad idea.

DONOVAN: Okay, okay. Bring him in again.

(ERICKSON takes a sip of coffee and goes off. DONOVAN

THE ESTABLISHMENT

finishes his danish and sips his coffee. ERICKSON reenters with BEN GRADY.)

DONOVAN: Haven't I seen you some place before?

BEN: You're the detective. You tell me.

ERICKSON: Okay, Ben. You're not gonna help yourself by being a smart ass.

BEN: Am I under arrest?

DONOVAN: No one's under arrest. You're here for questioning. Understand?

BEN: I understand perfectly.

DONOVAN: You're not gonna get anywhere with that attitude of yours.

BEN: I'm sorry.

DONOVAN: You think you're pretty clever, don't you?

BEN: Not really. I am well read. I read books.

> *(ERICKSON taps DONOVAN on the shoulder, takes him aside and they have a whispered conversation. DONOVAN goes off, and ERICKSON returns to BEN.)*

BEN: Wise move. There's something about that man.

ERICKSON: Okay. Now let's just relax. I think we both want to find out who killed your aunt. Or do we? *(HE picks up the pad on*

THE ESTABLISHMENT

the table.) I see your full name is Benjamin. Were you named after someone?

BEN: My mother reads the Bible a lot. Benjamin was the youngest son of Jacob. That's the old testament.

ERICKSON: Are you religious?

BEN: In what sense?

ERICKSON: Do you believe in God?

BEN: I'm a skeptic.

ERICKSON: Were you fond of your aunt?

BEN: Yes.

ERICKSON: Were you close to her?

BEN: I used to be, growing up. As a matter of fact, I liked her better than I did my mother.

ERICKSON: But you changed your mind about her.

BEN: Whatever gave you that idea?

ERICKSON: You said you used to be close to her. But you're relationship changed. Why?

BEN: I'm a big boy now.

ERICKSON: Did you know that she had two bank accounts?

THE ESTABLISHMENT

BEN: No, I didn't.

ERICKSON: You discovered the body, didn't you? There were two bank books on the floor, not far from the body. You didn't notice them.

BEN: I noticed them, yes.

ERICKSON: But you didn't inspect them. Did you?

BEN: No.

ERICKSON: You weren't curious?

BEN: There was a dead body on the floor. It was my aunt, Cleo, who I loved. Why in God's name would I bother about two bank books?

ERICKSON: Okay, okay. Did you find your aunt attractive?

BEN: Are you asking me if I had sex with her? No.

ERICKSON: Did you want to have sex with her?

BEN: No.

ERICKSON: You didn't think she was attractive?

BEN: Do you have sex with every woman you think is attractive?

ERICKSON: Then you did think she was attractive.

BEN: Aunt Cleo was a sexy woman.

THE ESTABLISHMENT

ERICKSON: You think she was faithful to your uncle while he was in prison?

BEN: You'll have to ask her.

ERICKSON: You didn't answer my question.

BEN: What was the question?

ERICKSON: Do you think your aunt was faithful to your uncle while he was in prison?

BEN: I hoped she was.

ERICKSON: You still haven't answered my question.

BEN: No. I mean I think that Cleo was faithful to my uncle. She was a good woman; a good wife and a good mother.

ERICKSON: Your mother had some doubts.

BEN: About what?

ERICKSON: About Cleo's fidelity. Did you know that?

BEN: My mother is a very bitter woman. The only thing she believes in is Jesus, and if Jesus came down to earth she'd have doubts about him.

ERICKSON: Did you know anything about your aunt's recent activities?

BEN: Not really, no.

THE ESTABLISHMENT

ERICKSON: You didn't know anything about this job she had with this catering outfit?

BEN: No.

ERICKSON: Did you speak to your cousins after you found the body?

BEN: You asked me that.

ERICKSON: I'm asking you again.

BEN: Yes, of course I did. I was concerned about them. Whoever killed Aunt Cleo might have hurt them, too.

ERICKSON: They said they heard voices and screams.

BEN: That's right.

ERICKSON: They identified their mother's voice. They couldn't identify the other voice.

BEN: That's right.

ERICKSON: Isn't that strange? They didn't even know if it was a man's voice or not. Don't you think they're trying to protect someone? Their father, perhaps?

BEN: It has occurred to me.

ERICKSON: Weren't you curious to find out?

BEN: Yes, of course.

THE ESTABLISHMENT

ERICKSON: You didn't question them?

BEN: Two hysterical children? Their mother lying dead on the floor?

ERICKSON: You were at the party, I gather.

BEN: Yes.

ERICKSON: Was there a lot of drinking?

BEN: Aunt Cleo keeps a tight ship. She never lets things get out of hand.

ERICKSON: You think she was a remarkable woman, don't you?

BEN: Did I say that?

ERICKSON: You think she was sexy.

BEN: Did I say that?

ERICKSON: Yes, you did.

BEN: Dead or alive, I think it was quite obvious. Don't you?

ERICKSON: Can you think of any reason why someone would want to kill your aunt? Was your uncle in love with his wife?

BEN: I think so, yes.

ERICKSON: Was he possessive? Was he the jealous type?

THE ESTABLISHMENT

BEN: He loved his wife. He wouldn't want any harm to come to her, if that's what you mean.

ERICKSON: That's not what I mean. Did he have a temper?

BEN: Don't we all?

ERICKSON: Did he have a temper?

BEN: He was human.

ERICKSON: Did he have a temper? *(After a moment)* Did he ever lose his temper?

BEN: He was a scrapper. He was able to defend himself.

ERICKSON: Did he ever lose his temper?

BEN: You'll have to ask him.

ERICKSON: I'm asking you.

BEN: He may have. I've never spent that much time with him.

ERICKSON: How well did you know your uncle?

BEN: He was my uncle. My mother's brother. I knew him from the day I was born. I was fond of him. I looked up to him. I felt closer to him than I did to my father.

ERICKSON: You would do anything to defend him.

BEN: He was a good man. I thought he was special.

THE ESTABLISHMENT

ERICKSON: Was?

BEN: Is.

ERICKSON: You changed your mind about him?

BEN: No.

ERICKSON: Where is he now? Do you know?

BEN: No.

ERICKSON: You have no idea.

BEN: No. I have no idea.

ERICKSON: Do you think he might be trying to find the man that killed his wife?

BEN: I don't know.

ERICKSON: Do you think he killed Cleo?

BEN: He loved her. Why would he want to kill her?

ERICKSON: In a moment of passion, jealous passion. *(After a moment)* You went home after the party. Why did you come back to the house?

BEN: I thought I left my wallet there.

ERICKSON: Did you?

THE ESTABLISHMENT

BEN: No. It was in my jacket pocket, but I never put my wallet in my jacket pocket.

ERICKSON: When did you discover it was in your jacket pocket?

BEN: When I went into the bedroom to talk to the kids. I was leaning over and I felt this lump, and there was my wallet.

ERICKSON: I don't believe you. Why did you go back to the house? I think you were concerned about your uncle. I think you knew that Cleo was unfaithful, and that your uncle knew, and you were afraid what might happen. I think, when you got there, you found Cleo on the floor and the bloody knife right next to her. I think you wiped the knife clean, then went in to see your cousins, telling them not to mention that they heard their father's voice, and then you called the police. Do you deny it?

BEN: Are you accusing me of being an accomplice to murder?

ERICKSON: Do you deny it?

BEN: Yes. I went back to look for my wallet.

    (DONOVAN enters. HE whispers something to ERICKSON.)

ERICKSON: Okay, Ben. Come with me.

    (BEN starts toward the door through which DONOVAN entered.)

ERICKSON: No. Not that way. Follow me.

    (BEN follows ERICKSON off, looking back at the door

THE ESTABLISHMENT

through which DONOVAN entered. DONOVAN opens the door.)

DONOVAN: Come on in.

(DICK JOHNSON enters wearing handcuffs.)

DONOVAN: Sit down.

DICK: What's this all about?

DONOVAN: You are Dick Johnson, aren't you?

DICK: Yeah.

DONOVAN: You live at 346 Carter Street?

DICK: That's right. Did I do anything wrong? I'm on parole. If I'm in trouble, I got real trouble.

DONOVAN: Believe me, brother, you've got real trouble.

DICK: What am I suspected of?

(DONOVAN removes the handcuffs.)

DICK: Thank you.

DONOVAN: Where were you headed for when you were picked up?

DICK: I was heading for a bar.

DONOVAN: You just came out of a bar.

THE ESTABLISHMENT

DICK: I was heading for another bar.

DONOVAN: Another bar, or a bus?

DICK: A bus?

DONOVAN: You were found near the bus station.

DICK: There's a bar next door.

(ERICKSON reenters.)

ERICKSON: Have you read him his rights?

DONOVAN: I was just about to. *(HE takes a form from a drawer and reads.)* "You have the right to remain silent and refuse to answer questions. Do you understand?"

ERICKSON: Answer yes or no.

DICK: Yes.

DONOVAN: "Anything you do may be used against you in a court of law. Do you understand?

DICK: Yes.

DONOVAN: "If you cannot afford an attorney one will be provided for you without cost. Do you understand?

ERICKSON: Answer yes or no.

DICK: Yes.

THE ESTABLISHMENT

DONOVAN: "If you do not have an attorney available you have the right to remain silent until you have had an opportunity to consult one. Do you understand?

DICK: Yes.

DONOVAN: "Now that I have advised you of your rights, are you willing to answer questions without an attorney present? Do you understand?"

DICK: Yeah, sure. Why not? I've got nothing to hide.

DONOVAN: You just got out of prison. Ain't that right?

DICK: That's right.

DONOVAN: So your first night back, you're out on the town?

DICK: I needed some air.

DONOVAN: You been away for how many years?

DICK: Two years, seven months, one week and three days.

DONOVAN: And you haven't seen your wife in all that time.

DICK: She came to visit me.

DONOVAN: How often?

DICK: Whenever she could. She's got two kids to take care of, and a job.

DONOVAN: What kind of a job?

THE ESTABLISHMENT

DICK: She works for this catering outfit.

DONOVAN: What does she do for this catering outfit?

DICK: I don't know. We never talked about it much. She said it was a good job, and paid pretty well.

DONOVAN: How well? *(After a moment)* How well?

DICK: I don't know exactly.

DONOVAN: She never discussed this job with you?

DICK: Not really, no. It was a job.

DONOVAN: Did you know how much she was getting paid?

DICK: No.

DONOVAN: Weren't you interested?

DICK: No. She made enough to take care of herself and the kids, and when I got out, I would take over.

ERICKSON: You didn't care?

DICK: About what?

ERICKSON: About what your wife was doing for this company?

DONOVAN: *(After a moment)* What did you and your wife talk about when you got home?

DICK: I don't know.

THE ESTABLISHMENT

DONOVAN: You don't know what you talked about?

DICK: Things. The kids. The family. Things like that.

ERICKSON: You didn't notice how nice the apartment was? How well dressed your children were?

>   *(DONOVAN places his hand on ERICKSON's arm. ERICKSON relaxes.)*

DONOVAN: Let me get this straight. You spent two years in the clink. It's been two years since you spent...some quality time with your wife, and you leave her behind and go out on the town.

DICK: I was edgy. I was nervous.

DONOVAN: What were you nervous about?

DICK: If I knew, I wouldn't be nervous.

DONOVAN: Maybe your wife didn't interest you anymore. Maybe you picked up another life style while in the can.

ERICKSON: *(After a moment)* What happened after the party broke up?

DICK: I helped my wife clean up the apartment.

DONOVAN: And then what?

DICK: I said I wanted to get some air. I've been cooped up for a long time. May I ask why I've been brought in?

DONOVAN: When did you last see your wife alive?

THE ESTABLISHMENT

DICK: What do you mean?

DONOVAN: You heard what I said?

DICK: Has something happened to Cleo?

ERICKSON: Cleo is dead.

DICK: What? What happened? How did she die?

ERICKSON: Your wife was murdered.

DONOVAN: You don't know anything about it.

DICK: I think I'm gonna be sick. How...?

DONOVAN: How...what?

DICK: How did it happen?

ERICKSON: That's what we'd like you to tell us.

DICK: You don't think... Oh, Christ! Why would I kill my wife? I love her. She was my whole life...my whole life. *(HE weeps.)* How could anyone...? Please... *(After a moment)* The kids, my little boy and girl... Are they all right? You don't think... Why would I kill the woman I love, the mother of my children? I love my family. That was the only thing that kept me alive. They were my whole life. My wife and my kids. Without them I couldn't have made it. I loved my wife. *(HE weeps.)*

ERICKSON: How **much** did you love her?

DICK: She was everything. She was my whole life.

THE ESTABLISHMENT

ERICKSON: Suppose she was unfaithful to you?

DICK: That's not possible.

DONOVAN: Why?

DICK: Because I know Cleo.

ERICKSON: Just suppose.

DICK: What?

DONOVAN: That she was unfaithful.

(HE shakes his head.)

ERICKSON: Why do you shake your head?

DICK: Because that's something I can't imagine. That's like asking someone...suppose your mother...

ERICKSON: What?

DONOVAN: What would you do?

DICK: *(HE shakes his head.)* It wouldn't be Cleo.

ERICKSON: It would be someone else.

DICK: That's right.

DONOVAN: And what would you do to that someone else?

THE ESTABLISHMENT

ERICKSON: *(After a moment)* Suppose we found the person that killed your wife?

DICK: Have you?

ERICKSON: How did your sister feel about Cleo?

DICK: I don't know.

DONOVAN: You don't know how your sister felt about your wife?

DICK: Well, you know women. Besides my sister's very religious. She wouldn't kill anyone.

ERICKSON: What about your nephew?

DICK: What about him?

DONOVAN: How did he feel about Cleo?

DICK: He loved her. She was his aunt.

ERICKSON: Is that all that she was?

DICK: What do you mean? You don't think that...

DONOVAN: What?

DICK: Ben's a nice kid. He wouldn't harm a fly.

ERICKSON: Ben is not a kid. He's a young man. A bright young man, and you know how young men are. They get aroused very easily.

THE ESTABLISHMENT

DICK: What are you trying to say?

DONOVAN: You figure it out.

DICK: What are you trying to tell me? *(HE shakes his head.)*

ERICKSON: What are you shaking your head for?

DICK: Nothing?

DONOVAN: You don't think your wife and your nephew had it on?

DICK: No.

ERICKSON: No, what?

DONOVAN: Suppose I tell you that your nephew's prints were on the knife?

(DICK shakes his head.)

ERICKSON: You don't believe it.

DONOVAN: What makes you so sure?

DICK: Because I know my nephew, and I know my wife.

ERICKSON: You been away a long time. Things happen.

DICK: I know my nephew. He's a good kid.

DONOVAN: What about your wife?

THE ESTABLISHMENT

DICK: I know my wife.

> *(ERICKSON whispers something to DONOVAN and goes off.)*

DONOVAN: *(HE shoves a piece of paper and a pencil in front of DICK.)* I want you to make a list of everyone you saw and everyone you spoke to since you got out.

DICK: What about my nephew?

DONOVAN: What about him?

DICK: You said his prints were on the knife.

DONOVAN: Did I say that?

> *(ERICKSON reenters with BEN.)*

ERICKSON: *(To BEN)* I want you to make a list of everyone that was at the party, and everyone you spoke to last night.

> *(ERICKSON provides BEN with paper and pencil. The two DETECTIVES look at one another and go off.)*

DICK: *(After a moment)* How are the kids? Do you know?

BEN: They're all right.

DICK: Where are they?

BEN: They're with my mother.

DICK: They said that Cleo was murdered.

THE ESTABLISHMENT

BEN: Let's not talk about it.

DICK: They said your prints were on the knife.

(BEN shakes his head.)

DICK: Why would they say that?

BEN: They wanna upset you. We shouldn't talk.

DICK: I've gotta get out of here.

BEN: You will, you will. You didn't kill Cleo. We know that.

DICK: Yeah, yeah.

BEN: And the less we talk about it, the better. Did they read you your rights?

(DICK nods.)

BEN: Don't say anything until you talk to your lawyer. You got a right to remain silent.

DICK: I've gotta get out of here. I don't care what happens to me, but first, I've gotta get out of here.

BEN: Uncle Dick, they have no proof. There were no fingerprints on the knife.

DICK: How do you know? *(After a moment)* Benny...

BEN: What?

THE ESTABLISHMENT

DICK: I was set up.

BEN: What do you mean?

DICK: That numbers bust. I was set up.

BEN: How do you know?

DICK: In the can. I found out about it. Mel Peters. He was the one. And she was in on it. She was working for him, and he was the one that set me up, so she had to be in on it..

BEN: I don't know what you're talking about, and you don't know what you're talking about, and let's not talk about it.

DICK: I'm gonna fry, I know that. You've gotta help me, Benny. They think that maybe you did it, but they'll never convict you.

BEN: What are you talking about?

DICK: You can help me out, help me to get out of here. There's something I gotta do, kid. That son of a bitch! And she was in on it.

BEN: Dick, please.

DICK: I didn't mean to do it. But I lost my head. I mean, when I found out that she was in on it. How could she do this to me? To set me up like that? On top of it all. And those kids. How could she do it. I worshipped that woman. *(HE sobs.)* I don't care what they do to me, Benny. I don't care.

(DONOVAN reenters, accompanied by ERICKSON.)

THE ESTABLISHMENT

DONOVAN: Okay, Johnson.

DICK: What?

DONOVAN: You know what.

DICK: What? I didn't do anything.

DONOVAN: Then everything you just said was a lie? Everything we've got on tape? Come on, Johnson. Let's go.

DICK: I didn't do anything. It was all a mistake.

    (DONOVAN takes DICK by the arm and leads him off.)

ERICKSON: Okay, Ben. You can go.

BEN: Where?

ERICKSON: Home. You got a home, don't you?

BEN: I used to have.

    (BEN goes off. After a moment DONOVAN reenters. The blues are heard softly in the distance.)

DONOVAN: What a night! Can you imagine? Killing your wife like that? He's an animal.

    (Blues music is heard.)

DONOVAN: Hey, in all the excitement I forgot to tell you.

ERICKSON: What?

THE ESTABLISHMENT

DONOVAN: We heard from Billy.

ERICKSON: Sometimes you forget there's a war going on. Your boy made sergeant, didn't he?

DONOVAN: You won't believe this. That little son-of-a-gun. He knocked out a machine gun nest single handed. Four men with one grenade. He's gonna be awarded the D.S.O.

> *(DONOVAN throws his arm around ERICKSON's shoulder, and THEY go off as the lights come down.)*

SCENE FOUR

SOLICITING

The police station. Three years later. Plaintive blues music is heard and fades. DONOVAN, now sporting a mustache, enters with ERICKSON. THEY hang up their outer jackets.)

DONOVAN: What?

ERICKSON: I didn't say a thing. Look, you're the one that asked for this transfer.

DONOVAN: The old lady kept complaining that I was never home.

ERICKSON: They gave us a choice, didn't they? You were the one that chose the vice squad.

DONOVAN: How was I supposed to know what vice we'd be assigned to? What are you smiling at? You're smiling. What's so funny?

ERICKSON: Nothing.

DONOVAN: You think it's funny, don't you? Well, the next time you're the bait.

ERICKSON Okay, okay. I gotta take a leak. Excuse me. *(HE goes off laughing.)*

DONOVAN: Son of a bitch!

> *(HE kicks a chair, goes off and reenters shoving BEN GRADY into the room.)*

THE ESTABLISHMENT

DONOVAN: Okay, Buster.

(BEN staggers slightly.)

DONOVAN: You're not drunk, are you?

BEN: That all depends, Lieutenant Donovan.

DONOVAN: You know me?

BEN: I do now. I didn't at first. Or I wouldn't have tried to make your acquaintance. *(HE stumbles.)*

DONOVAN: How much have you had to drink?

BEN: Not enough, Lieutenant, not nearly enough. You don't remember me, do you? Ah well, perhaps it was all a dream.

DONOVAN: What are you talking about?

BEN: I was just remembering.

DONOVAN: Remembering what?

BEN: A lovely lady with a wicked tongue and the heart of a Jezebel. I was remembering a prince who was cut to the quick.

DONOVAN: You writing some kind of story?

BEN: Ah, no, my friend. That story has been written...in blood, so to speak.

DONOVAN: You some kind of a writer?

THE ESTABLISHMENT

BEN: Nothing so extraordinary, I'm afraid. I'm just an ordinary faggot. As a matter of fact, I wouldn't even go that far. I'm what you might call a closet queen. You've heard of that expression, haven't you? And it even takes me three or four drinks to be that.

DONOVAN: You ever been picked up before?

BEN: For what?

DONOVAN: You know for what.

BEN: No, Lieutenant. I want to offer you my congratulations. You've got a cherry, Lieutenant.

DONOVAN: Are you sure you haven't been picked up before? Okay, okay. I think you need a little exercise. On your feet. You heard me. Get your ass off that chair. Now, why don't you start running around the room a few times. You heard me. Get moving.

   (BEN starts to trot around the room.)

DONOVAN: Pick up those feet, sister. Come on. You can do better than that.

   (ERICKSON enters.)

DONOVAN: I'm giving the flute player here a little exercise. *(To BEN)* Keep moving.

ERICKSON: You better fill out that report.

DONOVAN: I thought you were gonna fill it out.

ERICKSON: You made the arrest.

THE ESTABLISHMENT

DONOVAN: *(To BEN)* All right; keep moving, sister. *(HE goes off.)*

ERICKSON: Okay. You can stop.

BEN: Thank you.

ERICKSON: Take a seat.

BEN: Where?

ERICKSON: Over there. On that bench.

BEN: Thank you. You always were the more intelligent of the two, Lieutenant Erickson. Ah, yes. We've met before. You were on homicide once. It comes back to you now. But how lucky you are, to be able to forget. I've had no such luck, you see. I remember...everything. A woman's mutilated body, sprawled out on the kitchen floor. A bread knife dripping blood. And I remember whispering into his ear, in my drunken state...or was I really drunk? "Your wife has been unfaithful. You've been betrayed."

ERICKSON: Okay, kid, just relax. No one's going to hurt you.

BEN: Where it shows, you mean.

ERICKSON: As long as you tell the truth, no one's going to hurt you.

BEN: Ah, but you see, I want to be hurt, lieutenant. I deserve to be hurt.

ERICKSON: You'll probably get off with a fine, if this is your first offense.

THE ESTABLISHMENT

BEN: My first offense? My first offense was to abuse myself as we sat around in a circle. It's commonly known as a circle jerk. It was conducted like a symphony. And we were all concerned with one another, making sure we all followed the right procedure. I resisted all assistance. I wanted to do it all by myself. *(After a moment)* I'm due at work in half an hour.

ERICKSON: I doubt if you'll be working tonight.

BEN: But they're depending on me. I'm the knight in shining armor. I protect the building against all harm. The day man's waiting for me to relieve him.

ERICKSON: I'm afraid he'll just have to wait.

BEN: Can I phone him?

ERICKSON: You'll get a chance to make a phone call.

BEN: Will they keep me overnight?

ERICKSON: That all depends. Have you got someone to put up bail?

BEN: Well, there is my mother, but perish the thought.

ERICKSON: Why do you want to hang around toilets?

BEN: I don't, as a rule. I just happened to wander in.

ERICKSON: If you want to meet someone, there are all kinds of places. You don't have to go and make a nuisance of yourself.

BEN: I wasn't making anymore of a nuisance of myself than your

THE ESTABLISHMENT

partner was, displaying himself like that. Now why would he do a thing like that?

ERICKSON: It's our job to protect the public.

BEN: From someone like me? You must be kidding. You do remember me, don't you? And Dick Johnson.

ERICKSON: Dick Johnson...?

BEN: He was a man....

ERICKSON: I assumed as much.

BEN: That's a mistake, my friend. A masculine name does not a man make, nor does a phallus. A man is made of gentleness and strength. A man is made of courage...the courage to be what he is. True men are rare, Lieutenant Erickson.

ERICKSON: Was he your lover?

BEN: He was my uncle, but he filled my heart. He is the ghost to my Hamlet; the Othello to my Iago. And I wish I had the courage to avenge him.

ERICKSON: He ended up in jail, didn't he?

BEN: Manslaughter. Twenty five years for killing Guinevere.

ERICKSON: *(After a moment)* You're not queer, kid. Why don't you find yourself a nice girl and settle down?

BEN: Ah, but you see, I'm pursued by demons. Some, I must admit, of my own creation. Others have been thrust upon me.

THE ESTABLISHMENT

ERICKSON: What kind of demons?

BEN: Little green demons, with tails and pitchforks. They poke me with their sharp points. They make me weep at a sunset, and at the beauty of nature. And they give me no release. So I reach out, when I can, where I can, and here I am.

ERICKSON: Maybe you ought to see a psychiatrist. If you can't afford one they got all sorts of clinics.

BEN: Now why should I deprive myself of comfort?

ERICKSON: Comfort?

BEN: Yes, comfort. The assurance that affection can be had for the asking is my only source of comfort. That, and my two young charges. We play house, my mother and I, with two ready-made children.

ERICKSON: You responsible for two kids?

BEN: I most certainly am.

ERICKSON: Then you ought to be ashamed of yourself.

BEN: I am, my dear Erickson, I most certainly am. But for different reasons. You see before you a man with a white albatross around his neck, but unlike the ancient mariner, no one will listen to my tale of woe.

ERICKSON: Everyone's got problems, kid. And it's easy enough to feel sorry for yourself.

THE ESTABLISHMENT

BEN: Oh, but you see, it's not for myself I feel sorry for. I am weighed down by a world I did not create. This ready-made Society doesn't suit me at all. I blunder, I stumble and I bleed.

(DONOVAN reenters.)

DONOVAN: I thought I told you to keep moving.

ERICKSON: Let him alone.

DONOVAN: Those cocksuckers think they can do whatever they want.

ERICKSON: What time's the wagon leaving?

DONOVAN: We got another hour yet. *(To BEN)* C'mere, honeybunch. Stand right over here. How many tricks did you pick up today?

BEN: None.

DONOVAN: You were hangin' around that place for hours. I saw you.

BEN: I just walked in there.

DONOVAN: What other places do you hang out?

BEN: None.

DONOVAN: That's what you say. How many times you been arrested?

BEN: Just once. For running numbers, but I was released.

THE ESTABLISHMENT

ERICKSON: I'll be right back.

DONOVAN: Where you going?

ERICKSON: I'll be right back! *(HE goes off.)*

DONOVAN: You got a lot of friends?

BEN: Not really, no.

DONOVAN: You like little boys, don't you?

BEN: Sexually, no.

DONOVAN: Didn't I see you hangin' around the school playground the other day.

BEN: What time was that?

DONOVAN: Oh, about four o'clock or so.

BEN: Last week?

DONOVAN: Yeah, last week.

BEN: It couldn't have been me. I was working an early shift last week.

DONOVAN: Any of your friends hang around schools?

BEN: Not that I know of.

DONOVAN: You're just making it tougher for yourself, you know. You help us out, and I'll put in a good word for you.

THE ESTABLISHMENT

BEN: I can't tell you something I don't know.

DONOVAN: Where else do you hang out?

BEN: I told you. I don't hang out anywhere.

DONOVAN: How many orgies you been to?

BEN: I've never been to an orgy.

DONOVAN: You know Elyot Raymond, don't you?

BEN: No.

DONOVAN: He knows you.

BEN: I've never heard of him.

DONOVAN: Okay. Sit down over there. On second thought. I think you need a little more exercise. How many push-ups can you do?

BEN: I don't know.

DONOVAN: Well, why don't we start with ten. Okay, kid. Hop to it.

(BEN starts to do push-ups. ERICKSON reenters.)

ERICKSON: Why don't you leave the kid alone?

DONOVAN: I'm doin' him a favor. The cocksucker needs the exercise.

THE ESTABLISHMENT

ERICKSON: Leave him alone.

DONOVAN: Okay, kid. Sit down. Over there.

ERICKSON: We got almost an hour. Why don't we go out for some coffee.

DONOVAN: Hey, honeybunch. Go sit in that other room. Don't worry, we won't forget you.

BEN: How long will I be kept here?

DONOVAN: You'll be kept here as long as necessary.

BEN: I was told I could make a phone call.

ERICKSON: There's a pay phone in there. You got a dime?

BEN: Yes.

DONOVAN: Then what are you waiting for?

BEN: Thank you. *(HE goes off.)*

DONOVAN: Well, at least we got our fruit for the day.

> *(THEY start off as the lights start to dim, and blues music is heard playing softly.)*

DONOVAN: Did you ever let one of them blow you? They're better at it than most women.

> *(THEY are off as the lights come down.)*

BUCK JARVIS
(A Play in Two Acts)

CAST OF CHARACTERS

Stanley Blackstone, The Mayor
Larry Keefer, The Sheriff
Bart Warren, The Bartender
Jeff Calvin, A Cattleman
Edwin Spruce, The Mortician
Val Henderson, Editor of "The Freetown Weekly"
Henry Fowler, The School Teacher
Abigail Fowler, Henry's Mother
George "Doc" Hardy, The Town Doctor
Cornelius Morgan, The Reverend
Joe Costello, A Farmer
Fran Costello, Joe's Wife
Irv Cooper, A Young Handyman
Dora Brown, Proprietor of The Black Cow Saloon
Buck Jarvis, A Gunslinger
Jack Kegley, A Cattleman
Steve Kegley, Jack's Brother
John Kegley, Jack's Father

Abigail Fowler and Fran Costello can be played by one actress. Cornelius Morgan, Joe Costello and John Kegley can be played by one actor.

SCENE
The Black Cow, a saloon in Freetown, Nebraska

TIME
The Old West. A Sunday afternoon in August

ACT ONE

(The strains of the first verse of"The Streets of Laredo" is heard:
"As I walked out in the streets of Laredo,
As I walked out in Laredo one day,
I spied a poor cowboy wrapped up in white linen,
All wrapped in white linen as cold as the clay."
The lights come up on the main room of the saloon, The Black Cow. A door downstage right leads to the store room. A door upstage right leads to the apartment of DORA BROWN, the proprietor. A double door in the rear wall center leads to the street. There is a window on either side of the door high up on the wall. The bar runs along the stage left wall. A shelf on the wall contains the liquor bottles. Behind the bottles is a mirror and above the mirror hangs a large painting of a reclining nude. A door downstage left leads to an alleyway. Several tables and chairs are scattered about the room.
It is two o'clock in the afternoon, a hot, sticky day in August. STANLEY BLACKSTONE, the mayor, sits at a table playing solitaire. LARRY KEEFER, the sheriff, stands leaning against the bar. BART WARREN, the bartender is wiping the tables with a damp cloth.)

BLACKSTONE: You say you saw him ride out of town?

BART: That's right.

BLACKSTONE: What time?

BART: Around eleven, I guess.

BLACKSTONE: You guess?

BART: That's right, I guess. I didn't know I'd be questioned.

BUCK JARVIS

BLACKSTONE: How come no one else saw him?

BART: Maybe because everyone else was either asleep or at the funeral.

LARRY: Maybe we ought to postpone this whole thing.

BLACKSTONE: What do you think, Bart?

BART: Why ask me?

BLACKSTONE: You seem to know everything.

LARRY: I don't think anybody's gonna show up anyway. It's after one.

BLACKSTONE: We'll give 'em a few more minutes.

LARRY: It just doesn't seem right.

BLACKSTONE: Have you got a better solution?

LARRY: I like things out in the open.

BLACKSTONE: So do I, Larry. So do I. And that's why I called this meeting. I'm not trying to talk anybody into anything. All I want is a simple, open discussion. Bart, why don't you give the sheriff here a drink? Mark it on my bill.

(BART pours a drink.)

BLACKSTONE: Let's face it, Larry, Buck Jarvis is not in his right mind. If this town had a nut house, he'd be in it. Look, no one's

BUCK JARVIS

fonder of Buck than I am. He was a fine man once, and now he's a menace. It's as simple as that; and something has gotta be done.

(There are two knocks on the door. It's pushed open and JEFF CALVIN, a dark, handsome, well-dressed man in his early forties, enters and looks around.)

JEFF: Where is everyone?

BLACKSTONE: They're still at the funeral.

JEFF: Didn't you go?

BLACKSTONE: Well, of course, I did, and I paid my respects.

JEFF: All right. Let's get this over with.

BLACKSTONE: What's your rush?

JEFF: My wife's giving a dinner party, and if I'm late she'll start asking questions.

BART: What's the matter, Jeff? You afraid of that sweet, gentle creature?

JEFF: You serving drinks?

BLACKSTONE: Give my friend here a drink.

JEFF: Not right now, thank you. How long is this gonna take?

BLACKSTONE: That all depends.

JEFF: On what?

BUCK JARVIS

BLACKSTONE: On how soon we come to an agreement.

JEFF: I thought we were in agreement.

BLACKSTONE: We are, Jeff, up to a point that is.

JEFF: What point is that?

BLACKSTONE: We're all agreed that something's gotta be done about Buck. The question is...what and how?

JEFF: I thought that was all decided. We've gotta shoot him down. How else can we get rid of him?

LARRY: Are you willing to take on the job?

JEFF: I wouldn't be here if I wasn't.

LARRY: Yes, well, not everyone's as eager as you are.

JEFF: That poor little girl. It might have been anyone's child. Yours or mine.

LARRY: I'm quite aware of that, Jeff. But the law happens to be the law.

BLACKSTONE: Which law are you referring to, Larry?

LARRY: Stanley, the judge ruled that the little girl's death was an accident.

JEFF: No one's saying he killed her on purpose.

LARRY: Then...

BUCK JARVIS

JEFF: The fact of the matter is Buck is irresponsible. He's drunk all the time. Rides around town like a maniac, shooting his gun off whenever he feels like, scaring people half to death.

BLACKSTONE: Now, look, no one is denying the great service Buck has done for this community, but you cannot deny the fact that the man's just gone to pieces. Let me ask you this? Are we gonna let things slip back to way they were before Buck came to town?

LARRY: Oh, come now, Stanley.

BLACKSTONE: What?

LARRY: Don't you think you're exaggerating just a little?

BLACKSTONE: Buck Jarvis is nothing more than a killing machine gone wild. Well, go on, say it.

> *(There are two knocks on the door and EDWIN SPRUCE, the mortician, a small, neat man in a black suit, and GEORGE "DOC" HARDY, a doctor in his seventies, enter.)*

EDWIN: Sorry I'm late. I couldn't get away.

BLACKSTONE: That's quite all right, Mr. Spruce. Doc. Where are the others?

EDWIN: They're on their way. It sure is hot out there. I can't remember a summer as hot as this.

BLACKSTONE: What we need now is a nice spell of rain.

EDWIN: We're certainly due for one.

BUCK JARVIS

BLACKSTONE: That's something we can't count on, is it? What I wanna know, Mr. Spruce, is how you manage to look so cool, even in that black suit of yours.

EDWIN: It's very simple. I ignore the heat.

BLACKSTONE: Mind over matter. Very wise, Mr. Spruce, very wise. Now tell me, how do you stand in regard to the question before us?

EDWIN: I'm not quite sure what the question is.

BLACKSTONE: One way or another we have got to get rid of Buck Jarvis.

EDWIN: One way or another? Yes, well, I've gotta think about that.

JEFF: Good Lord! Are we gonna be here all day?

LARRY: A man's life's at stake, Jeff.

JEFF: We have lived with this situation long enough; and we have certainly talked about it long enough.

LARRY: You may not remember what this town was like before Buck Jarvis came here.

EDWIN: And he came here at our invitation.

BLACKSTONE: No one's disputing that, Mr. Spruce.

JEFF: If you were the sheriff you ought be, there wouldn't be any call for this meeting.

BUCK JARVIS

BLACKSTONE: Now, now, Jeff.

LARRY: If you're so smart, young man, why didn't you run for sheriff?

BLACKSTONE: Jeff's not a politician, Larry. Jeff is a business man.

LARRY: Well, before you can conduct any business, there's gotta be peace.

JEFF: I'll agree with you there.

BLACKSTONE: Now, Larry. Jeff has always pulled his weight, and, to his credit, he's volunteered to continue to do so. Haven't you, Jeff?

JEFF: That's right.

EDWIN: Maybe we oughta keep that door open and get some air.

BART: It's cooler in here with the door shut.

EDWIN: And there used to be a fan.

BART: The fan broke down.

EDWIN: Can't you fix it?

BART: It just broke down this morning. And besides, we've gotta send for a new one.

(Two knocks on the door are heard. The door is opened

BUCK JARVIS

and VAL HENDERSON, the editor of The Freetown Weekly, and HENRY FOWLER, the school teacher enter.)

VAL: Jack Kegley's right behind us.

HENRY: Is this all there is?

BLACKSTONE: I would have liked to have invited the entire population, but that would get us nowhere, since there are some poor fools in this town who've turned a blind eye to the way things are.

LARRY: Well, we've certainly got to give serious consideration to what Buck has accomplished.

JEFF: Now look here, Sheriff, you're the one that's been raisin' all this fuss.

LARRY: That doesn't mean that I wanna see him dead.

JEFF: What does it mean?

BLACKSTONE: Exactly what point are you trying to make?

LARRY: All right. I'll speak my piece. For one thing, I consider this meeting illegal.

BLACKSTONE: Do you now?

LARRY: I most certainly do.

BLACKSTONE: Well, since I just happen to be the mayor of this town, I think I have the right to form a vigilante committee.

BUCK JARVIS

LARRY: Let's put our cards on the table, Stanley. We're here to pick the man that's going to gun down Buck Jarvis. That's what we're here for, and we all know who we're going to end up choosing.

> *(There are two knocks on the door and JACK KEGLEY, a straight-forward looking young cowhand, followed by his brother STEVE, a pleasant looking young man a couple of years younger.)*

BLACKSTONE: I guess we're all here now. Jack. Steve. How's your family, Jack?

JACK: Fine, thank you.

BLACKSTONE: We haven't seen very much of you lately.

JACK: I've been pretty busy on the ranch.

BLACKSTONE: You're gonna be as rich as Jeff here, pretty soon.

JACK: I hope so.

BLACKSTONE: Everybody's mighty proud of the way you turned out, Jack.

JACK: I don't think we're here to discuss the way I turned out, Mr. Blackstone.

STEVE: Well, it's certainly been a relief to a lot of us, Brother.

BLACKSTONE: I'm not gonna try to make this any sort of a formal meeting. If we just show a little respect for one another, I

BUCK JARVIS

think we can settle this in no time. Who'd like to start us off? Mr. Spruce? You can be quite articulate when you wanna be.

EDWIN: I pass.

HENRY: What about you, Mr. Fowler? You're used to conducting a class. Why don't you start us off?

HENRY: Well, I...ah...

LARRY: Why don't you start us off, Mr. Mayor, since you're the one that called this meeting?

BLACKSTONE: And I'm ready to call it off. Day and night, night and day, that's all I hear, "Something's gotta be done. Something's gotta be done." And then when I suggest that we form a committee, people start hemming and hawing. "Oh, yes. You're quite right." And then they change the subject. Abe Foster keeps telling me how much Buck owes him for all the food he helps himself to in his store, and then when I tell him I'm calling a meeting, he tells me he can't be here this afternoon. It's his little grandson's birthday. Oh, now look here. I don't want to do all the talking. Val, you're always shooting your mouth off in that paper of yours.

VAL: I'm here as a reporter.

BLACKSTONE: All right then. It looks like I'm gonna have to speak for all of you, since suddenly everybody here's got lockjaw. When we hired Buck to come and clean up this town he was a fine, brave man. But, even then, there was something peculiar about him. There was a job that had to be done, and he did it. But even so, you can't respect a man for enjoying a job like that, and let's face it, Buck Jarvis enjoys killing. Okay, okay. The town is

BUCK JARVIS

clean right now, and Buck has a right to stay and enjoy the fruit of his labor, but there's no one else to kill, and the trouble is, that's what Buck lives for; he lives to kill. There are four innocent people dead in this town because of Buck Jarvis, and one is crippled. Is that a fact or isn't it? I'm talking to you, Mr. Spruce, since you're the one that had to bury them all.

EDWIN: That is a fact, sad to say.

HENRY: But that doesn't mean that we have to use violence, does it?

JACK: Isn't it the sheriff's job to keep law and order?

LARRY: You want the job, Jack Kegley, you can have it.

STEVE: Take it easy, Jack.

JACK: I'm not trying to be nasty. I'm just asking a simple question.

EDWIN: He's right, Sheriff.

LARRY: All right then. As far as that goes there is now law and order in this town.

JACK: Then why are we holding this meeting?

JEFF: You call the death of four people law and order?

LARRY: Buck Jarvis has never been accused of committing a crime. No one knows who fired those shots during that free for all. And that little girl's death was ruled an accident.

BUCK JARVIS

BLACKSTONE: Henry, you are an erudite young man. I'd like to hear what you have to say?

HENRY: I'm a patient man, Mr. Blackstone. I think we oughta wait.

JEFF: Wait? Wait for what?

HENRY: Eventually Mr. Jarvis is going to commit a crime.

JEFF: In other words we've got to live in double fear? We've got to be afraid that he's going to commit a crime, and then again, we've got to be afraid that he's not gonna commit a crime?

BLACKSTONE: Henry, Buck Jarvis commits a crime every day, and we know it. He is stealing Abe Foster blind. He takes up a room at the hotel, which he doesn't pay for.

HENRY: Then put him in jail. But I don't see that's any reason to kill a man for stealing food, for not paying his bills.

JEFF: This town is supporting him, and it isn't as if he hasn't been paid. He got his money.

VAL: And you think our debt ends there?

JEFF: You're the one that's been writing all those snide little articles. What do you want, Mr. Henderson? Can you tell us that?

VAL: There are two sides to every question.

JEFF: That's right. And there comes a time when you've gotta make a choice.

BUCK JARVIS

VAL: We paid Buck to kill, didn't we?

JEFF: Are you trying to say that it's our fault that he's gone berserk?

VAL: Maybe it is, and maybe it isn't. We hired a man that was fast with a gun, and when you're geared up like that, you can't expect a man to change, just like that.

JEFF: That's his responsibility, not ours.

JACK: What difference does it make whose responsibility it is? The point is there's a job to be done. And who's going to do it?

HENRY: Which job are you referring to?

JEFF: Don't be a fool, Henry. There are two good shots in this town, me and Jack here.

JACK: Count me out. I've put my gun away. I gave my wife my word.

> *(The door downstage is opened and ABIGAIL FOWLER, a stern, middle-aged woman, enters. SHE is followed by CORNELIUS MORGAN, a minister. EVERYONE rises.)*

BLACKSTONE: Hello, Abigail. Here for a snort?

ABIGAIL: You know what I'm here for, Stanley.

CORNELIUS: I'm ashamed of you Stanley Blackstone.

BLACKSTONE: Now Reverend, you're not in the pulpit now.

BUCK JARVIS

CORNELIUS: Why, Mr. Mayor, why isn't this meeting being held where all public meetings are held?

ABIGAIL: Edwin Spruce and you, Jeff...I never expected to find you two here.

BLACKSTONE: We might say the same for you, Abigail.

CORNELIUS: The whole town's going to know about this meeting.

BLACKSTONE: Calm down, Reverend, calm down. We're not in church right now.

CORNELIUS: And you, Doc Hardy, you of all people.

DOC: Don't look at me, Cornelius. I'm just here to mend the cuts and bruises.

BLACKSTONE: You don't mind if we all sit down, Abigail, do you?

ABIGAIL: Not at all. As a matter of fact, I hope you won't let me interfere with the proceedings.

CORNELIUS: This is shocking, absolutely shocking. Haven't you men seen enough bloodshed in your lifetime?

BLACKSTONE: As a matter of fact, that's why we're here, Reverend.

CORNELIUS: Murder begets murder, Mr. Blackstone. Where is it going to stop?

BUCK JARVIS

BLACKSTONE: We'll leave those long-winded sermons to you, Cornelius.

CORNELIUS: Religion isn't just words, Mr. Blackstone. It isn't just sermons and attending church on Sunday. Religion is something we live by.

BLACKSTONE: I think we'll all agree that the church has had its share in murder, Reverend Morgan, as well as death.

CORNELIUS: Let's not change the subject, Stanley.

BLACKSTONE: What, exactly, is the subject?

CORNELIUS: This country has come a long way since it was first settled. Are we to continue living like the beasts in the field?

BLACKSTONE: Unfortunately, Reverend, I'm afraid, that human nature is human nature, and we are still the same creatures that we've always been.

CORNELIUS: We're to cater to our basest instincts? Is that what you're trying to tell me?

BLACKSTONE: All I'm saying, Reverend, is that these bodies are still the same bodies the Lord above has given us.

CORNELIUS: He also gave us souls, and the ability to distinguish between right and wrong.

BLACKSTONE: We're living in a democracy, Reverend, and in a democracy the majority rules. Now, there are twelve of us here, and of that twelve, two of you seem to be moved by some holy spirit. And that's the way it would read if the whole town were lined up right now.

CORNELIUS: Stanley, I beg of you, dismiss these men.

BLACKSTONE: You dismiss them, Reverend.

CORNELIUS: Do you men know why you're here?

JACK: I gather we're here to deal with a matter that...has to be dealt with.

CORNELIUS: I see. So you've all gone ahead and set yourselves up as court and executioner. Is that it?

STEVE: Well, Reverend, you must admit, something has got to be done.

CORNELIUS: Stanley, why don't you let me talk to him?

BLACKSTONE: You have talked to him, Cornelius, and where did it get us?

ABIGAIL: Jeff Calvin, you're a God fearing man. You have a family.

JEFF: That's why I'm here.

ABIGAIL: And does your wife know you're here?

JEFF: I don't tell my wife how to cook, and she doesn't tell me how to run things.

BUCK JARVIS

CORNELIUS: This happens to be a matter that concerns every single person in this community, male and female.

ABIGAIL: If I recall, Buck Jarvis saved your wife considerable embarrassment at one time, and physical harm.

JEFF: And I'm grateful to him for that. He did his job, and he was paid for it.

ABIGAIL: I have no respect for Buck Jarvis, but he helped us when we needed help.

DOC: That's right, Stanley.

BLACKSTONE: I thought you were here, Doc, to mend the cuts and bruises.

DOC: If I can prevent them, better yet.

ABIGAIL: You're the one that's responsible for all of this, Val Henderson. You and that paper of yours.

VAL: I didn't think you subscribed to my paper, Abigail. Or maybe you just borrow someone else's copy. Is that it?

HENRY: Mother, you promised not to interfere.

BLACKSTONE: You've learned a very important lesson, Son.

HENRY: And what might that be?

BLACKSTONE: Never put your faith in a woman's word.

BUCK JARVIS

ABIGAIL: I'm sure Margaret would be interested in your attitude towards women, Mr. Mayor.

BLACKSTONE: I happen to have the greatest respect for my wife, and my wife has the greatest respect for me. All right, all right. I must admit that the Reverend does have a point. Why don't we put this to a vote. How many people here believe that nothing should be done about Buck Jarvis. Raise your hands.

(There is silence. No one raises their hand.)

BLACKSTONE: I rest my case.

CORNELIUS: All right, Stanley, like you say, this is a democracy. Let's call a town meeting, and hear what everyone in this town has to say.

BLACKSTONE: All right. When do you want to call this meeting?

CORNELIUS: Wednesday, Thursday. Whenever you say.

BLACKSTONE: Let's make it Thursday. On one condition.

CORNELIUS: And what might that be?

BLACKSTONE: Not a word of this meeting to anyone else.

CORNELIUS: Fair enough. I hope to see you all at our special service this evening.

ABIGAIL: Coming, Henry?

HENRY: I'll be home shortly, Mother.

BUCK JARVIS

(ABIGAIL goes off with CORNELIUS.)

EDWIN: Maybe it's better this way.

BLACKSTONE: Don't be a fool. I just said that to get rid of him. Whatever we're gonna do has got to be done before this evening's service.

JACK: Why before the service?

BLACKSTONE: Because that's how long we can trust Abigail to keep her trap shut. I'm sorry, Son, but your mother loves to hear herself talk.

EDWIN: Maybe we ought to wait until Thursday, Stanley.

BLACKSTONE: And give Buck a chance to get all worked up about this?

JEFF: It's ridiculous for a whole community to be afraid of one man.

DOC: There was a time when we were all very grateful for the fear that Buck Jarvis inspired.

JACK: We've been through all that, Doc.

DOC: He taught you how to shoot.

JACK: He taught me lots of things it's taken me a long time to forget.

STEVE: That's right, Doc.

BUCK JARVIS

DOC: You all go right ahead. I'm not going to say another word. I'm just going to sit here with Mr. Spruce. We'll just wait until the killing's over and then we'll do our job...and wait for the next one...and the next one.

JEFF: There's only going to be one more.

(IRV, a pale, wiry boy of sixteen enters from the outside.)

IRV: Mr. and Mrs. Costello are heading this way.

BLACKSTONE: Fine, boy. You send 'em right in.

IRV: Yes, sir. *(HE goes off.)*

VAL: I don't know why you have that kid out there, standing guard.

BLACKSTONE: There are several reasons, Val, which I don't intend to go into for the present.

VAL: It seems to me there are a lot of things you don't intend to go into.

BLACKSTONE: Like what?

HENRY: No one said anything about the Costello's being here.

BLACKSTONE: I think they've got as much right to be here as anyone of us; even more so. I think we can all agree to that.

(The door is opened and JOE COSTELLO, a gaunt man of forty, and his wife, FRAN, a faded blond in her late thirties, enter. The MEN rise.)

BUCK JARVIS

FRAN: Please. Don't get up.

JOE: Sorry to keep you all waiting like this.

BLACKSTONE: We didn't expect you any sooner, Joe. Sit down, sit down. We're grateful that you've come at all. Would you care for a glass or water, Mrs. Costello?

FRAN: No, thank you.

JOE: Have you decided who its going to be?

BLACKSTONE: We haven't decided anything yet.

JOE: We don't want to see anymore people hurt, but he's got to be put away. Now. Before he has a chance to kill anymore.

FRAN: We know he's done a great deal for this town, but he's undone all the good that he's done. I wish there was a legal way, but if there isn't... Well, it's gotta be done, that's all. Maybe we were wrong in using evil to fight evil, but we had no choice, and it isn't as if he's not going to get a fair chance. He's going to get more of a chance than my baby did.

DOC: That was an accident, Fran.

JOE: He was drunk, Doc, and you know it.

DOC: He didn't do it deliberately.

JOE: He ran my baby down, and he didn't even stop. And what about Frank Emery? That poor kid'll be hopping around on a wooden stick for the rest of his life.

BUCK JARVIS

DOC: Frank asked for it, and you know it.

FRAN: And what about those three other people? Did Mrs. Jackson ask for it? And Samuel Peters? And Waldo Finch?

DOC: That was a free-for-all drag down fight, and no one knows who fired those shots.

JOE: And no one ever tried to find out.

LARRY: That's not true.

JOE: Why are you sticking up for him, Doc?

DOC: I'm sticking up for you, Joe, and for every one else in this town. We fought for law and order. Didn't we, Joe?

JOE: And we're still fighting for it.

DOC: No, Joe. That's not true. Now we're fighting for respectability.

BLACKSTONE: Let's not start splitting hairs, Doc.

DOC: And you, Stanley, are responsible for all this.

FRAN: I have the greatest respect in the world for you, Doc. You know that. I didn't know what I was going to say before I came into this room. But this town has got to be made safe for little kids to grow up in, and, as long as Buck Jarvis is running around loose, it won't be. I don't want to say anymore. Take me home, Joe. Jack, you're a good shot. We'll be grateful to you for the rest of our lives.

BUCK JARVIS

(JOE and FRAN go off.)

DOC: Don't you believe it, Jack?

HENRY: Does anyone mind if I open the door?

BLACKSTONE: Sit down, Mr Fowler.

HENRY: It's suffocating in here.

BLACKSTONE: I said, sit down.

DOC: You heard the mayor, Henry.

BLACKSTONE: What are you trying to do, Doc? You know as well as I do that something's gotta be done about Buck.

DOC: How are you gonna collect all the money he owes you, if you kill him?

STEVE: You're had your say, Doc.

DOC: No, sir. Not by a long shot. We all know who elected you mayor, Stanley; and now you're tired of paying off.

BLACKSTONE: Buck did some campaigning for me, when I was first elected. I was re-elected on my own.

DOC: That's what hurts, doesn't it, Stanley.

BLACKSTONE: Buck is bleeding me, just like he's bleeding the people in this town. I'm ashamed to admit it, and so is everyone else. I could just as well accuse you of wanting Buck around so that there'll be more work for you to do.

BUCK JARVIS

JEFF: No one's thinking about money, Doc.

BLACKSTONE: Let's take a vote, and quit all this arguing.

JEFF: We just took a vote.

BLACKSTONE: Well, let's take another one. All those opposed to immediate action, raise your hands.

(DOC and HENRY raises their hands.)

BLACKSTONE: That settles it. He'll be here for the poker game this afternoon, and the only fair way is to call him. Unless someone has a better idea. Now, who's it gonna be.

LARRY: Jeff volunteered.

EDWIN: We can't afford second best, with all apologies to Jeff.

VAL: Second best is better than nothing.

STEVE: Buck isn't the man he used to be.

EDWIN: He's still pretty quick.

VAL: Of course, we all know there's only one man in this town that can really stand up to him.

JEFF: Jack gave his word to his wife.

JACK: It's not only that, Jeff. It just doesn't seem right. Buck taught me how to shoot.

BLACKSTONE: What about the other things he taught you, Jack?

BUCK JARVIS

Do you want your sons growing up with Buck as their idol, just like you did? There's no need to tell you the harm Buck Jarvis is doing, just by being alive.

STEVE: Jeff is pretty quick, Mr. Blackstone.

JACK: Stay out of this, Steve. I don't need no nursemaid.

BLACKSTONE: You still carry it, Jack. Obviously you still think there's a need for it.

VAL: He's not the only one that carries a gun, Stanley. Jeff volunteered, and Jeff's a good shot.

LARRY: No one should be talked into this.

BLACKSTONE: I guess Jeff's our man, then. That right, Jeff?

JEFF: I guess so.

BLACKSTONE: We get together around three for poker. Why don't you drop by around three thirty or so?

JEFF: Okay.

BLACKSTONE: And from there on in, it's up to you.

JEFF: If I'm a little too slow, I want my family to know the truth.

BLACKSTONE: You'll be back home in time for that dinner party.

JEFF: I hope you're right.

HENRY: Good luck, Jeff.

BUCK JARVIS

JEFF: Thank you, Henry.

EDWIN: *(HE rises.)* Gentlemen.

BLACKSTONE: You're usually more articulate, Edwin.

EDWIN: If I said anymore it might be thought in bad taste.

BLACKSTONE: We're not that sensitive, Edwin.

EDWIN: I guess I'm just used to working with people that don't talk. All this conversation gets my head in a muddle.

BLACKSTONE: Give my regards to the wife, Jeff.

JEFF: I don't think I'll mention my seeing you this afternoon.

BLACKSTONE: Good idea.

> *(JEFF goes off, followed by EDWIN and HENRY. IRV enters.)*

IRV: I guess the meeting's over, ain't it?

BLACKSTONE: Just about, Son, just about.

LARRY: I'm not lookin' forward to that poker game, I'll tell you that.

DOC: Sure. Now it's easy to speak up.

LARRY: The cards haven't been dealt yet, have they?

DOC: Where've you been?

BUCK JARVIS

LARRY: You know what I mean.

DOC: Yes, I know what you mean. Well, I've got to go and bring another poor sucker into this world. If he knew what was in store for him, he'd stay right where he is.

BLACKSTONE: It might be a girl, Doc.

DOC: Whatever the gender, I shall be back.

BLACKSTONE: Now, we wouldn't want you to get hurt, Doc. You're the only doctor we've got.

(DOC goes off.)

BART: And he's a damn good one, too.

VAL: You're not going to hang around till the poker game, are you?

BLACKSTONE: We can't all leave at once.

VAL: That's quite all right, Stanley. You've always got a good reason for everything you do. Only one of these days you might just go and outsmart yourself.

BLACKSTONE: Talk about me nice in that next editorial of yours. See you later, Larry.

LARRY: That's right, Stanley.

BLACKSTONE: What's the matter now?

BUCK JARVIS

LARRY: Nothing. Everything's just fine, Stanley. Everything's just fine.

(LARRY goes off, followed by VAL.)

BLACKSTONE: Let's have a couple of drinks here.

JACK: Not for me, thanks.

BLACKSTONE: How about you, Steve?

STEVE: I'll have a short one.

BLACKSTONE: Make that two, Bart. What's the matter, Jack. What's eatin' you?

JACK: Nothing. Nothing at all.

BLACKSTONE: How's that beautiful wife of yours? You're a lucky man, Jack. It isn't easy for a woman out here.

JACK: Babs is more than a woman. She happens to be the better part of me.

BLACKSTONE: She certainly helped to straighten you out. I will say that. And your charming mother...how is she?

JACK: Ma's fine.

BLACKSTONE: I guess we know how your Dad feels about all this.

JACK: Dad's always been sorta strict. You gotta admire him for that.

BUCK JARVIS

STEVE: Ain't that the truth!

JACK: Steve here's the one that can get away with anything.

STEVE: You just gotta know how to handle him, that's all.

BLACKSTONE: In a country like this you've gotta have something to cling to. With your father, it happens to be religion. What do you think drives a man like Buck to behave the way he does?

JACK: How should I know?

BLACKSTONE: Except for Dora, you've been as close to that man as any of us. It just seems to me that that man doesn't believe in anything, except his gun. And I think he's beginning to doubt even that. As a matter of fact, I think we'll be doing him a favor, Jack.

JACK: How do you mean?

BLACKSTONE: Buck's a lost soul, Jack, and all he wants is somebody to put a bullet through his head, and he hasn't got the nerve to do it himself. I mean, think about it. What has he got to look forward to? If it wasn't for Dora, he'd be dead by now. Ain't that right, Bart?

BART: You're doin' the talkin', Mayor.

BLACKSTONE: And maybe Irv, there. Ain't that right, Irv?

IRV: No one's putting a bullet through Buck's head, except maybe from behind his back.

BLACKSTONE: That's the way you felt about him once. Wasn't it, Jack?

BUCK JARVIS

JACK: Maybe Irv is right, Mr. Blackstone. Jeff's no match for Buck.

BLACKSTONE: Say, Bart, how about walkin' over to my place and bringin' back that case of Irish Whiskey? Dora said she wanted to buy it from me. Here's something for your trouble. *(HE hands him some money.)*

BART: In all this heat?

BLACKSTONE: *(HE hands him more money.)* Is that better?

BART: Keep an eye on the place.

BLACKSTONE: We'll be here till you get back.

BART: Come on, Irv.

(BART goes off, followed by IRV.)

BLACKSTONE: I'm a true politician, Jack. I'm always up to something, but that doesn't mean that I don't care about people. I may have cut a few corners now and then, but I do care about what happens to the citizens of this town.

JACK: I guess that's why you were re-elected.

BLACKSTONE: Doc's a fine man, we all know that. But he's not very practical. He's in his seventies, and he still walks around with his head in the clouds. This town is living under a cloud of fear, just the same as we were when we were over-run with killers and thieves and whores. You're not living in town, now. You don't know what it's like. Ever since that brawl people have been snappin' at each other. No one knows when it might happen again.

BUCK JARVIS

Buck is drunk, most of the time, and he's always arguin' with somebody. He's itchin' to use his gunon someone, but there's no one to use it on. People were patient with him up until that brawl, but three innocent people dead, just like that, for no reason at all. That's pretty hard to take, especially now, when we thought we were beginning to be a decent town. And he ain't gonna leave Jack, ever. He knows he's not wanted, and that makes him even madder. He's gonna keep on drinking and carousing, Jack, until he picks a fight with somebody and kills him deliberately.

STEVE: Why are you telling us all this, Mr. Blackstone? You don't want Jack to start usin' his gun again, do you?

BLACKSTONE: Jack's grown up now, Steve. He knows when to stop. He's got a balance wheel inside of him now, not like Buck.

STEVE: A balance wheel is a delicate thing, Mr. Blackstone. Jack doesn't drink anymore, because when he starts, he can't stop drinkin'. And he's still proud of the fact of how good a shot he is, and how fast he is on the draw.

JACK: I still carry my gun, Steve, and I'll use it only if I have to.

STEVE: Is that what you tell Babs?

JACK: I don't have to, because she knows it. The time ain't come to put our guns away, not yet.

BLACKSTONE: We're just talkin', Steve.

STEVE: Well, it's bad talk.

JACK: Mr. Blackstone's right. You're actin' worse than Ma.

BUCK JARVIS

STEVE: All right, Jack. Go ahead and shoot Buck Jarvis down. Then you'll be top gun, won't you? And won't Babs be proud of you, and the kids and all of us. Except, maybe, at night when Babs'll be wonderin' who's gonna shoot you down. It won't be worryin' me none, because Nancy and I'll be married then and I'll have my own family to think about. But who's gonna look after Babs and those kids of yours? Maybe the Mayor would like that job.

JACK: Jeff has a family, too you know.

STEVE: Jeff Calvin's a rich man. He's got money in the bank.

JACK: What am I, a pauper?

STEVE: How about a drink, Jack. Just one little shot.

JACK: Will you leave me alone?!

BLACKSTONE: Maybe Steve's right, Jack. Maybe we have no right. I want to see Buck destroyed, not you. And I know that your father will never forgive you.

JACK: That don't worry me none. We never seen eye to eye, my Pa and me. There's gotta be a right, and there's gotta be a wrong, and I wish I could see it.

STEVE: Why has there gotta be a right, and why has there gotta be a wrong?

JACK: You ain't makin' any sense.

STEVE: You don't even come to town anymore. You got a ranch to run.

BUCK JARVIS

JACK: My kids'll be comin' to town some day. They'll be goin' to school here.

STEVE: The judge said that was an accident. The little girl just ran into the street. She didn't even look where she was goin'. She might have been run down by anyone, Jack, anyone.

BLACKSTONE: Yes, well there are gonna be a lot more accidents like that, while Buck Jarvis is around.

STEVE: Besides it's all been settled. Jeff's gonna take it on.

BLACKSTONE: The game starts at three. Jeff won't get here till three thirty.

STEVE: You had it all figured out, Mr. Blackstone.

BLACKSTONE: No, Steve. I thought, and everyone as well thought, that Jack was gonna take on the job.

STEVE: At least Buck got paid for cleanin' up this town.

JACK: You're talkin' too much.

BLACKSTONE: I ain't gonna say no more. It's up to you, Jack. You do what you have to do.

STEVE: Remember what Babs said.

JACK: Babs said lots of things, but she'll stick by me, no matter what I do.

STEVE: You go after Buck, Jack, and you've lost yourself a brother, because I won't go through all that again.

BUCK JARVIS

JACK: C'mon, Steve.

STEVE: No, I mean it, Jack. I got other things to think about. After all you been through, and you ain't learned your lesson yet.

JACK: I'm not a kid anymore.

STEVE: You're the same man you always been. Leave sleeping dogs lie, Jack.

JACK: Boy, you sure started something, Mr. Blackstone.

BLACKSTONE: You think it over, Jack. You got till three o'clock.

JACK: That's not much time, is it?

STEVE: Time enough to draw up a will.

JACK: You just keep at me, Steve, and I'll go through with it, just to spite you.

BLACKSTONE: Don't you have any faith in your brother, Steve?

STEVE: This ain't go nothin' to do with faith, Mr. Blackstone. I know what Jack can do. He went out on that drive, year after year, and he saved every penny, and he went out and bought that ranch. He lived on nothin' but hope for all those years. That's one side of him. But there's another side of him, Mr. Blackstone.

BLACKSTONE: There are many sides to all of us, Steve.

STEVE: I know that, Mr. Blackstone. But the higher we climb, the longer the fall. There ain't many people that's seen Jack the way I seen him, so drunk he couldn't make it to the privy, and I was the

BUCK JARVIS

one that had to carry him all the way home, smellin' of crap. Now, if you want that job, you're welcome to it.

BLACKSTONE: Seems to me you're talkin' about one thing, and we're talkin' about another.

STEVE: Okay, I've said my piece. Maybe I've said too much already.

JACK: You're actin' as if I wanted to get mixed up in this. I don't know what to say, Mr. Blackstone. All right, let me put it this way. If Buck's gotta go, I wouldn't want to see him get a send-off by a second best, someone that might not be able to pull it off.

BLACKSTONE: Look, I'm not sayin' a word about this to anyone. If you don't show up, no one'll know anything about this except for the three of us.

JACK: I'll be here at three. And I don't want you saying a word about this to Dad, or Ma.

STEVE: Are you gonna tell Babs?

JACK: No use worryin' her about this, unless there's a need.

STEVE: And then it'll be too late.

JACK: Are you gonna tell her?

STEVE: You wrestle with your problems, Jack, I'll wrestle with mine.

JACK: I'd better get going. Babs'll be wonderin' where I disappeared to.

BUCK JARVIS

STEVE: I hope you're not sorry one day for what you've done, Mr. Blackstone.

BLACKSTONE: I didn't make this situation, boy, and the final decision is your brother's.

STEVE: I'll buy that last part.

JACK: No one'll ever blame you for this, Mr. Blackstone.

BLACKSTONE: I'm hoping they'll thank me for it, Jack. But if there is any blame, I'll carry my share of it.

STEVE: Let's go, Jack.

JACK: You still talkin' to me?

STEVE: You don't hear me, whether I talk to you or not, so what's the difference?

JACK: I wonder who'll do the worryin' when you've got your own family.

(JACK and STEVE go off.)

BLACKSTONE: See you later, boys. *(HE lights a cigar, then walks over to the door upstage right and tries it.)*

(BART enters, carrying a case of whiskey.)

BART: Lookin' for somethin', Mayor? Dora always keeps that door locked. You know that.

BLACKSTONE: Even when she's here?

BUCK JARVIS

BART: Yup. The sun sure is blistering.

BLACKSTONE: Where's Irv?

BART: Oh, he's around.

BLACKSTONE: Did you have any trouble gettin' that liquor?

BART: Nope. As a matter of fact, your wife seemed glad to get rid of it.

BLACKSTONE: Margaret's a very fastidious woman. I sometimes I envy you your bachelorhood.

BART: Marriage never seemed to stop you none.

BLACKSTONE: It makes things rather uneasy, especially with a mess of kids around. Poor Bart.

BART: What's that?

BLACKSTONE: Whenever someone talks about you, they always say, "Poor Bart." I wonder why that is.

BART: Why do you think that is?

BLACKSTONE: Maybe it's because you give the appearance of strength, and have nothing to back it up. And maybe that's why Buck's so fond of you? No competition.

BART: You think so? Yeah, well, anyway I'm not workin' for Buck.

BUCK JARVIS

BLACKSTONE: You're workin' for Dora. Same thing, isn't it? What do you think she sees in him?

BART: He brings out the mother in her.

BLACKSTONE: He claims he never had a mother. He claims he stepped full-grown, like Minerva, out of the head of his father. I suppose there is something godlike about Buck Jarvis. Or is it that he just makes more noise than anybody else? He must have been a man of principle once. What do you think, Bart?

BART: Why ask me? You've known him longer than I have.

BLACKSTONE: I don't think anybody knows Buck Jarvis, not even Dora. But somebody must have known him once.

BART: Maybe. Maybe not.

BLACKSTONE: What do you do with yourself in your spare time?

BART: You writin' a song about me?

BLACKSTONE: No. But I may be able to fit you into the one I'm writin' about Buck. Only I haven't quite decided where you fit in.

BART: Are you gonna be in that song of yours?

BLACKSTONE: Maybe. Maybe not. I'm not very important, you see. What are you smilin' at?

BART: Your modesty.

BLACKSTONE: Thank you, Bart. Can I buy you a drink?

BUCK JARVIS

BART: When I want a drink, I help myself. That's part of my salary.

BLACKSTONE: What a depressing place this is."The Black Cow." This town needs a new saloon.

BART: You got big plans for this town, ain't you, Stanley?

BLACKSTONE: That's right, Son. And I'll see them carried out. Most of 'em, at any rate.

BART: Gonna clean out all the riff-raff?

BLACKSTONE: Oh, not necessarily. We've got to have some local color.

BART: Gonna open up a place of your own?

BLACKSTONE: If I did, it'd have to be a classy one. And even then, I'd have to have a front. Someone I could trust.

BART: That lets me out.

BLACKSTONE: We're all sentimental, I guess. And, I guess, we all respect the almighty dollar, even Jack Kegley, who's about as honest as they come. No, Bart, I don't think I'd hold it against you, if you went and told Buck about this meetin'. Or, even if you tipped him off beforehand, and he was planted right behind that door, all this time. You and Buck have got to stick together. But I feel sorry for you, Bart.

BART: And why is that?

BLACKSTONE: Because Dora belongs to Bart.

BUCK JARVIS

BART: Your wife wanted to know if you're comin' home to supper.

BLACKSTONE: Ah, the joys of domestic bliss! You know, it just occurred to me.

BART: What?

BLACKSTONE: If Buck should happen to leave us rather sudden like, Dora'd find herself all alone. I'll be back shortly. Ought to be an interesting poker game, don't you think?

>*(BLACKSTONE goes off. BART locks the outer door, then unlocks the door, upstage right and opens it. HE clears the table and brings the glasses back to the bar. BUCK JARVIS, a solidly built man in his early forties, with a tired, weather-beaten face, enters and sits at a table.)*

BUCK: Don't say a friggin' word.

>*(The lights slowly dim as we hear the first verse of "The Streets of Laredo."*
>*"As I walked out in the streets of Laredo,*
> *As I walked out in Laredo one day,*
> *I spied a poor cowboy wrapped up in white linen,*
> *All wrapped in white linen as cold as the clay.")*

ACT TWO

Scene One

(The strains of a verse of "The Streets of Laredo" is heard.
"'I see by your outfit that you are a cowboy'
These words he did say as I proudly stepped by.
'Come sit down beside me and hear my sad story,
I'm shot in the breast and I know I must die.'"
The action is continuous. BUCK is seated. BART is at the bar.)

BUCK: Just bring me a bottle and a glass.

(BART brings a bottle and glass to the table. BUCK pours a drink and downs it.)

BUCK: What are you tryin' to do, poison me? Break out that case of Irish Whiskey.

(DORA BROWN, a handsome woman in her forties, appears in the doorway, upstage right.)

DORA: That whiskey ain't paid for yet.

BUCK: So you'll pay him.

(DORA nods to BART and HE fetches a bottle and places it on the table.)

BUCK: So you ain't workin' for me, eh?

BART: That's right.

BUCK: You son-of-a-bitch! If it wasn't for me, you'd be dead.

BUCK JARVIS

DORA: Okay, Buck, okay.

BUCK: Okay, is it? Everything's okay! The way this town's been treatin' me. That's okay, isn't it? Sons of bitches! That little kid runs under my horse, and the fault is mine. Somebody goes crazy and fires some shots, and the fault is mine. Everything that goes wrong in this town, the fault is mine.

DORA: So what are you gonna do about it?

BUCK: I ain't leavin' town, if that's what you're getting at?

DORA: I didn't ask you what you're not gonna do. I'm askin' what you're gonna do.

BUCK: All the trouble they're goin' through. Why don't they just shoot me in the back? Those sons of bitches! I wouldn't put it past them.

BART: Blackstone's the one.

BUCK: That two-timing son-of-a-bitch!

BART: What's he got against you?

BUCK: I remind him of what he was when he started out.

BART: What was he?

BUCK: A chicken-livered, skinny good-for-nothing.

BART: Ain't he the one that sent for you?

DORA: I was the one that sent for him, God help me.

BUCK JARVIS

BART: But he was the one that hired you, wasn't he?

BUCK: Yeah. He hired me. So what? *(HE takes a drink.)* This stuff's awful.

DORA: So, don't drink it.

BUCK: Bring me some of that other rot-gut. The one I usually drink; and a clean glass.

DORA: *(SHE sips the whiskey.)* There's nothing wrong with this stuff.

BUCK: So you drink it.

DORA: Your days here are numbered, Buck, and you know it.

BUCK: I'm not leavin' this town.

DORA: You're leavin', Honey, one way or another.

BART: Why don't you get a job, Buck? That might solve the problem. It'd show 'em that you've settled down.

BUCK: You friggin' idiot! Who's gonna hire me?

BART: Have you tried? If you settled down and got a job, everything'd be okay. *(HE turns to DORA.)* Don't you think so? I mean not everybody's so hot to get rid of you.

BUCK: This town is mine. It's my baby.

DORA: Now who's the idiot?

BUCK JARVIS

BUCK: I went through all the trouble of cleaning it up, and now that's it's a decent place to live, I think I have a right to live here.

DORA: Anybody's got a right to live here, if they live like a human being. Look at yourself.

BUCK: If I'm such a mess, why do you bother with me?

DORA: That's what I keep asking myself.

BART: It's the liquor, Buck.

BUCK: Don't.......

BART: If you stopped drinkin'...

(DORA signals BART by shaking her head.)

BUCK: *(HE drinks and pours himself another.)* I sunk my life into this town.

DORA: You got paid for it, Buck.

BUCK: Paid for it? What are you, some kind of comedian? Paid for it! You remember when I rode into town that first day, the way they crowded around me. You'da thought I was Jesus Christ come down from the cross. "Welcome, Mr. Jarvis. Welcome, Mr. Jarvis." I gave my life's blood for these people. You remember that?

DORA: Yes, Buck, I remember.

BUCK: And that's when it started. When I was laid up, when that bastard Willie Jones, snuck up on me behind my back and got me

BUCK JARVIS

in the shoulder. But I got him, didn't I? Blood pouring outa me, I got that bastard.

DORA: Yes, Buck. You got him.

BUCK: And, everyone made such a big fuss about me being laid up, but the truth was out. I was just an ordinary guy, who was a pretty good shot. And that's when it started.

DORA: You shoulda quit while you were ahead. You got too much pride, Buck.

BUCK: What do you know about pride? The way you suck up to everybody. Pride! I got self respect, that's what I've got. I know what I did for this town, and I know what I'm entitled to. And if they think they can buy me off... Oh, I didn't tell you that, did I? Stanley came and offered me some money to get out of town.

DORA: When was this?

BUCK: A couple of weeks ago.

DORA: How much did he offer you?

BUCK: A thousand bucks.

DORA: That's a lotta money, Buck.

BUCK: Yeah, well, I told him what he could do with his thousand bucks. He's the one behind it all. Treating me like some whore.

DORA: None of the whores in this town get a thousand bucks.

BUCK JARVIS

BUCK: Well, I'm not some whore. I know too much. That's what the trouble is.

DORA: You gonna stand up to Jack Kegley?

BUCK: What?

DORA: Jack Kegley. You don't want to put that boy in a spot like that, now do you?

BUCK: Jack Kegley's not a boy. And I'm not putting him anywhere. He's the one that volunteered.

BART: He didn't volunteer, Buck.

BUCK: Who's askin' you? And besides, I don't think he's got the guts to go through with it.

DORA: You two were like...

BUCK: Okay, okay.

DORA: You two were like brothers, like father and son. You kept telling me there was this bond between the two of you.

BUCK: Well, he ain't my son.

DORA: He does have your eyes.

BUCK: You're talkin' like a crazy woman. John Kegley's his Pa, and that boy's an arrogant son of a bitch. The trouble with you is you're too sentimental. The kid I used to know, he doesn't exist anymore. The Reverend got hold of him, and that Pa of his, and now he's an upright, god-fearing hypocritical snot.

BUCK JARVIS

DORA: And you're not the shot you used to be. Okay, okay. I've said my piece.

BUCK: Jack Kegley! He was like a son to me.

DORA: *(After a moment.)* What are you gonna do when I sell this place?

BUCK: What?

DORA: You heard me.

BUCK: You thinkin' of selling this place?

DORA: As a matter of fact, I've been thinking about it for quite some time.

BUCK: And then what are you gonna do?

DORA: Yeah, I've been thinking about selling the place for almost a year now. This town's beginning to get on my nerves.

BUCK: Where you gonna go?

DORA: I've been looking over this place in Redwood City. It's got lots of potential.

BUCK: How come you never mentioned this before?

DORA: I don't have to tell you everything, do I?

BUCK: I was just wondering, that's all.

BUCK JARVIS

DORA: Well, business here ain't been so hot lately, ever since this town's gotten so respectable.

BUCK: When?

DORA: When what?

BUCK: When you thinking of moving?

DORA: I don't know exactly. Sometime soon. I was planning to ride over to Redwood this afternoon, and look the place over.

BUCK: This afternoon?

DORA: It's Sunday, ain' it? And I'm not needed here.

BUCK: What's the rush?

DORA: I don't know what you're getting so upset about.

BUCK: I'm not getting upset. I just thought...

DORA: What?

BUCK: If you're going over to Redwood, I thought I might ride along with you.

DORA: I don't need your help, Buck. Besides, you got a poker game.

BUCK: I don't got no poker game.

DORA: You mean you're not gonna play?

BUCK JARVIS

BUCK: I can play poker any time I want.

DORA: It's up to you, Honey.

> *(There is a knock at the outer door. BART opens it and IRV enters.)*

IRV: What's goin' on? You back already?

BUCK: Back from where?

IRV: I thought you rode out of town somewhere.

BUCK: I ain't been anywhere.

BART: You heard him. He ain't been anywhere.

BUCK: We've been in the apartment.

IRV: Then you must have heard.

BUCK: What? Oh. Yeah, yeah, we heard.

IRV: Jeff Calvin!

BUCK: What about him?

IRV: He's the one they're putting up against you, Jeff Calvin.

BART: It's not Jeff Calvin.

IRV: Who is it then?

BART: Jack Kegley.

BUCK JARVIS

IRV: Jack Kegley? After all you done for him?

DORA: What did he do for him? Teach him how to drink?

IRV: And how to shoot.

BUCK: Yeah, well, that's the way the cookie crumbles.

IRV: Jack Kegley! What a rat!

BUCK: You wouldn't turn on me like that, would you, kid?

IRV: Yeah, well, I ain't no good shot like Jack Kegley.

DORA: That's not what he asked you.

IRV: But I will be someday, and, no sireee, I wouldn't turn on you like that.

BUCK: *(To DORA)* What was that all about? That look?

DORA: What look?

BUCK: That look, like when some deadbeat says he's gonna pay his tab any day now. You don't have any faith in anybody, do you?

DORA: I call it as it is.

BUCK: You're a cynic, Dora.

DORA: Maybe I am, and maybe I ain't. The trouble with you, my dear, is you really believe this picture people have of you. Or used to have. You live in a dream world, Buck. You're stuck in those

BUCK JARVIS

stupid books you read. Or used to read, when you were sober enough to read.

BUCK: You have no soul, Dora. That's the trouble with you. You got a heart, and you got a brain, and some other things, too, but you ain't got no soul.

DORA: And you have.

BUCK: Yeah. Me...and...

DORA: Who else?

BUCK: Jack Kegley, once.

DORA: Oh?

BUCK: Yeah, well, he used to have.

DORA: And just exactly what is this soul you're talkin' about?

BUCK: It's not something you can put your finger on. My Ma had it.

DORA: What about your Pa?

BUCK: I never really knew my Pa. I was a baby when he was shot. I was told he was a good shot, but apparently he wasn't good enough.

DORA: And what, exactly, does this soul of yours do for you?

BUCK: It gives me a reason to get out of bed in the morning. You think that's funny?

BUCK JARVIS

DORA: No, Buck, I don't think it's funny. I think it's pathetic. You're still a little kid inside.

BUCK: You think so, huh?

DORA: You're not talkin' about a soul, Honey.

BUCK: What am I talkin' about?

DORA: You're talking about all that romantic stuff you read in those books of yours. Knights in shining armor. Ladies in distress. That's what you're talking about.

BUCK: Yeah, well, there sure ain't no ladies in distress in this town.

DORA: That's the trouble, Buck. You got no one to rescue. But you still dream about it.. Who was that Spanish guy?

BUCK: Spanish guy? You mean Don Quixote?

DORA: Yeah. Don Quixote.

BUCK: Maybe you're right. Maybe I am Don Quixote, and you're my Dulcinea.

DORA: Your who?

BUCK: The lady in distress, with a shady reputation.

DORA: Thank you, Buck. I appreciate that.

BUCK: Well, you're certainly no lily of the field.

BUCK JARVIS

DORA: Keep going. You're doing just great.

BUCK: I'm just teasing you.

DORA: Maybe you are, and maybe you ain't.

BUCK: Now don't get sore. I'm your lover boy. You know that.

DORA: Lover boy! You don't know what love is. Lover boy. *(To IRV)* What are you starin' at? Did you clean out the store room?

BUCK: Leave the boy alone. This is Sunday.

DORA: Did you?

IRV: I started to.

DORA: Well, go on and finish it.

IRV: It's almost finished. Okay, okay.

DORA: And you butt out. He's workin' for me, not for you. Well, don't just stand there. Move.

IRV: Okay, okay. *(HE goes off.)*

BUCK: You sure are a hard woman.

DORA: You keep spoiling that kid, and he's gonna grow up to be a good-for-nothing, just like you.

BUCK: All right, all right. I apologize

DORA: For what?

BUCK JARVIS

BUCK: For saying that you're not a lily-of-the-field.

DORA: *(SHE laughs.)* Oh, Jesus!

BUCK: You know you're the love of my life. I was thinking...

DORA: Uh, oh!

BUCK: No, I'm serious. I was thinking, maybe we oughta adopt that kid. Why not?

BART: You gotta be married to adopt someone, don't ya?

BUCK: So we'll get married.

(SHE laughs.)

BUCK: Well, at least I'm givin' you a laugh. Don't you wanna marry me?

DORA: Is that a proposal?

BUCK: It was just a question.

DORA: So was mine.

BUCK: What?

DORA: I asked you if that was a proposal.

BUCK: I guess so. What do you think?

DORA: I think you're crazy.

BUCK JARVIS

BUCK: Is that your answer?

DORA: You wanna marry me so you can adopt that boy? Is that it?

BUCK: Well, yeah. Is there anything wrong with that?

DORA: Bart, are you listening to this?

BUCK: Did I say something wrong?

BART: Ladies are sensitive, Buck. If you ask someone to marry you, you gotta do it in a nice way.

DORA: Think about it, Honey.

BUCK: I always wanted a son.

BART: Buck!

BUCK: What?

BART: You're not goin' about this the right way.

BUCK: I don't know what the fuss is all about. I mean we're...bed partners. No? Is that the wrong word? Words?

DORA: I guess I should be grateful that you didn't put it more crudely.

BUCK: I didn't know you were that sensitive.

DORA: Well, now you know. Well?

BUCK JARVIS

BUCK: Well, what?

BART: Do you wanna marry her, or don't you?

BUCK: Well, first we gotta talk to Irv. I mean, the only reason for us to get married is for us to adopt Irv.

DORA: And if he doesn't wanna be adopted?

BUCK: Then I don't see the point in our getting married, do you?

DORA: Are you asking me or telling me?

BUCK: Both.

DORA: You sure are one for the books.

(IRV reenters.)

DORA: That was quick.

IRV: I told you it was almost finished.

BUCK: How would you feel about being adopted?

IRV: By who?

BUCK: By who? By the king of the gypsies. By me and Dora, you idiot.

IRV: *(To DORA)* Do you wanna adopt me?

DORA: This was Buck's idea.

BUCK JARVIS

BUCK: So what do you say?

IRV: I never thought about it.

BUCK: Well, think about it.

IRV: What would be the point?

BUCK: We'd be responsible for you. We'd be like your parents, and you'd be like our son.

IRV: Is that good?

BUCK: Well, screw you.

IRV: Well, don't get mad. I just don't see the point of it.

BUCK: Forget it. Forget I ever said anything.

IRV: I never had any parents. I mean I always had to look after myself.

BUCK: If that's the way you want it, fine.

IRV: I didn't say that that was the way I want it. I'm just saying that that was the way it was. It's something to think about.

BUCK: Why don't you talk it over with Mr. Fowler, the next time you go to class. Or better yet, why don't you ask the Reverend what to do?

IRV: I don't know what you're getting so mad about. I mean...it's a big step...to have parents, I mean. Somebody you gotta answer to.

BUCK JARVIS

BUCK: Forget it. Forget the whole frigging thing.

IRV: Gee, Buck. You been like a father to me. I like you and all of that, except when you get mean drunk. And you been teaching me how to shoot, and all. It's just that...that's a very serious step.

BUCK: Forget I ever brought it up. It was a rotten idea to begin with.

IRV: I didn't mean to hurt your feelings. It's not that I don't like your company...when you're sober that is.

BUCK: What are you trying to say? You want me to stop drinking? Is that what you're trying to say?

IRV: Please don't put words in my mouth. You can drink all the hell you want.

BUCK: Hey, hey. Watch your language.

DORA: You take your time and think about it, Irv.

IRV: How do you feel about being my mother, Miss Brown?

DORA: That's a good question.

BUCK: Well?

DORA: It never occurred to me, being a mother I mean. Oh, I used to think about it when I was young, but raising a kid, in a country like this...at least out here.

IRV: It's not as if you had to raise me. I'm fifteen years old.

BUCK JARVIS

Around that anyway. Maybe sixteen. I don't know exactly. What I mean to say is, I'm not a kid anymore.

BUCK: Yeah, yeah, you're a big man.

IRV: And, well, I did sort of envy the kids who had a Pa and a Ma. But I got sort of used to it. Especially since I started hanging out with you, Buck. And I guess, really, you have been sort of a Pa to me. And I like the fact that you don't try to boss me around. Not that I don't feel that I have to do my job, and earn my keep, Miss Brown. So, I guess, in a way, the two of you have sort of been my Pa and my Ma. And, I guess, if you adopted me, it would make it sort of official.

BUCK: Maybe you gotta read some history books about what it feels like to have a Pa and a Ma.

DORA: Leave him alone, Buck.

BUCK: What'd I say? I'm just giving him some advice.

IRV: What I mean to say is, I guess it would be sort of an honor for the two you to adopt me...if you want to, Miss Brown.

DORA: You can call me Dora.

IRV: I'd feel funny callin' you Dora.

DORA: Well, since nothing is final why don't you...

IRV: What?

DORA: Don't call me anything.

BUCK JARVIS

IRV: I gotta call you something.

DORA: Ma'am's okay, I guess.

IRV: Yes, ma'am. But don't you two have to get married first?

BUCK: Yeah, we've been thinking about it.

IRV: When?

BUCK: That's up to Dora. Ma'am?

DORA: A wedding needs arranging. You don't rush into a wedding.

IRV: And I can be best man.

DORA: Well, we'd have to talk to the Reverend. And I'd have to send away for a dress from one of those catalogues.

IRV: A wedding? That'd be really something. And I could be the best man.

BUCK: We're just talking about it.

IRV: You mean you might change your mind?

BUCK: I didn't say that, did I? As a matter of fact, Dora and me are planning to ride over to Redwood this afternoon to look over another saloon.

IRV: Another saloon?

BUCK JARVIS

DORA: Yeah, I'm thinking of selling the place and opening up that place in Redwood.

IRV: You going over there this afternoon?

DORA: You can come along, if you like.

IRV: What about the poker game?

BUCK: What about it?

IRV: You gonna skip out?

BUCK: What do you mean skip out?

IRV: Well, you heard what was going on.

BUCK: What? You think I'm afraid of going up against Jack Kegley?

IRV: You said it, not me.

BUCK: You know me better than that, kid.

IRV: Sure I do, Buck. I was just wonderin'...

BUCK: What?

IRV: Well, people been sayin' that Jack Kegley's just as good a shot as you are, maybe even better, and I'm just wonderin' what everybody else'll think.

DORA: What difference does it make what everybody else thinks, since nobody knows that Buck knows anything about it?

BUCK JARVIS

BART: I think Blackstone knows.

DORA: Who asked you?

BART: I didn't mean...

BUCK: Well, we don't have to go to Redwood this afternoon, do we? We can go next Sunday, can't we?

DORA: You can go whenever you want to, Buck. I'm going this afternoon.

BUCK: Then go if you want to.

DORA: What are you gonna do?

BUCK: I'm going over to the hotel and wash up.

DORA: Does that mean you're not comin' with me? Does that mean you're gonna go up against Jack Kegley?

BUCK: I'm not gonna go up against anyone. I'm just gonna play a game of poker. If that little snot wants trouble, that's okay with me, 'cause he don't mean anything to me anymore. You comin', Irv?

IRV: Sure, Buck.

(BUCK goes off, followed by IRV.)

DORA: You hadda open your big mouth.

BART: I'm sorry, I...

DORA: Oh, shut up, and let me think. First I want you to ride over

BUCK JARVIS

to Jeff Calvin's place, and tell him things have changed, and Jack Kegley'll be taking his place.

BART: You think that'll do any good?

DORA: Don't ask questions, and do as I say.

BART: Okay, okay. I'm goin'.

DORA: Just a minute. And then I want you to ride over to the Kegleys and tell Mrs. Kegley all about this.

BART: Jack's wife's in town.

DORA: I didn't say his wife. His mother.

BART: His mother?

DORA: That's right, his mother.

BART: You really think Buck's Jack's father?

DORA: Beth Kegley and Buck were lovers once, and Buck's still in love with her. I know that.

BART: There is some resemblance around the eyes.

DORA: Well, there you are, and there's only one way of finding out. I want you to tell Beth Kegley what's going on, and if Buck's the father she's not gonna stand by and let it happen.

DORA: What are you gonna do?

DORA: Me? I'm gonna sit here and worry. Well, get going.

BUCK JARVIS

BART: Okay, okay.

(BART goes off. DORA sits and pours herself a drink as we hear "The Streets of Laredo" and the lights come down. "Oh beat the drum slowly and lay the fife lowly, And Play the dead march as you carry me along. Take me to the valley and lay the earth o'er me, For I'm a poor cowboy, and I know I've done wrong.")

Scene Two

(A couple of hours later. The saloon is empty. Someone tries to open the outer door. It's locked. There's banging on the door. The banging grows louder. DORA enters from her apartment and opens the door. BLACKSTONE enters.)

BLACKSTONE: What's goin' on?

DORA: Can't you read English?

BLACKSTONE: What are you tryin' to pull?

DORA: I'm not trying to pull anything. The place needs cleaning, and that sign says that we're closed for the day.

BLACKSTONE: The place looks fine to me.

DORA: You may be runnin' this town, but I'm the one that's runnin' this saloon.

BLACKSTONE: Now Dora, you wouldn't want me to close you down, now would you?

DORA: Oh me, oh my. Please don't do that to me, Mr. Mayor.

BLACKSTONE: Are you trying to get us to cancel the poker game, because if that's what you're aimin' at, forget it. If we don't hold it here, we'll find some other place.

DORA: Why don't you go and do that?

BLACKSTONE: Don't be a fool, Dora. Buck's days here are numbered, and there's nothing you can do about it.

DORA: Why are you so afraid of Buck?

BUCK JARVIS

BLACKSTONE: I'm not afraid of Buck.

DORA: No?

BLACKSTONE: No, I 'm afraid for the people of this town. That's what I'm afraid of, Dora. Now why don't you just relax, and leave that door open, cause the poker game's goin' on, no matter what you try to pull. *(HE pushes the door open, takes down the notice, and tears it up, then takes a seat.)* Now, how about serving me a drink, like the great little hostess that you are?

(SHE makes a note of it then serves him a drink.)

BLACKSTONE: For the life of me, I can't figure out why you waste your time on that bum. You could have your pick, you know.

DORA: Why, Mr. Mayor, you're not tryin' to flirt with me, are you?

BLACKSTONE: You know me better than that. I'm a married man.

DORA: So I hear, from every girl you've plowed. "I don't get no lovin' at home."

BLACKSTONE: Always let them hear what they wanna hear. I'm a politician, my love.

DORA: Well, as far as Buck is concerned, you can rest easy.

BLACKSTONE: Oh?

DORA: That's right. I'm pulling up stakes, and Buck is coming with me.

BUCK JARVIS

BLACKSTONE: That's something new, and kind of sudden, isn't it?

DORA: Not really, no. This town's dying, as far as I'm concerned, and Redwood City's still pretty lively.

BLACKSTONE: You thinking of selling the place?

DORA: That's right.

BLACKSTONE: You got a buyer?

DORA: That's right, and don't ask me who, 'cause I'm not at liberty to say, right now. Why? You interested?

BLACKSTONE: What are you asking?

DORA: Ten thousand dollars, cash.

BLACKSTONE: That's pretty steep, ain't it?

DORA: You asked, and I'm telling you.

BLACKSTONE: And Buck's coming with you? I find that hard to believe.

(BART enters hurriedly, and stops short at the sight of BLACKSTONE.)

BLACKSTONE: What have you been up to, Bart?

BART: What makes you think that I've been up to something?

BUCK JARVIS

BLACKSTONE: Well, your employer here's been anxious to sabotage our poker game, and I thought maybe she's been using you to help her.

BART: I don't know where you got that idea. I just went back to my place to take a little nap.

BLACKSTONE: Did you really? And on the way, didn't I see you talking to the Kegleys?

BART: That's right. I ran into them coming from the funeral.

BLACKSTONE: And how are the Kegleys?

BART: Fine, as far as I can tell.

BLACKSTONE: Weren't Beth Kegley and Buck kind of friendly once?

BART: How should I know?

BLACKSTONE: Weren't they, Dora? Wasn't that some kind of a romance? Kind of serious, from what I gather.

DORA: Buck and me don't discuss ancient history.

BLACKSTONE: She was real pretty once, too, according to Buck. What a shame people have to grow old. Though I must say, Dora, you're sure holding up well.

DORA: You trying to cadge a free drink?

BLACKSTONE: I can afford to pay for my drinks.

BUCK JARVIS

DORA: And a lot more than that. How rich are you, Mr. Mayor?

BLACKSTONE: I never discuss money on a Sunday.

DORA: Or the rest of the week either.

(JEFF CALVIN enters.)

JEFF: What's goin' on?

BLACKSTONE: Why, Jeff!

JEFF: Hello, Dora.

DORA: Nice to see you, Jeff.

JEFF: I understand there have been some changes made.

BLACKSTONE: Changes? What sort of changes?

JEFF: The last I heard, Jack Kegley wasn't available.

BLACKSTONE: Well, we're not quite sure whether Jack's going to show up or not.

JEFF: Then I've been misinformed.

BLACKSTONE: Maybe you misunderstood.

DORA: How about a drink, Jeff? It's on the house.

JEFF: Don't mind if I do?

BART: The usual?

BUCK JARVIS

JEFF: That'll be fine.

(JEFF goes to the bar and BART pours him a drink.)

JEFF: How ya been, Dora? Haven't seen you in quite a spell.

DORA: That's not my fault, Honey. How's the family?

JEFF: Just had a new addition. A little boy.

DORA: Good for you. This town's really growin', ain't it, since things quieted down. Folks can raise a family now, without worrying about all the gunplay and all those shenanigans.

BLACKSTONE: Not quite, Dora. Unless you haven't heard about that poor little Costello child.

DORA: That was an accident, wasn't it? From what I heard, or have you heard differently? And now we got a real good teacher runnin' the school house, all the way from Chicago. Your little boy's gonna get some good schoolin' now, Jeff.

BLACKSTONE: If things here are so great, how come you movin' out on us?

JEFF: You leavin' us, Dora?

DORA: I'm thinking about it. Yesiree, Buck and me are thinking of moving to Redwood.

JEFF: How come?

DORA: It's all your fault, Honey. All the men are going home to their wives. Used to be they came here, looking for a good time, looking for companionship. Now they get all that at home. Ain't that so, Honey?

JEFF: Well, yeah, up to a point that is.

DORA: Gotta watch your Ps and Qs?

JEFF: Well, I must say, family life does have its rewards.

DORA: I will say, it certainly seems to agree with you.

JEFF: Why, thank you, Dora. So you and Buck are movin' out on us.

DORA: Looks that way.

JEFF: Did you know about that Mr. Blackstone?

BLACKSTONE: As far as I know, it's not down in black and white, now is it, Dora? I mean, as far as Buck is concerned?

(LARRY KEEFER, VAL HENDERSON and HENRY FOWLER enter.)

LARRY: Well, now, is the lady of the house going to be joining us?

VAL: What an unexpected pleasure.

HENRY: Are you going to be joining the game, Miss Brown?

DORA: No, Honey. I'm just here and watch.

BLACKSTONE: Actually, our poker games are really boring.

BUCK JARVIS

DORA: Then why do you play?

BLACKSTONE: To watch, that is.

DORA: A room full of attractive men couldn't possibly be boring. How's the new school room, Mr. Fowler?

HENRY: It's fine. Couldn't be better.

DORA: Got all the books you need?

HENRY: I certainly do, and I've been meaning to thank you for all your help.

DORA: Well, the mayor did have something to do with it.

BLACKSTONE: Don't be so modest, Dora.

DORA: Val, honey, how come there's nothing in your paper about The Black Cow lately? Is it because there's been no violence here?

VAL: You hit the nail on the head, Dora. My readers are always looking for something sensational.

DORA: I guess Buck did too good a job.

VAL: You got something there. What do you think, Stanley?

DORA: Things keep going the way they are we won't be needing a sheriff anymore.

LARRY: That'd be fine with me.

BUCK JARVIS

DORA: Step up to the bar, gentlemen. Today the drinks are on the house.

LARRY: How come this generosity, Dora?

DORA: I thought we oughta celebrate how peaceful this town's become. Pour one for me, too, Bart.

>   *(BART pours a drink for VAL, LARRY, HENRY and DORA.)*

DORA: *(SHE lifts her glass.)* To Buck Jarvis, who tamed this hell hole, and made it livable.

>   *(There is an awkward silence. DORA drinks. VAL, LARRY and HENRY follow suit. DOC HARDY and EDWIN SPRUCE enter.)*

DORA: Just in time, gentlemen. Drinks are on the house.

DOC: That's mighty thoughtful of you, Dora. Any special reason for this sudden generosity?

DORA: I just thought we oughta celebrate what Buck's done for this town.

DOC: You got something there.

DORA: And how are you Mr. Spruce, now that your business has slowed down considerably?

EDWIN: That's fine with me, Miss Brown. No matter how things turn out, I'll always be in business. Death's a habit nobody seems to be able to break.

BUCK JARVIS

(Several gun shots are heard. LARRY and JEFF reach for their guns.)

BLACKSTONE: Relax, gentlemen. That's just Buck letting us know that he's on his way.

JEFF: He's still carrying on like that?

BLACKSTONE: You know, Buck.

LARRY: I'll never get used to it.

JEFF: I guess he'll never come to his senses.

BLACKSTONE: You got something there, Jeff.

HENRY: Has anyone ever sat down and had a talk with him?

BLACKSTONE: Talkin' to Buck is like talkin' to the wall.

(Gun shots are heard from a closer distance.)

BLACKSTONE: The gun's his special toy, and he'll never stop playin' with it.

HENRY: Isn't there some kind of law, like disturbing the peace?

LARRY: It wouldn't do any good.

HENRY: Have you tried it?

LARRY: Look, Son. Buck's gonna do as he pleases. The fact of the matter is, he thinks he owns this town.

BUCK JARVIS

(IRV enters.)

BART: His drink's all ready.

IRV: Cancel it. Buck's not drinking.

BART: Are you sure?

IRV: That's what he said.

VAL: That's news enough to make the front page.

(BUCK enters. He is all cleaned up, and changed into his best clothes.)

BUCK: And what might that be, Val?

VAL: Well, look at you. All duded up? You got a special date?

BUCK: Quite possibly, gentlemen, quite possibly. Dora, my love, are you joining us today?

DORA: I thought I might just stick around. You look quite presentable for a change.

BUCK: I don't know whether to take that as a compliment or an insult. How are you doin', Jeff?

JEFF: I'm doin' fine.

BUCK: We seldom see you anymore.

JEFF: Well, I've got a growin' family now. As a matter of fact, I've just had me a little boy.

BUCK JARVIS

BUCK: Good for you, Son. Well, gentlemen, are we ready to play poker?

BLACKSTONE: It's still early yet.

BUCK: Who you expecting, Mr. Mayor?

BLACKSTONE: Jack Kegley said he might be joining us.

BUCK: Ah, the esteemed young Kegley. And here I thought he'd deserted us forever. Mr. Fowler!

HENRY: Yes, sir?

BUCK: Where's that book you promised me?

HENRY: Which one was that, Mr. Jarvis? I'm sorry, I've been so busy making repairs on the school room.

BUCK: Well, why didn't you say so? I would have come and helped you. When would you like me to come?

HENRY: Well, I've just about finished. It was the windows. They needed some caulking. And the doors. And the floor needed sanding and polishing.

BUCK: Seems to me the mayor ought to provide you with some help, since the school is the government's responsibility. Ain't that so, Mr. Mayor?

HENRY: Oh, that's all right. I was able to manage it on my own. Now what was the book I promised to find for you?

BUCK: It was a biography.

BUCK JARVIS

HENRY: Oh, yes. Boswell's Life of Samuel Johnson. I know just where it is. You drop by tomorrow, any time after three and I'll put it aside for you.

BUCK: Thank you.

DOC: What are you gonna do with all that learning, Buck?

BUCK: You never know when it might come in handy. In case I decide to run for mayor.

DOC: Oh?

BUCK: Then again I might decide to run for sheriff.

LARRY: I wish you would, Buck. It would be a great relief.

BUCK: How long are we supposed to wait for young Mr. Kegley?

BLACKSTONE: What's your rush, Buck? You're not going anywhere, are you?

BUCK: Not that I know of.

BLACKSTONE: That's what I thought.

BUCK: Oh? Have you heard differently?

DORA: I was telling the mayor about Redwood.

BUCK: Ah, yes. Well, that's all speculation, ain't it, Dora? I mean nothing's really settled, is it? As a matter of fact, you've been talking about moving on for years, and here we still are.

BUCK JARVIS

(STEVE KEGLEY enters and looks about.)

BLACKSTONE: Looking for something, Steve?

STEVE: Yes. I'm looking for my brother.

BLACKSTONE: We've been expecting him.

STEVE: I know that Mr. Blackstone.

BLACKSTONE: Well, you two are as thick as thieves.

STEVE: Not always, Mr. Blackstone. Not always. Hello, Mr. Jarvis.

BUCK: Hello, Son. Are you joining us for poker?

STEVE: I don't know how to play poker. And besides, my Pa doesn't like me to play.

BUCK: Your Pa's pretty strict I gather.

STEVE: There's nothing wrong with that, is there?

BUCK: Life's not all fun and games, Son, that's true. But there are times when it's good just to let go and relax.

STEVE: Up to a point, that is.

BUCK: Why, yes. Up to a point. I sense a note of disapproval.

STEVE: Of you, sir. I wouldn't dare.

BUCK JARVIS

BUCK: Well, well, well. You are Jack's brother, and your father's son, I might add.

STEVE: I won't disturb you.

(STEVE starts off, when JACK strides in, slightly dishevelled and a bit unsteady.)

JACK: What are you doing here?

STEVE: Looking for you.

JACK: Well, now you've found me. You can go tell Pa.

STEVE: You can go to hell! *(HE strides off.)*

JACK: You must forgive my brother, gentlemen. He gets very emotional some times.

(STEVE reenters.)

STEVE: And for your information, I don't care what you do. I'm just concerned about Ma.

JACK: Ma is perfectly fine.

STEVE: She's anxious to have a talk with you.

JACK: You tell Ma that I'm fine, too.

STEVE: You don't give a damn about anybody, do you? I don't know why I bother.

JACK: Go on home, Steve.

BUCK JARVIS

(STEVE goes off.)

JACK: *(HE goes up to the bar.)* Pour me a drink. My usual.

BART: I don't remember what your usual is, Jack. It's been a long, long time.

JACK: It hasn't been that long.

DORA: Hello, Jack.

JACK: Hello, Dora. Haven't seen you in ages. How have you been?

DORA: I'm fine, Jack. How's married life?

JACK: Married life is just great. Now how about that drink, Bart? Do I have to ask for it twice?

DORA: Take it easy Jack.

(SHE nods and BART pours a drink.)

JACK: *(HE raises his glass.)* To your health, gentlemen. *(HE drinks.)* Isn't that my old friend, Buck Jarvis, over there?

BUCK: Mr. Kegley. It's been quite a while.

JACK: Can I buy you a drink, Mr. Jarvis?

BUCK: You doing that well?

JACK: That I am, sir, that I am. *(HE reaches into his pocket.)*

BART: The drinks are on the house.

BUCK JARVIS

JACK: Why thank you, Dora.

DORA: I thought you'd given it up.

JACK: What's that?

DORA: Liquor. I thought you'd swore off.

JACK: So I did, and now I'm swearing on.

BART: Would you like a drink, Buck?

BUCK: Not right now. But thank you, Jack.

JACK: Do my ears deceive me, or is Buck Jarvis refusing a drink?

BUCK: I'd like to keep my mind sharp for our poker game.

JACK: Ah, yes. Our poker game.

BLACKSTONE: Well, gentlemen, shall we commence?

JACK: If Buck ain't drinking, I'll take his.

BLACKSTONE: Jack?

JACK: Yes? What is it?

BLACKSTONE: We're getting ready to start.

JACK: Who's stopping you?

BLACKSTONE: Bart, can we have the cards please?

BUCK JARVIS

JACK: I'll take that drink first, Bart.

BART: Sure, Jack, sure. Just let me get the cards.

JACK: I said, I'll take that drink first.

DORA: Take it easy, Jack.

BUCK: Jack's a little nervous tonight. What's the matter, Jack? That Pa of yours been giving you another lecture?

JACK: I don't remember addressing you, Mr. Jarvis.

BUCK: "Mr. Jarvis."

JACK: So my drink ain't good enough for you.

BUCK: For you, neither. Because, if I remember correctly, you never could hold your liquor.

JACK: Ha! You're sure one to talk.

BLACKSTONE: Bart, can we have those cards? And a fresh deck, please?

BART: Yes, sir. Yes, sir.

BLACKSTONE: Who's playing tonight? Jeff?

JEFF: Count me in.

BLACKSTONE: Val? Larry? Doc? Edwin?

(They each shake their heads.)

BUCK JARVIS

BLACKSTONE: Jack, are you playing tonight?

JACK: You know damn well, I'm playing.

BLACKSTONE: Okay, Son, okay.

BLACKSTONE: Buck, are you playing?

BUCK: Well, of course, I'm playing, Stanley.

BLACKSTONE: How about you, Henry?

HENRY: Sure. Why not?

IRV: Can I play, too?

BLACKSTONE: Now, Irv, son, you know perfectly well you're too young to play.

IRV: How old do you have to be?

BLACKSTONE: Twenty one.

BUCK: Why don't you sit beside me, Irv? You can give me advice.

BLACKSTONE: Can we take our seats, please.

>   *(JEFF, BLACKSTONE, HENRY, BUCK and JACK sit around the table. IRV draws up a chair beside BUCK. BART approaches the table with a deck of cards and a box full of chips. HE hands the deck to BLACKSTONE, then goes around the table, selling chips to the five players.)*

BLACKSTONE: Does anyone mind if I deal?

BUCK JARVIS

BUCK: If it's a new deck, I have no objection.

BLACKSTONE: It is.

BUCK: Then go right ahead.

BLACKSTONE: Thank you.

BUCK: You're quite welcome.

JACK: *(HE turns to BUCK.)* You look mighty spiffy tonight, Mr. Jarvis. What's the occasion?

BUCK: The word was out that Jack Kegley was joining us, my old friend, Jack Kegley.

JACK: Run over anymore little girls lately?

BUCK: Are we playing poker or ain't we?

BLACKSTONE: Okay, Buck. Don't get so excited. Has everyone got their chips?

(HE deals a hand to the five players.)

JACK: Are you ignoring me, Buck?

BUCK: What's that?

JACK: I asked you a question?

BUCK: That was not a question.

JACK: What was it then?

BUCK JARVIS

DORA: Are you gonna talk, Jack, or are you gonna play poker?

JACK: I wasn't aware that I was addressing you, ma'am.

DORA: Well, I'm addressing you.

JACK: I didn't know that Buck needed a woman to speak up for him.

BUCK: You itching for a fight, Jack?

JACK: I'm just asking a simple question? Is there anything wrong with that?

BUCK: *(HE rises.)* Because if you are...

JACK: *(HE rises.)* Then what?

(JOHN KEGLEY, enters. BLACKSTONE rises.)

BLACKSTONE: Mr. Kegley, can I help you?

JOHN: I'm sorry to interrupt your game, gentlemen, but I'd like a word with Buck.

BUCK: What is it, John?

JOHN: I'd like to speak to you in private.

BUCK: I'm in the middle of a game. If you have anything to say to me, you can say it here and now.

JOHN: This is private, Buck.

BUCK JARVIS

BUCK: I don't know of anything private between you and me.

JOHN: Well, actually, Buck, it's my wife that wants a word with you. I don't think you'd want me to bring her in here for a private conversation. Now would you?

JACK: What's Ma got to do with this?

JOHN: I wasn't addressing you, boy.

JACK: I don't know why you had to drag Ma into this.

JOHN: You shut your mouth, son, or old as you are I'll whip the living daylights out of you. Buck? Would you please step outside? Beth would like a word with you.

(BUCK rises and goes off.)

JOHN: Not another word out of you. *(HE goes off.)*

BLACKSTONE: What have you been up to, Jack?

JACK: Nothing.

BLACKSTONE: Doesn't seem like nothing to me.

JACK: My Pa and me have never seen eye to eye.

LARRY: Maybe we oughta call this game off.

BLACKSTONE: Why?

LARRY: I think the reason's pretty obvious.

BUCK JARVIS

JACK: And what might that be, sheriff?

LARRY: Things may turn out quite differently from what was intended.

JACK: You think so, Sheriff?

LARRY: Yes, I do.

JACK: Well, that's one man's opinion. I'll take Buck's drink now, Bart.

DORA: The bar is closed.

JACK: Now that's not very friendly of you, Dora.

DORA: I think you've had enough.

JACK: Well, I'm not thinking of myself. I was just thinking of Buck's drink, which now goes undrunk.

DORA: Bart, pour Buck's drink. Bart, I said, "Pour Buck's drink."

(BART pours a drink. DORA downs it.)

DORA: So, there we are. Never let it be said, that Dora Brown would let a drink go to waste.

JACK: You're a tough woman, Dora.

DORA: And you're a foolish boy.

JACK: I'm not a boy anymore.

BUCK JARVIS

DORA: That's a matter for debate. Why don't you go on home?

BLACKSTONE: Take it easy, Jack. You don't wanna start any trouble?

JACK: *(HE laughs.)* Say that again.

BLACKSTONE: You heard me.

JACK: I'm a little confused.

JEFF: Obviously.

JACK: What's that?

JEFF: Come on, Jack. You never could hold your liquor.

HENRY: Maybe this poker game wasn't such a good idea.

JACK: Then don't play poker, Mr. School Teacher. Maybe you'd like to play, Pussy In The Corner.

HENRY: I don't know that game.

JACK: He doesn't know that game. What kind of a teacher are you?

   (BUCK reenters.)

JACK: Ah, the white knight returns. Our savior, gone to pot. Why don't you do us all a favor and put a bullet through that thick head of yours?

BUCK: *(Gently)* Had a little too much to drink, Son?

BUCK JARVIS

JACK: Not really, no, since I can still see your ugly face. Why don't you face the facts?

BUCK: And what are they, Son?

JACK: What's that?

BUCK: What are these facts you want me to face?

JACK: The fact is, my friend, and you used to be my friend...the fact is, your life is over. It's been over for quite some time now. You have nothing to live for, Buck. You've done what you've been meant to do...and there's nothing left. *(HE snaps his fingers.)* I have it.

BUCK: What's that?

JACK: Why don't you do like the Indians do? When the old man's dying, they put him out to pasture. They leave him out there on the mountain top, so that he can die alone. It saves us all a lot of trouble...'cause dying is ugly, Buck. And you...are an ugly man, Buck. An ugly man.

BUCK: I gather the poker game's been called off. Is that it, gentlemen?

JACK: No, it's not been called off. Whatever gave you that idea?

BUCK: Well, you're certainly not fit to play.

JACK: And you? What are you fit for?

IRV: Are you gonna take it, Buck? Why don't you shut him up?

BUCK JARVIS

JACK: Oh, oh, oh. Another voice is heard from, another young apprentice. Teaching him how to shoot, Buck? Teaching him how to hold his liquor. That's is, obviously, one thing you never taught me.

BUCK: And what did I teach you, Jack?

JACK: You taught me where to keep my eye. You taught me how to be quick on the draw, how to take proper aim, and how to watch my back. You taught me that, sir, and you taught me well.

BUCK: Jack, old boy, I told your Ma and Pa that you'd be joining them. Why don't you go on home?

JACK: Since when, Mr. Jarvis, did you get the right to speak for me?

BUCK: I'm trying to be patient, Son.

JACK: Oh, oh, oh! He's threatening me, gentlemen. Did you hear that? I'm actually trembling. Our washed-up hero, is threatening me. Lord have mercy.

BUCK: Go on home, Jack.

JACK: You goddamned son of a bitch! You're afraid of me.

IRV: Have it out with him, Buck.

BUCK: I'm not gonna take you on, Jack. You are drunk.

JACK: Drunk or not, you are a washed up good for nothing. And a coward, to boot.

BUCK JARVIS

IRV: Buck!

BUCK: All right, Jack. Okay. Let's go outside.

JACK: Be my guest.

>(*JACK bows, making room for BUCK, who goes off. JACK follows him off unsteadily.*)

JEFF: That ain't right. The man is drunk.

DORA: Someone stop 'em. Blackstone. You're the one to blame for this. Go out there and stop 'em.

BLACKSTONE: I'm afraid it's too late for that.

JEFF: Well, go out there and see that it's fair. That's the least you can do. This is wrong, all wrong.

>(*BLACKSTONE goes off, followed by LARRY, JEFF, VAL, DOC and EDWIN.*)

HENRY: I don't think Buck'll hurt him bad. They used to be buddies.

DORA: You don't understand.

>(*HENRY goes off.*)

BART: Something's gotta be done.

>(*BART goes off. DORA goes to the bar and pours herself a drink. After a long silence, two shots are heard. DORA downs the drink. After a moment BART reenters.*)

BUCK JARVIS

DORA: Is he dead?

BART: No, but he's been hurt bad. It's Buck. Not Jack. He never came near the boy.

> *(JEFF and HENRY enters carrying BUCK. THEY lay him on a table as DOC follows them on.)*

JEFF: Kegley passed out. He's laying there on the ground, fast asleep. He didn't even know where he was firing.

> *(DOC examines BUCK, then looks at DORA and shakes his head.)*

DOC: Try and make him comfortable.

DORA: I'd like to be alone with him.

> *(DOC nods and goes off, followed by JEFF, HENRY and BART. BART closes the door behind them.)*

BUCK: Dora?

DORA: Yes, Honey?

BUCK: He's my son.

DORA: I sorta guessed.

BUCK: *(HE is silent for a moment.)* The first time I ran into him, I couldn't believe it. He was the spittin' image of his Ma, and I thought to myself, he coulda been my son. He oughta have been, and now it turns out that he is. *(HE coughs.)* He's a fine boy, isn't he?

BUCK JARVIS

DORA: Yes, dear.

BUCK: When I first met her she was such a pretty thing, and I knew right away, she was the one. We'd meet late at night, after her family'd gone to bed. And then she started talkin' about marrying, and having a family, and that scared the shit outa me, and I ran off. *(HE coughs and is silent for a moment.)* But I couldn't stop thinkin' about her, and then I began to think how great it would be to have a son, and I decided that one day, I was gonna go back, but I kept puttin' it off, and puttin' it off. *(HE coughs, and is silent for a moment.)*

DORA: Buck?

BUCK: After I ran off she found out she was pregnant. She thought she'd never see me again, and then John came acalling, and she told him the truth, and he married her anyway. *(HE coughs.)* We had some great times together, Jack and me.

DORA: Yes, dear, I know.

BUCK: But then, when the two of us drank too much, we'd get into fights, and he got disgusted with me. *(HE coughs.)* She never told the boy, you know. *(HE is silent for a moment.)* And there's no point in telling him now, is there?

DORA: If that's what you want.

BUCK: 'Cause I ain't gonna make it, I know that; and makin' him feel bad... *(HE coughs, and is silent.)*

DORA: Buck? Honey?

(Red River Valley is heard softly.

BUCK JARVIS

*"From this valley they say you are going,
We will miss your bright eyes and sweet smile;
For they say you are taking the sunshine
That has brightened our pathways awhile."*

IRV: *(Offstage)* Lemme in, lemme in. *(HE bursts into the room.)* Buck! Buck!

DORA: He's gone.

IRV: Buck!

(IRV weeps. DORA embraces him, as he clings to her.)

IRV: He was off his mark. He missed by a mile. He was gonna adopt me.

DORA: Yes, I know.

IRV: Jack Kegley... I can be just as good as he is. And I will be. One of these days, I will be. And he better watch his step, Jack Kegley.

*(The lights dim slowly as we hear the final verse of Red River Valley.
"They will bury me where you have wandered,
Near the hills where the daffodils grow.
When you're gone from the Red River Valley,
For I can't live without you, I know."*

THE HAIRCUT
(A Play in Two Acts)

CAST OF CHARACTERS

Claude Fairchild, A High School Principal

Deborah Fairchild, His Wife

Ethan Fairchild, His Son

Amanda Klotz, Ethan's Friend

Walter Ambrose, A Colleague

SCENE
The action moves fluidly between the Fairchild Home, Amanda's Apartment and the Office of the Principal.

TIME
The 1960s

ACT ONE

(The Fairchild home, early Monday morning. CLAUDE FAIRCHILD, a distinguished looking man in his mid-forties, enters. HE helps himself to breakfast on the sideboard then sits at the table.)

CLAUDE: Almighty God, I thank you for your past blessings. Today I offer myself...whatever I do, say, or think, to your loving care. Continue to bless me, Lord. I make this morning offering in unison with the divine intentions of Jesus Christ.

(CLAUDE proceeds to eat as DEBORAH FAIRCHILD, an attractive woman in her forties, enters and goes to the sideboard.)

DEBORAH: You're up early this morning. *(SHE helps herself to some food and sits at the table.)* Claude? I'm sorry. *(SHE starts to eat.)*

CLAUDE: *(After a moment)* You know I need some time after my morning prayer.

DEBORAH: I'm sorry, dear. Did you sleep well?

CLAUDE: Not really.

DEBORAH: I thought heard you call out.

CLAUDE: I had a nightmare.

DEBORAH: I really think you should see a therapist.

CLAUDE: I have Father Donovan. I don't need a therapist.

DEBORAH: Kenneth?

THE HAIRCUT

CLAUDE: He won't let go of me.

DEBORAH: His death was not your fault.

CLAUDE: I know that. I keep telling him that. He was a degenerate, a hopeless degenerate. I tried to show him the evil of his ways. I tried to persuade him to come to church with me. He was a fine man...fine boy, and, of course, I was just a boy as well, and maybe I didn't go about it the right way. Maybe I should have been gentler, and maybe I did mislead him, because I was just as confused. I really thought I was in love with him and, of course, I mistook a brotherly love for that...of something deeper. But I've paid for my sins, I really have. But why does he continue to haunt me? Father Donovan says it's the penance for my sins. It's my hair-shirt, something I must wear to the grave.

DEBORAH: It was all so long ago.

CLAUDE: I know, I know. Yet there he is. This time he hung himself. "Watch me, Claude," he said, "I'm going to kill myself, and it's all your fault." And he stood there, with this long thick rope, tying it into a noose and attaching it onto a beam. Then he stood on a chair, placed the noose around his neck. "Watch me, Claude," he said. "Watch me carefully." Then he kicked away the chair and hung there, making the most awful noises. And he swung there, in the air, back and forth, back and forth. *(HE sighs.)* I'm sorry. I'm sorry to burden you with all of this. I can go on for months, for years without him haunting me and then suddenly, when things go wrong, and I find myself in a crisis, there he is.

DEBORAH: Is it that business with Jenny Fletcher? I thought that was over and done with.

CLAUDE: It is, as far as I'm concerned. The Board of Education,

THE HAIRCUT

however, seems to think otherwise. They held a special meeting on Friday.

DEBORAH: They're questioning your decision?

CLAUDE: Apparently.

DEBORAH: And what did they decide?

CLAUDE: I don't know. Walter said he would drop by this morning and tell me.

DEBORAH: You were certainly within your rights. She had absolutely no right to conduct those discussions. And, from what you said about her appearance, it was an absolute disgrace. And you certainly weren't responsible for the way the students behaved. Disturbing the peace like that. Destroying school property. They behaved like little monsters.

CLAUDE: That, my dear, is the world we live in. The animals have taken over.

DEBORAH: I should think the Board of Education would support you. After all you've done for that school. You've set standards that ought to be a model for schools around the country.

CLAUDE: And I intend to maintain those standards.

DEBORAH: Of course, there is such a thing as private morality...

CLAUDE: Scholastic standards and moral standards go hand in hand. The mind cannot absorb if it is filled with garbage. Students come to school to learn, not to be sexually provoked. *(HE continues to eat.)* Walter's a member of your book club, isn't he?

THE HAIRCUT

DEBORAH: No, but Lily is, and she asked about you.

CLAUDE: And what did you tell her?

DEBORAH: I said you were a little on edge.

CLAUDE: And what did she say?

DEBORAH: That's understandable, she said. She did say you could have been a little more diplomatic.

CLAUDE: I refuse to play games. As a matter of fact, I think that's one of the reasons I was chosen for my position. I say what I think, and I do what I think is right.

DEBORAH: *(After a moment)* I know Father Donovan is a fine man, but I really wish you would consult a therapist. I noticed the other day, while you were reading, your hand was trembling. And it's happened once before.

CLAUDE: It's nothing. It's just a nervous twitch. It comes and goes. *(HE continues to eat.)* I see where Ethan's bed hasn't been slept in.

DEBORAH: He spent the week-end with a friend.

CLAUDE: The young man he refers to as his lover?

DEBORAH: He doesn't refer to him...

CLAUDE: Debbie, they are lovers, and he's proud of it. He glories in it.

DEBORAH: I thought you were going to have a talk with him.

THE HAIRCUT

CLAUDE: You can't talk to someone who won't listen. That son of yours is so full of himself that nothing one says has any effect whatsoever.

DEBORAH: Did you bring up Kenneth?

CLAUDE: Debbie, you cannot bring up anything, if someone turns a deaf ear. And besides, I really don't think it would have any effect, he's so full of himself. All this nonsense about the Greeks, and Margaret Mead. I tried to point out that we are living in the twentieth century, that we are Christians, not pagans.

DEBORAH: At any rate, dear, there's no longer any need to concern yourself. I understand they're no longer lovers.

CLAUDE: Since when?

DEBORAH: Since a few weeks ago.

CLAUDE: Oh? Then why are they parading about the schoolyard holding hands like Romeo and Juliet? I saw them just the other day.

DEBORAH: In Europe it's quite common to see men walking about holding hands.

CLAUDE: Then perhaps they ought to move to Europe.

DEBORAH: The fact of the matter is Ethan has decided that he loves Carl, but that he's no longer in love with him, or maybe he never was in the first place. I don't understand it myself.

CLAUDE: I see. Has he found himself another young man?

THE HAIRCUT

DEBORAH: No, dear.

CLAUDE: That's a relief.

DEBORAH: It's young woman this time.

CLAUDE: I suppose we should be grateful. Your son is unique, I will say that for him.

DEBORAH: He's your son too, my dear.

CLAUDE: Not really, Debbie.

DEBORAH: How can you say that? It's just that he does have a mind of his own.

CLAUDE: A child has to be disciplined. We're born with the instincts of an animal, and we all need guidance. He's defied me at every turn, rejecting Christ at the age of fourteen. As a matter of fact, he seems to have rejected everything that we stand for, and you have done nothing but encourage him.

DEBORAH: That's not true. I just think he needs room to grow, to find things out for himself. He's a very intelligent boy.

CLAUDE: I would hardly call him a boy. He's almost nineteen. The fact is, Ethan is a great disappointment to me, a great disappointment.

DEBORAH: Well, I am confident that one day you're going to be very proud of him.

CLAUDE: I'm glad you think so.

THE HAIRCUT

(THEY continue to eat.)

CLAUDE: Has he cut his hair?

DEBORAH: What's that, dear?

CLAUDE: I said, has he cut his hair?

DEBORAH: Why, no. I don't think so. Why do you ask?

CLAUDE: I spoke to him about it on Thursday.

DEBORAH: About his hair?

CLAUDE: About his hair. I insisted that he cut it. He looks ridiculous with his hair down to his shoulders.

DEBORAH: And what did he say?

CLAUDE: He said he would give the matter some thought, after giving me an argument that in certain periods of history men wore their hair long, and it was considered quite proper.

DEBORAH: Which is true, of course.

CLAUDE: There you go again, always taking his side.

DEBORAH: I'm sure that eventually, when he goes to college, he'll get around to cutting it.

CLAUDE: He said he may not go to college.

DEBORAH: That's not what he told me.

THE HAIRCUT

CLAUDE: At any rate, I've issued an ultimatum. Any one who shows up at class with long hair this morning, will either get their hair cut or they will be expelled.

DEBORAH: Ethan isn't the only one, dear. All the boys are wearing their hair long these days. It seems to have caught on.

CLAUDE: I beg to differ with you. All the boys are not wearing their hair long. There are exactly four boys at Central High who feature those long locks, and they will suffer the same fate.

DEBORAH: Since Ethan's almost nineteen, if he's not attending school he might be eligible for the draft.

CLAUDE: You need have no fear on that account. They don't take homosexuals into the army.

DEBORAH: Ethan is not a homosexual.

CLAUDE: At any rate, whatever he is, he's a disgrace to the name of Fairchild. If my father were alive today he would insist that, either Ethan pulls himself together or he finds himself another home. And now, if you will excuse me. *(HE rises.)*

DEBORAH: Will you be home for lunch?

CLAUDE: I'm not quite sure.

> *(CLAUDE goes off. DEBORAH goes to the phone, consults a note pad and dials a number. The light comes up on the apartment of AMANDA KLOTZ. The phone is ringing. ETHAN FAIRCHILD, a fresh faced boy of eighteen, enters in his shorts and picks up the phone.)*

THE HAIRCUT

ETHAN: Hello?

DEBORAH: Ethan? Is that you?

ETHAN: Yes, Mother.

DEBORAH: Have you had your hair cut?

ETHAN: I beg your pardon?

DEBORAH: I said...

ETHAN: I heard you the first time. Is that why you called me?

DEBORAH: Ethan, I've just had a talk with your father. He said that unless you get a haircut, you will be expelled.

ETHAN: He's going to expel me?

DEBORAH: Not only you, dear. Every student who has long hair will be expelled, unless they get a haircut. I understand he spoke to you about it on Thursday.

ETHAN: He kept insisting that I get a hair cut, but he didn't say anything about being expelled.

DEBORAH: Well now, you know. I suggest you get a haircut before you go to class, or, at least, let the teacher know you will the first chance you get. Ethan? Did you hear me?

ETHAN: Let me think about it.

DEBORAH: Ethan!

THE HAIRCUT

(AMANDA KLOTZ, a rather pleasant looking girl in her early twenties, enters.)

ETHAN: I can't talk now. I'll be home in a few minutes to pick up my books.

DEBORAH: Ethan!

ETHAN: I'll see you soon. Good-bye.

(ETHAN hangs up. The lights come down on the Fairchild home.)

AMANDA: What was that all about?

ETHAN: That was my mother.

AMANDA: What did she want?

ETHAN: She wants me to get a haircut.

AMANDA: Is that why she called?

ETHAN: According to my Dad, unless I get a haircut, I'll be expelled.

AMANDA: Is he serious?

ETHAN: You've never met my Dad, have you?

AMANDA: Not personally, no.

ETHAN: He's very serious, and very uptight.

THE HAIRCUT

AMANDA: That's quite understandable.

ETHAN: What's that supposed to mean?

AMANDA: He's got Central High to run, and you for a son. Well, Ethan, you must admit that you are...unusual to say the least.

ETHAN: On the contrary. I'm a child of nature. I listen to my heart. As a matter of fact, come to think of it, I suppose that is unusual. Now where did I put my shirt?

AMANDA: It's on the chair. Ethan we have got to talk.

ETHAN: Thank you. *(HE picks up his shirt.)* I could have sworn I left my shoes here. Ah, there they are.

AMANDA: You'll have to put on your trousers before you put on your shoes.

ETHAN: Good thought.

AMANDA: I'll get them for you.

> *(ETHAN puts on his shirt while AMANDA goes off. SHE reenters moments later with the trousers and a toilet article kit. SHE hands ETHAN his trousers and sets down the kit.)*

ETHAN: Thank you. *(HE gets into his trousers.)* What are you doing with my kit?

AMANDA: I think you'd better take this with you. I don't want to hurt your feelings, Ethan, but this is not gonna work.

ETHAN: Are you kicking me out?

THE HAIRCUT

AMANDA: No, I'm not kicking you out.

ETHAN: What then?

AMANDA: It's just that I don't think we should spend so much time together.

ETHAN: You're kicking me out.

AMANDA: Frankly, Ethan, we're just not on the same wave length.

ETHAN: Okay, let's have it. You want me to marry you.

AMANDA: Don't be ridiculous.

ETHAN: Than what?

AMANDA: I really don't think you understand, what life is all about. There is such a thing as commitment, you know.

ETHAN: You want me to swear on a Bible that I won't look at another woman? Is that it?

AMANDA: I just don't think you're ready for a relationship.

ETHAN: If you're referring to me and Carl, I explained all that to you. It was fun for a while, and then we both decided that we wanted to move on. I guess it was sort of an experiment.

AMANDA: Well, for your information, I'm not particularly interested in being a part of an experiment.

ETHAN: You want an insurance policy. Is that it?

THE HAIRCUT

AMANDA: If that's what you want to call it.

ETHAN: But you can't take out on insurance policy on love.

AMANDA: You're in love with me?

ETHAN: I like you. I like to be with you, and you're great in bed and so, for that matter, am I. Isn't that enough?

AMANDA: And besides, you'll be going to college at the end of the year.

ETHAN: I'm not quite sure that I want to go to college.

AMANDA: The fact of the matter is you're still a boy.

ETHAN: Okay, and you are a girl.

AMANDA: No, I am a woman.

ETHAN: I beg your pardon. You're two years older than I am. Actually one and a half.

AMANDA: It's not a matter of years. But then again, yes, I am years older than you are.

ETHAN: I beg your pardon. I'll buy you a cane, or would you prefer a walker?

AMANDA: I'm serious, Ethan. I feel very insecure and very uncomfortable about our relationship. That doesn't mean that we have to stop seeing each other.

THE HAIRCUT

ETHAN: In other words, you want to put an end to our sexual relationship. Is that it?

AMANDA: Let's just say a hiatus.

ETHAN: You want to be friends.

AMANDA: Is there anything wrong with that?

ETHAN: But I don't think of you as a friend.

AMANDA: Exactly.

ETHAN: Well, can't we be friends and lovers, too?

AMANDA: The point I'm trying to make...

ETHAN: Look, I've got to get going. Can I call you, and then we can talk this over? I'll call you this evening. I've got to pick up my books, and I haven't had my breakfast yet. *(ETHAN kisses her and runs off.)*

AMANDA: Oh, Lord!

> *(AMANDA sinks into a chair and sighs as the lights come down on the apartment and up on the office of the principal of Central High. CLAUDE escorts WALTER AMBROSE, a solidly built man in his mid forties, into the room.)*

WALTER: I'm sorry I'm late.

CLAUDE: That's quite all right, I just got here myself. Have a seat, and excuse me for a moment. I've got to water my plant. If I

THE HAIRCUT

don't do it, it won't get done. *(HE goes off and returns with a glass of water and proceeds to water the plant on his desk.)*

WALTER: *(HE stands looking out the window.)* What a beautiful morning. So peaceful here.

CLAUDE: It's always peaceful, except when the students are around.

WALTER: I should think that being around young people would keep you young.

CLAUDE: One would think so.

WALTER: They do keep one on one's toes.

CLAUDE: Quite true.

WALTER: How's Ethan these days. I haven't seen him in ages. I envy you, you know. I've always wanted a son. Not that Julie isn't a sweet child. But it's not the same, as having a boy.

CLAUDE: Can we get down to business?

WALTER: Yes, of course. May I offer you a bit of advice? A little charm goes a long way, Claude. I know you take your work very seriously, but one can accomplish a great deal by making people feel at ease.

CLAUDE: You think I make people feel uncomfortable?

WALTER: I know you don't mean to, but there's something so...austere about you. Whenever I'm with you, I feel that I'm in a classroom and I'm being judged. I'm boring you.

THE HAIRCUT

CLAUDE: No, no, no. It's just that I'm on edge of late, as Lily must have told you.

WALTER: Lily?

CLAUDE: She and Debbie had a long talk about me this past week-end. Didn't she mention it?

WALTER: No. You're not the only one with problems, Claude.

CLAUDE: Oh? I wish you'd sit down, Walter. You're making me very nervous, and I'm nervous enough as it is.

WALTER: Yes, of course, if it will make you happy. *(HE sits.)*

CLAUDE: Have you and Lily had a quarrel?

WALTER: Lily and I have been living an armed truce for the past ten years. I had gotten sort of used to it, but now she's decided that she wants a divorce. I suspect she's found someone else, though she insists on denying it. As a matter of fact, if I had any sense, I'd be relieved, but it's rather late in life to be starting all over again.

CLAUDE: I never could understand why you married her in the first place. You never seemed to care that much about her.

WALTER: Didn't you know? Well, I suppose it was a well kept secret. I knocked her up.

CLAUDE: Did Debbie know about this?

WALTER: Yes. Yes, of course.

THE HAIRCUT

CLAUDE: I see. So that's why you never married her. I did think it was odd. The two of you seemed to be so much in love.

WALTER: So now you know.

CLAUDE: Yes, now I know.

(The phone rings.)

CLAUDE: Excuse me. *(HE answers the phone.)* Hello? Yes, George. We need a new lock. That's right. Well, as soon as you can. Thank you. *(HE hangs up.)* Someone broke into the gym over the week-end.

WALTER: Did they take anything?

CLAUDE: There wasn't that much to take. A couple of bats, some balls and a few other things.

WALTER: That's the second time this year.

CLAUDE: Third. And people seem to think I'm an alarmist.

WALTER: Claude, I'm with you all the way. You know that. I have the greatest respect for your integrity. But some people think that you're a stick in the mud, that you're somewhere back in the Middle Ages.

CLAUDE: Walter, I refuse to compromise.

WALTER: I'm not asking you to. When it comes to major issues, I will back you up to the hilt. But, for God's sake, don't get sidetracked. Don't make a mountain out of a molehill, if you'll pardon the metaphor.

THE HAIRCUT

CLAUDE: You're referring to Jenny Fletcher, I take it.

WALTER: At the moment, yes.

CLAUDE: Jenny Fletcher was a demoralizing influence on the students in this school.

WALTER: Claude, most schools have classes on sex education.

CLAUDE: This school does not. It's up to the parents to deal with that issue. Why doesn't the PTA hold classes on sex for the parents?

WALTER: An interesting suggestion. I shall bring it up at the next meeting. But back to Jenny Fletcher. She was not teaching sex.

CLAUDE: She allowed these discussions to take place in her classroom.

WALTER: And she allowed the students to draw their own conclusions. She did not force her own morality down anyone's throat.

CLAUDE: Ostensibly, no. But it wasn't only the discussions, and you're well aware of that.

WALTER: Her appearance.

CLAUDE: She dresses like a tart; a cheap one at that. You could actually see the nipples on her breast.

WALTER: We went through all of that. She appeared in class one afternoon without a bra. The strap broke and she couldn't fix it in time.

THE HAIRCUT

CLAUDE: And that was only one example. Her clothes are too tight and much too short.

WALTER: Claude, Jenny Fletcher is a young woman. You may not be aware of it, but that's the way young women dress nowadays.

CLAUDE: Not in my school they don't.

WALTER: You want to change women's fashion?

CLAUDE: Fashion, my foot! There is such a thing as modesty and good taste.

WALTER: You acted arbitrarily and highhandedly. This school is a tinder box, as it is, what with the civil rights issue and a war going on and a shortage of funds.

CLAUDE: And the lack of discipline. Since when do children know what they're supposed to be taught? There are radical elements in this school trying to stir things up.

WALTER: It just so happens that Jenny Fletcher was very popular.

CLAUDE: I see. And I suppose that excuses what took place.

WALTER: No, it does not. The violence and the destruction was shameless, and I said as much, if you will remember. Look, Claude, I have defended you.

WALTER: I'm well aware of that, and I appreciate it. But, as long as I'm the principal of Central High, I will continue to do my job as I see fit. And if the Board of Education sees fit to replace me, that's their affair.

THE HAIRCUT

WALTER: All right, Claude, all right. But I think you ought to know, that if it wasn't for me, they would have started a search for another principal.

CLAUDE: I see.

WALTER: One word of advice. One more...quote...crisis...unquote, and I'm afraid you've had it. Now, is there anything else I can do for you?

CLAUDE: I want police locks on all the outside doors, and iron bars on all the first floor windows.

WALTER: I'll see what I can do. Anything else?

CLAUDE: Not at the moment. Oh, yes. Now that you're free, or will be shortly, I sincerely hope you're not thinking of taking up with my wife again.

WALTER: Good Lord, Claude, that never even occurred to me.

CLAUDE: It's just that this climate we live in nowadays, people seem to have lost all sense of decency. I'll see you out. I keep the door locked until my secretary shows up.

> *(CLAUDE escorts WALTER off as the lights come down on the office and up on the Fairchild home. ETHAN is seated at the table, eating his breakfast.)*

DEBORAH: *(Offstage)* Ethan, is that you?

ETHAN: Yes, Mother.

> *(DEBORAH enters and stands studying ETHAN.)*

THE HAIRCUT

DEBORAH: You have no intention of cutting your hair. I'm talking to you.

ETHAN: I heard you, Mother.

DEBORAH: You know, my dear, you really do look ridiculous. May I ask you a question? What on earth prompted you to let your hair grow long?

ETHAN: Let me see. I think It was after seeing Errol Flynn in one of those old movies. I thought it looked rather dashing.

DEBORAH: That was in the movies, my dear. I really think you did spend too much time at the movies.

ETHAN: It did make my childhood more interesting.

DEBORAH: It seems to me you haven't left your childhood. In real life, my dear, Errol Flynn didn't have long hair.

ETHAN: I gather he was much too busy to think about his hair.

DEBORAH: What do you think you accomplish by wearing your hair long?

ETHAN: I'm not trying to accomplish anything.

DEBORAH: It's another one of your experiments.

ETHAN: Do I criticize you for tinting your hair, though I do think it doesn't accomplish very much?

DEBORAH: I think I've made a great mistake in allowing you to indulge in all your idiosyncrasies. You know, Ethan, we do not live

THE HAIRCUT

in this world all by ourselves. We share this universe with others, and we do have certain responsibilities. And sometimes, by indulging our whims, we can do great harm. I don't think you understand what a remarkable man your father is. He has many demons to contend with, and yet he's forged ahead and accomplished remarkable things.

ETHAN: If you're referring to Central High, I don't know what's so remarkable about it.

DEBORAH: Central High is a highly respected school.

ETHAN: With all sorts of problems.

DEBORAH: Which are not of your father's making.

ETHAN: On the contrary.

DEBORAH: When and if you apply to a university, you will find out how remarkable, and how highly rated Central High is.

ETHAN: That's because we just happen to have a very intelligent body of students, who are stifling under an antiquated scholastic system. Who ever heard of teaching Creationism alongside of Evolution? And poor Miss Fletcher.

DEBORAH: And you think your behavior, and the behavior of your fellow students was justified?

ETHAN: Well, it did get a little out of hand, and I did not participate in the destruction of any school property. But Dad just asked for it, the highhanded way he treated that poor woman.

DEBORAH: Under tremendous pressure, he did what he thought

THE HAIRCUT

was right, and you've got to respect him for it. And the fact of the matter is, his position is now in jeopardy. If there are anymore incidents like that last one, your father will be out of a job.

ETHAN: If this is leading to my getting a haircut, forget it.

DEBORAH: Why?

ETHAN: Because my body belongs to me, and no one has any right to tell me how to care for it. I know it may come as a great shock but I, too, have a certain amount of integrity.

DEBORAH: And your integrity involves letting your hair grow long?

ETHAN: Among other things.

DEBORAH: And you have no concern for your father who's worked hard all his life so that we can live comfortably; who has provided you with the clothes on your back, with the food you're eating now.

ETHAN: Dad has been working to earn a living for himself as well. Whether I was here or not he'd still have to work.

DEBORAH: If I asked you, as a personal favor...

ETHAN: No, Mother. And besides, I'm not the only one. Harold and Irving have long hair too.

DEBORAH: Harold and Irving have cut their hair.

ETHAN: How do you know?

THE HAIRCUT

(DEBORAH consults a note pad then picks up the phone and dials.)

DEBORAH: Margaret, is Harold still there? Please. Hello, Harold? Just a moment. *(SHE hands the phone to ETHAN.)*

ETHAN: Have you cut your hair? Why? I thought we had agreed... I see. There's no need to apologize. You're a traitor and a weakling. Nevertheless... Good-bye.

(ETHAN hangs up. DEBORAH picks up the phone and dials a number.)

DEBORAH: Hello, Edna. Is Irving there? Well, I was wondering. Did he cut his hair? I see. Just a moment. *(SHE turns to ETHAN.)* Would you like to speak to Mrs. Hauser? *(SHE hands the phone to Ethan.)*

ETHAN: Hello, Mrs. Hauser. Did Irv cut his hair? When? I see. No, no, no. Thank you. *(HE hangs up.)*

DEBORAH: That leaves you and your ex-friend, Carl.

ETHAN: Carl is still my friend, and Carl cut his hair on Saturday. As a matter of fact, he shaved his head in protest.

DEBORAH: I'm sure that's very brave of him. Well? Are you satisfied?

ETHAN: Mother, I don't care what other people do. I am me. I am not going to shave my head, nor am I going to cut my hair.

DEBORAH: Well, for your information, since you are living on the money that your father earned, since you're eating the meals that

THE HAIRCUT

I have cooked for you, and since you are wearing the clothes your father paid for, as along as you live in this house you will abide by the rules that we set down. So, you will cut your hair if you want us to continue to feed and clothe you. Is that perfectly clear?

ETHAN: Perfectly. *(HE continues to eat.)*

DEBORAH: Did you hear what I said?

ETHAN: Yes, Mother. I heard you, loud and clear. It's just that I'd like to be allowed to finish this breakfast Dad paid for, and you prepared so handsomely, since I'd hate to see this good food go to waste. *(HE finishes his coffee and sets down the cup.)* Now, may I kiss you good-bye?

DEBORAH: What is that supposed to mean?

ETHAN: It means good-bye. I'm leaving behind my childhood home, and facing the cold cruel world. Unless, of course, you've changed your mind. Very well. Farewell, my love. I hope we shall meet again under far better circumstances. *(HE kisses her.)*

DEBORAH: Aren't you going to pack?

ETHAN: I intend to take nothing that isn't mine. I'd give you the clothes I'm wearing, but I wouldn't want to cause you and Dad any further embarrassment.

DEBORAH: Where will you go?

ETHAN: I haven't decided yet?

DEBORAH: The home of your paramour?

THE HAIRCUT

ETHAN: Quite possibly. May I take these books that Dad's money paid for?

DEBORAH: Don't be ridiculous.

ETHAN: But I am ridiculous mother. You've raised a ridiculous son. *(HE picks up his books and goes off.)*

DEBORAH: Ethan! Oh, God!

> *(DEBORAH sinks into a chair and sits thinking. SHE rises, paces about, consults a pad and starts to dial a number. The lights come up on AMANDA's apartment. The telephone is ringing. AMANDA enters and picks up her phone.)*

AMANDA: Hello?

DEBORAH: Is this Amanda?

AMANDA: Yes, it is.

DEBORAH: This is Mrs. Fairchild, Ethan's mother. I hope I'm not disturbing you.

AMANDA: Not really, no. What can I do for you?

DEBORAH: I need your help.

AMANDA: In regard to Ethan?

DEBORAH: It's of the utmost importance. Could you possibly spare me some time?

AMANDA: When?

THE HAIRCUT

DEBORAH: Well, right now as a matter of fact. Will you be home for a while?

AMANDA: Well, if it's that important.

DEBORAH: It is.

AMANDA: Do you have my address?

DEBORAH: No. No, I don't.

AMANDA: It's One Sixty Tyler Place. I'm just a couple of blocks away from you, and I'm one block South of Central High. Apartment two "B".

DEBORAH: I'll be right over. Thank you. I really appreciate this.

> *(DEBORAH hangs up and goes off as the lights come down on the Fairchild home.)*

AMANDA: Oh, Lord! *(SHE goes off and reenters a moment later without the towel around her head. SHE picks up the phone and dials.)*

AMANDA: Hello, Mr. Watermark, it's Amanda. I know I'm late. As a matter of fact, I'm not feeling very well. I meant to call you earlier, but... It's my stomach. I've been throwing up, and I've got a slight fever. I think it may be something I ate. I think I should be all right by tonight, and I'm sure I'll be able to come in tomorrow. I'll call you tonight. Thank you. *(SHE sits with a sigh, then feels her hair.)* Oh God!

> *(SHE goes off and a moment later the phone rings. SHE reenters.)*

THE HAIRCUT

AMANDA: What now? *(SHE picks up the phone.)* Hello? Yes, Mr. Watermark. If it's the article about Truman Capote, it's on my desk and it's been proof read. The short story about Vietnam? No, we haven't received that yet. Thank you. No, I'll be all right. See you tomorrow.

(AMANDA goes off. A moment later the doorbell rings.)

AMANDA: *(Offstage)* The door's open.

(DEBORAH enters.)

AMANDA: *(Offstage)* Did you hear me?

DEBORAH: Yes. Yes, I heard you.

AMANDA: *(Offstage)* I'll be out in a minute.

(DEBORAH walks about examining the room. SHE runs her hand over the back of a chair as AMANDA enters, hair combed and wearing a nice dress.)

AMANDA: It's second hand.

DEBORAH: I'm sorry.

AMANDA: That's quite all right. And it does need a dusting.

DEBORAH: I hope I'm not intruding.

AMANDA: Actually I've taken the day off.

DEBORAH: What sort of work do you do?

THE HAIRCUT

AMANDA: I work for a small literary magazine.

DEBORAH: Are you a writer?

AMANDA: Fledgling. I've written a couple of short stories.

DEBORAH: Were they published?

AMANDA: One was.

DEBORAH: Congratulations.

AMANDA: Thank you. Can I get you some tea...or coffee? I do have some coffee. It's quite fresh.

DEBORAH: That'd be fine. Milk. One sugar.

AMANDA: It'll only take a minute or two.

(AMANDA goes off. DEBORAH sits and takes off her hat.)

DEBORAH: Where did you get this furniture?

AMANDA: *(Offstage)* That little thrift shop on Maple Street.

DEBORAH: Oh, yes.

(AMANDA reenters.)

AMANDA: It'll just take a second or two. I suppose you want to talk about Ethan.

DEBORAH: Not really, no.

THE HAIRCUT

AMANDA: Excuse me.

(AMANDA goes off. DEBORAH rises and walks about. AMANDA reenters with two cups of coffee, which SHE sets down.)

AMANDA: I do have some biscuits.

DEBORAH: That's...

(AMANDA has gone off. DEBORAH heaves a sigh and sits. SHE picks up her coffee stirs it and takes a sip. AMANDA reenters with the biscuits.)

AMANDA: Is the coffee all right? I can brew some more. Or I can get you some tea.

DEBORAH: No, no, no. This is fine.

AMANDA: What did you want to talk about?

DEBORAH: My husband, Ethan's father.

AMANDA: Oh?

DEBORAH: Ethan is well equipped to take care of himself. Are you in love with him?

AMANDA: I'm not quite sure what love is.

DEBORAH: I think it has something to do with pity. What drew you to my son?

AMANDA: I hate to say this, but I think it was the mother in me.

THE HAIRCUT

DEBORAH: That's quite all right. I don't think we can have too many mothers. But you're not much older than Ethan, are you? You certainly don't look it.

AMANDA: I'm twenty one.

DEBORAH: Ah, yes.

AMANDA: Were you in love with your husband when you married him?

DEBORAH: I married my husband on the rebound. I am, however, in love with him now.

AMANDA: All this business of romantic love, love at first sight. It's all a lot of hooey, isn't it? In the old days...I mean there was a time when one didn't meet one's husband until the wedding day, and there were probably less divorces. My mother does not approve of my way of life. She's a firm believer in finding one man and marrying him. *(After a moment)* Then you don't regret your marriage?

DEBORAH: I don't see the use of regrets. I don't see the use of looking back.

AMANDA: I think Ethan's very lucky, having a mother like you.

DEBORAH: I'm not so sure about that. I was never allowed to think for myself, and I vowed that if I had any children, I would see to it that they were permitted to find their own way. My husband is a very complicated man, and I think I've done him a great disservice. Is there anything more complicated than the relationship between a parent and a child? With a lover or a husband there are only two people to deal with. With a child there

THE HAIRCUT

are three, three individuals minds, three individual egos. I had the impossible task of protecting a very fragile man from an aggressively curious child. And an aggressively curious child from a from a very inhibited, close-minded man.

AMANDA: Ethan never talks about his father.

DEBORAH: They're not close, and the fault is partially mine. My husband's a man who's been crippled by well meaning parents. If you were to meet him... Have you, by the way?

AMANDA: Not personally, no.

DEBORAH: He gives the impression of a very gentle, but stern man who knows exactly what he wants, and how he wants to achieve it. His parents were ultra-conservative Catholics. Hellfire and damnation were very real and an imminent threat. My husband lives from day to day with that threat hanging over him. At the age of seventeen, he had a nervous breakdown. A few years ago, he suffered another one, a minor one, thank God.

AMANDA: Does Ethan know all this?

DEBORAH: I didn't think it was fair to burden a growing child with such heavy duty problems.

AMANDA: Why have you come to me?

DEBORAH: Ethan won't listen to me. As a matter of fact he's left home. At least, he said that he has, and I thought that he might come here.

AMANDA: But, if you can't talk any sense into him, I'm not sure

THE HAIRCUT

that I can do any better. Is this in regard to his hair, by any chance?

DEBORAH: I'm afraid so. It's ironic. The two of them, my husband and my son, are at loggerheads, and yet they're so much alike. It's ridiculous, I know. But with all this uproar about Jenny Fletcher, if Ethan is expelled, and he will be if he doesn't cut his hair, it's going to start all over again, the protests and the violence. And if it does... He doesn't show it, I know, but I'm afraid my husband's nerves are at the breaking point. The fact of the matter is, if there is a disturbance like the last one, my husband is bound to lose his job, and if he does...I'm afraid it might drive him over the edge; and if that should happen, Ethan will be the cause of it, and, even though he's at odds with his father, at the moment, he will never forgive himself.

AMANDA: I'll do what I can, when I see him again, But I'm not sure that I can do very much.

DEBORAH: Thank you, Amanda. Do you mind if I call you, Amanda?

AMANDA: Please do.

DEBORAH: May if I use your phone?

AMANDA: Yes, of course. Go right ahead.

> (DEBORAH picks up the phone and dials, as AMANDA picks up the cups and goes off. The phone rings as the lights come up in the principal's office. CLAUDE enters and picks up the phone.)

CLAUDE: Hello?

THE HAIRCUT

DEBORAH: Claude?

CLAUDE: Yes, Debbie?

DEBORAH: I was wondering. You will be home for lunch, won't you?

CLAUDE: At the moment, I'm not quite sure.

DEBORAH: You will let me know.

CLAUDE: Yes, of course.

DEBORAH: By the way, is Ethan there?

CLAUDE: Yes. Yes, he is.

DEBORAH: Has he cut his hair?

CLAUDE: No.

DEBORAH: Claude...

CLAUDE: I really can't talk now. I'll call you later.

> *(CLAUDE hangs up. DEBORAH hangs up and sinks into a chair as AMANDA reenters. THEY exchange looks as the lights come down on the apartment. CLAUDE goes to the doorway.)*

CLAUDE: Ethan, you can come in now.

> *(ETHAN enters.)*

THE HAIRCUT

CLAUDE: Sit down.

ETHAN: I prefer to stand.

CLAUDE: Did you have a pleasant week-end?

ETHAN: Reasonably.

CLAUDE: You spent it with your lady friend?

ETHAN: With Amanda, yes.

CLAUDE: And how long have you been seeing her?

ETHAN: A few weeks now.

CLAUDE: Is she a student?

ETHAN: No. She works for Wisdom's Child. It's a literary magazine.

CLAUDE: Yes, I know the publication. Very avant garde. Is she a writer?

ETHAN: She hopes to be. She's had one short story published.

CLAUDE: I didn't know you were interested in writing.

ETHAN: I'm interested in everything, but it wasn't her talent that attracted me to Mandy.

CLAUDE: I see. Sit down, please.

(ETHAN sits. CLAUDE sits on the edge of the desk.)

THE HAIRCUT

CLAUDE: What are you interested in, Ethan?

ETHAN: Do you really want to know? Well, actually I'm interested in everything.

CLAUDE: I mean as a profession.

ETHAN: I really don't know. I'm interested in literature, politics, music, poetry.

CLAUDE: How do you expect to earn a living?

ETHAN: Since I'm not sure that I'm really capable of anything, I may end up teaching.

CLAUDE: What?

ETHAN: I don't know. Philosophy, perhaps. Psychology.

CLAUDE: Do you feel it's necessary to experience everything in order to understand it, to teach it, perhaps. I mean, if you're going to delve into the psychology of a murderer, do you think it's necessary to commit murder to understand the subject?

ETHAN: What are you getting at?

CLAUDE: I'm trying to understand you, Son.

ETHAN: Isn't it kind of late in the day?

CLAUDE: Just because we've never had any deep philosophical discussions, doesn't mean that I'm not interested in you. But it seems to me that everything you've done, everything you've said is completely contrary to the way I think, to the way I feel. As a

THE HAIRCUT

matter of fact, I have the feeling that you've been going out of your way just to...I don't know...defy me.

ETHAN: Why on earth would I do that, since it's quite obvious that you don't really care what I think or what I do?

CLAUDE: If I ever gave you that impression, I'm sorry. But I will say that I've been under the impression that you had no respect whatsoever for my opinion. I was hoping that one day you would come to me with any problem you were having, but you never have.

ETHAN: Maybe it's because you didn't really seem interested in what I thought or what I felt. You're a cold fish, Dad. Even when you kiss Mother on the way out, or on the way in, it's a cold, passionless peck. As a matter of fact, I'm quite puzzled about how I ever came into existence. I think that's the first time I've ever seen you smile.

CLAUDE: Just because I'm not effusive, like Aunt Bertha, or tell off color jokes like cousin Joe, does not mean that I'm not human. I don't believe in making a spectacle of my feelings.

ETHAN: It comes as a surprise to me that you have any feelings. Have you ever once put your arms around me? Have you ever shown me one bit of affection. And, oh, yes. I've always been meaning to ask you. Up until the age of eight or ten maybe, you used to kiss me. And then suddenly you stopped. Can you tell me why?

CLAUDE: You were approaching manhood.

ETHAN: What has that got to do with it?

THE HAIRCUT

CLAUDE: Really, Ethan!

ETHAN: Yes, really. Why did you stop?

CLAUDE: Is that why you resent me, because I stopped kissing you?

ETHAN: I was still a child. I thought at first you stopped kissing me because I'd done something wrong.

CLAUDE: I should think it would have been obvious. I stopped kissing your cousin, Paul, and yet I continued to kiss his sister.

ETHAN: It gradually dawned on me. And I thought, how ridiculous. I mean, after all, all kisses are not necessarily erotic.

CLAUDE: You are not a child any longer, Ethan. You live in a Society, a Society that has certain customs, certain rules. Tell me this. Why have you stopped coming to church?

ETHAN: I told you, Dad. I don't believe in prayer.

CLAUDE: You don't believe in Jesus? You don't believe in God?

ETHAN: For one thing, I'm not convinced that Jesus was the son of God, and I'm not quite sure there is a God, whatever he or she is supposed to be like. As a matter of fact, I'm not really that much concerned about Jesus, and I'm not really concerned about the existence of a God. I have enough things to deal with right here on earth.

CLAUDE: You think you're wise enough, and know enough so that you have no need of any guidance.

THE HAIRCUT

ETHAN: I think I'm a good person, Dad, and I think it's my privilege to be allowed to make my own mistakes.

CLAUDE: To indulge in your basest desires? To live like a beast in the field? Ethan, you are not the first man on earth. There are others that have come before you, and they might...they just might...have some advice to give you that will make life more bearable.

ETHAN: More bearable? You think that life is a burden?

CLAUDE: You live in a real world, Ethan. You live among people. There are some things that are acceptable, and some things that are not.

ETHAN: Does that make it right? Whatever is acceptable is right?

CLAUDE: If there are rules, Ethan, there are reasons for those rules. There is a right, and there is a wrong.

ETHAN: And who makes these decisions?

CLAUDE: People wiser, and older than yourself. Whether you're aware of it or not, I do love you, Son. I want the best for you; and so does your mother. Let me ask you this? Do you think that everything you do is right? Do you think that every impulse you have should be followed? We all have all sorts of desires. We sometimes have a desire to kill someone or, or to commit obscene and perverted acts. Suppose we gave into all those impulses? What would the world be like? We are born into a sinful world and we go through life at war with the evil that we're born with.

ETHAN: I don't believe we're born evil.

THE HAIRCUT

CLAUDE: You think Man is inherently good?

ETHAN: Yes, I do.

CLAUDE: Not too long ago... I believe you must have been about ten or eleven or so. Your mother sent you to the drugstore to pick up a prescription. You returned with the prescription, but also you had in your hand a little chocolate wafer wrapped in gold tinfoil which, she believed, you had pilfered.. She spoke to me about it and I asked you, "Where did you get that?," I asked. "Ethan, where did you get that?," I asked. You blushed and said that the druggist had given it to you. "Did you help yourself to that chocolate?" I asked, and finally you admitted you had actually stolen the article. I escorted you to the drugstore and made you return the article, and confess your sin. Do you think that I did the right thing? Do you think you should not have been shown the evil of your ways?

ETHAN: Oh, Dad...

CLAUDE: Oh, Dad, what?

ETHAN: That was just a harmless, minor little incident.

CLAUDE: I beg your pardon, Ethan, theft is not a minor incident.

ETHAN: I still don't see what that has to do with me wearing my hair long.

CLAUDE: It's unseemly.

ETHAN: Unseemly? What does that mean?

CLAUDE: It's a style that's followed by degenerates.

THE HAIRCUT

ETHAN: Well, maybe I am a degenerate.

CLAUDE: Do you intend to go through life giving in to all your evil impulses? You made a big show of your so-called love affair with your friend, Carl. And now, I understand this big love affair has bitten the dust. What did you accomplish by this foolish display of yours?

ETHAN: It was an experience that I don't regret. Even if Carl and I are no longer lovers, it has brought us closer together.

CLAUDE: Am I to understand then that this is a process you intend to go through life pursuing? Do you intend to investigate all unacceptable behavior?

ETHAN: No, of course not. But as long as I don't hurt anyone...

CLAUDE: All right, Ethan. That's enough. I have done my best to be patient with you, Son. You are my flesh and blood, and I do feel obligated to do the best I can in regard to your upbringing. But I will not have you, or your comrades, parading around this school like a bunch of degenerates. Either you cut your hair or you will not be permitted to attend your classes.

(The phone rings.)

CLAUDE: Excuse me. *(HE picks up the phone.)* Hello? Yes? What is it? I see. *(HE hangs up.)* That was your friend, Carl. He's given me fair warning. If you are expelled, he said, the entire student body intends to walk out and hold a demonstration. Are you aware of this?

ETHAN: We spoke about that possibility.

THE HAIRCUT

CLAUDE: So, in order to indulge this foolish whim of yours, you're willing to turn this school into a fiery cauldron.

ETHAN: I think it is debatable, Dad, who's being foolish, who is responsible for a "fiery cauldron."

CLAUDE: It's up to you, Son. Either you cut your hair, or you will not be permitted to enter the building.

ETHAN: You mean I'm expelled.

CLAUDE: Until you're presentable.

ETHAN: Until I cut my hair.

CLAUDE: Exactly.

ETHAN: Okay.

CLAUDE: What does that mean. okay?

ETHAN: I guess I'm expelled.

CLAUDE: Don't you want to think it over?

ETHAN: I have thought it over, and I've come to the conclusion that you are a tyrant.

CLAUDE: The interview is over. You may go.

> *(ETHAN hesitates, looks at his father, and goes off. CLAUDE sits at his desk, lost in thought. After a moment, he rises and stands looking out the window. Shouts are*

THE HAIRCUT

heard in the distance, whistles and catcalls. Then a chant is heard, softly at first, then grows louder and louder.)

CROWD: *(Offstage)* No haircut! No haircut! No haircut!

(The chant continues as the lights come down.)

ACT TWO

(Two hours later. The Fairchild home. The doorbell rings. DEBORAH enters from the kitchen and goes off to answer the door.)

DEBORAH: *(Offstage)* Oh, Walter. Come in.

(WALTER enters followed by DEBORAH.)

DEBORAH: I thought you might be Claude. I was just preparing his lunch.

WALTER: I don't think he'll be home for lunch. It's started, all over again, and I think, this time, it's going to be worse, much, much worse.

DEBORAH: I was afraid of that.

WALTER: This time it's the entire student body. They're picketing in front of the school, and refusing to let anyone enter the building. Someone attempted to, a fight broke out, and the police were called.

DEBORAH: Was anyone hurt?

WALTER: No one seriously, as yet, but there were a few bloody noses. In addition to that, the entire faculty has left the building. Claude is the only there and he has no intention of leaving.

DEBORAH: Have you spoken to him?

WALTER: I spoke to him earlier this morning, and then again on the phone just now. And, I'm sorry to say, he's acting very strangely. He's going to remain in his office until, quote, "Those animals come to their senses." I was hoping you might be able to

THE HAIRCUT

talk some sense into him, or Ethan, perhaps. It's going to mean his job. That's for sure. If this were the Midwest somewhere, or some ultra conservative community, it might be a different story. He would probably be a hero. But there've been so many upheavals. And the board, I'm afraid, is made up of a group of young liberals. There's his insistence that Creationism be taught in addition to Evolution. And there's still Jenny Fletcher who, I'm afraid, is a very popular young lady, with a number of friends in high places.

DEBORAH: Is Ethan there?

WALTER: Ethan is there in spades. He's a hero now, a Cause Celebre. I am really concerned. The word is that, eventually, the students plan to take over the building. They've given Claude an ultimatum. Either Ethan is admitted to class or they "storm the barricade." They've set five o'clock as their deadline.

DEBORAH: Does he know that?

WALTER: Oh, yes.

DEBORAH: What did he say?

WALTER: "Let them come," he said. "I'm ready for them." I'm really in a pickle. Since I'm head of the board, I'm being held responsible, and my phone hasn't stopped ringing. I don't know. Sometimes, with the war and all, it seems to be that this whole world is coming apart. Could I trouble you for a drink? I really need one.

DEBORAH: Yes, of course. *(SHE pours a drink and hands it to WALTER.)*

THE HAIRCUT

WALTER: Thank you. *(HE drinks.)* You haven't spoken to Lily lately, have you?

DEBORAH: I ran into her on Saturday.

WALTER: Has she told you?

DEBORAH: What?

WALTER: She wants a divorce.

DEBORAH: I'm so sorry.

WALTER: Actually it's a great relief. We're like oil and water. Julie's the only thing that's kept us together, and now that Julie's a lovely young lady, this is the best thing that could have happened... for the both of us. I suspect she's found someone else.

DEBORAH: And I'm sure you'll find someone else as well. You're still young, my dear.

WALTER: Not that young. Debbie?

DEBORAH: What?

WALTER: You're not really in love with him, are you? I said...

DEBORAH: Now Walter, please. Claude and I are man and wife, for better or worse.

WALTER: You couldn't possibly be happy, living with that...martinet.

THE HAIRCUT

DEBORAH: I'm at peace, and our marriage does have its rewards. I was in love with you once.

WALTER: And I with you.

DEBORAH: But it didn't work out.

WALTER: And believe me, Honey, I've paid for it in spades.

DEBORAH: But that was once, and we're two different people now. Subject closed. I want you to do me a favor?

WALTER: Yes, of course. What is it?

DEBORAH: Will you come with me to the school. I want to bring Claude his lunch, and maybe I can talk some sense into him.

WALTER: It's quite a messy scene out there.

DEBORAH: That's why I'd like you to come with me. Will you, please?

WALTER: Yes, of course. We'll go through the back way.

DEBORAH: No. I'm not going to sneak around. I want them to make way for me. I want them to see that my husband has some support.

WALTER: If that's what you want.

DEBORAH: It is. Thank you. I've got to pack his lunch. It won't take me a minute.

THE HAIRCUT

WALTER: I'll need to use your phone meanwhile. I've got to cancel a couple of appointments.

DEBORAH: Help yourself.

(DEBORAH goes off. WALTER finishes his drink, picks up the phone and dials.)

WALTER: Nancy, call Mrs. Bradford and tell her something's come up, and set up something for tomorrow. And then call Jeff Collins and tell him I won't be able to meet him for lunch. What's that? It's a mess, from what I gather. I'm taking Debbie over to bring Claude his lunch. When did she call? Okay. Thanks. *(HE hangs up and dials another number.)* Yes, Lily? What is it? This afternoon? That's impossible. Look, we've put up with each other for fifteen years, so one more day will not make that much difference. So we'll meet next week. When's he due back? All right, next month. I'm sorry. Then get another lawyer, damn it!

(WALTER slams down the phone as DEBORAH enters with a lunch basket.)

DEBORAH: Ready?

WALTER: As I'll ever be. Come on, let's go.

(THEY start off, then DEBORAH stops.)

DEBORAH: Just a minute. *(SHE goes off, returning a moment later. SHE sets down the lunch basket.)*

WALTER: What is it? What's the matter?

THE HAIRCUT

DEBORAH: The gun, Claude's gun. He bought one last year when someone tried to break into the house. It's not there now.

WALTER: You think...?

DEBORAH: No one knew about that gun, except for Walter and myself. It was locked away.

WALTER: Oh, Lord!

DEBORAH: I've never told this to anyone. When he took that leave of absence... Very well, when he had that nervous breakdown, I was lucky enough to stop him from taking his own life.

WALTER: You think he may have taken it?

DEBORAH: I don't know.

WALTER: Well, there's only one way of finding out.

> *(DEBORAH picks up the lunch basket and goes off, followed by WALTER as the lights come down on the Fairchild home and up on Amanda's apartment. AMANDA is eating her lunch and watching television.)*

TV REPORTER: So far there's been no violence, but some of the students have been quite vociferous. Things may come to a head if the students make true on their threat to take over the building. And now for the local weather.

> *(AMANDA rises, shuts off the television set, picks up the dish and silverware and starts off when ETHAN enters from the outside.)*

THE HAIRCUT

AMANDA: Well, if it isn't the man of the hour himself!

ETHAN: I hope I'm not intruding. What are you doing home?

AMANDA: I called in sick. What can I do for you?

ETHAN: I'm starved. Can you feed a hungry man?

AMANDA: I've got some chili left.

ETHAN: I love chili.

AMANDA: And some fruit.

ETHAN: Perfect.

AMANDA: Have a seat.

ETHAN: Thank you.

(AMANDA goes off to the kitchen.)

ETHAN: Am I still welcome?

AMANDA: *(Offstage)* You're always welcome.

ETHAN: As a friend. Were we on the news?

AMANDA: *(Offstage)* Oh, yes, indeed.

ETHAN: Did they show my interview?

AMANDA: *(Offstage)* Oh, yes, indeed.

THE HAIRCUT

ETHAN: Well?

AMANDA: *(Offstage)* Well, what?

ETHAN: How'd I come off?

AMANDA: *(Offstage)* Rather pompous.

ETHAN: Oh, come on.

AMANDA: *(Offstage)* You asked me, and I'm telling you. Are you actually going to take over the building?

ETHAN: It wasn't my idea.

AMANDA: *(Entering with bowl of chili and some crackers)* But you are responsible for all of this.

ETHAN: Not from my point of view. Talk about pompous.

AMANDA: There's not that much chili, but you can fill up on the crackers and the fruit.

ETHAN: Thank you.

> *(AMANDA goes back to the kitchen. ETHAN eats the chili and the crackers. AMANDA reenters with some fruit.)*

AMANDA: Don't eat too fast, you'll give yourself indigestion.

ETHAN: You sound just like my mother.

AMANDA: She paid me a visit a little while ago.

THE HAIRCUT

ETHAN: Oh? Really? Why?

AMANDA: She thinks I may have some influence over you. Ha!

ETHAN: What did she say about me?

AMANDA: Apparently it's not you she's concerned about. It's your father.

ETHAN: Oh?

AMANDA: You're not really close to your father, are you?

ETHAN: We live in two different worlds. I feel sorry for him though. There's no joy in the man, no love, no fun. Life for him is a burden.

AMANDA: Did you ever try to understand him?

ETHAN: He's opaque. It's impossible for anyone to see beyond this veneer of religion and ultra-conservative morality. Actually I don't think there is anything more. I often wonder why my mother married him.

AMANDA: She married him on the rebound.

ETHAN: How do you know?

AMANDA: She told me.

ETHAN: Amazing.

AMANDA: What's so amazing about it?

THE HAIRCUT

ETHAN: Why on earth would she tell a thing like that to a perfect stranger?

AMANDA: Sometimes it's easier to talk to a perfect stranger, to someone who can be objective. Did you know your father had a nervous break-down?

ETHAN: It wasn't a nervous break-down. He was just tired and overworked.

AMANDA: Or so you were told. And he had one when he was a boy.

ETHAN: My mother told you all this?

AMANDA: She also told me what effect all this mess might have on him.

ETHAN: And what would that be?

AMANDA: It might push him over the edge, and if that should happen, you may regret it for the rest of your life. Tell me why are you doing this?

ETHAN: To make a point, my dear.

AMANDA: "My dear." Oh, you're so sophisticated Ethan. Why don't you grow up? Isn't it time you started to think about other people?

ETHAN: One's first responsibility is to oneself.

AMANDA: You really are a selfish little beast.

THE HAIRCUT

ETHAN: Is that why you're madly in love with me?

AMANDA: Selfish, conceited and destructive. All you think about is yourself.

ETHAN: I suppose you think my father's right.

AMANDA: I never said that.

ETHAN: Then what?

AMANDA: Don't you have any affection for him at all?

ETHAN: I did, as a child, when he showed an interest in me. As soon as I developed a mind of my own, as soon as I started to think for myself suddenly the interest stopped. I was not a toy any longer. I didn't agree with everything he said, everything he did.

AMANDA: So you're going to spite your father because he wasn't as affectionate as you thought he should have been. Why are you shaking your head?

ETHAN: Psychology 101. You can do better than that.

AMANDA: Ethan, grown-ups are people, too. And sometimes we've got to stop thinking as a child and take a good look at our parents. We owe them that much.

ETHAN: Look who's talking. You and your mother have battle royals continually.

AMANDA: At least there's still affection, underneath it all. There's love. I never told you about my father, did I?

THE HAIRCUT

ETHAN: Were you close to him?

AMANDA: He was a mess. He drank like a fish. And he would poke fun at me. I was a slob. I was a lazy good-for-nothing, which was exactly what I thought of him, and I told him so. When he died, he was fifty three years old, and when they read his will, I found out that he left me his insurance policy. It was worth twenty thousand dollars. He knew I wanted to write, and that would give me the time to try my wings. I was able to take this apartment, and just work on my writing for over a year. And I keep thinking back. Maybe the fault wasn't always his. Maybe he didn't get the love from us that he should have gotten. I mean there must have been a reason why he drank so much.

ETHAN: Maybe he just liked to drink.

AMANDA: Very funny. That's one thing I've learned, Ethan, it's almost impossible to understand one's parents. But I think if we could understand our parents we might just be able to understand ourselves.

ETHAN: That's very profound.

AMANDA: I think back to the way I treated my father, and I wish I could do it all over again. Ethan, you said yourself you don't know what's going on inside of him. If you're responsible for another breakdown, a serious one, perhaps, you may regret it, like your mother said, for the rest of your life.

ETHAN: You think I should cut my hair.

AMANDA: I think you ought to have a heart to heart talk with your father.

THE HAIRCUT

ETHAN: The martinet of Central High? *(HE sits lost in thought for a moment.)* Can I see you tonight?

AMANDA: Tonight is a long way off. Now finish your lunch and get out of here.

> *(ETHAN continues to eat as the lights come down on the apartment and up on the office. In the distance a chant can be heard, "No haircuts, no haircuts." CLAUDE is seated at his desk, his head buried in his arms which are resting on the desk. HE raises his head, listens to the chant, then opens the desk drawer and pulls out a gun. A knock is heard.)*

CLAUDE: Who's there?

DEBORAH: *(Offstage)* It's me, Claude. Open the door.

> *(CLAUDE puts the gun in the drawer and goes off. DEBORAH enters a moment later with the lunch basket, followed, a moment later, by CLAUDE.)*

DEBORAH: I've brought you your lunch.

CLAUDE: How did you get into the building?

DEBORAH: I came through the back door. I was going to come through the front, but there was such chaos, and the police couldn't guarantee my safety.

CLAUDE: You shouldn't have come.

DEBORAH: You've got to eat. I've brought you some soup, and I've heated up the meat loaf you liked so much.

THE HAIRCUT

CLAUDE: Thank you.

(DEBORAH sets out the food on the desk.)

DEBORAH: I even brought you some wine. There was still some left in the bottle. We've got to order some more.

CLAUDE: I don't have much of an appetite.

DEBORAH: Well, I did not make this trip for nothing.

CLAUDE: Have you spoken to Ethan lately?

DEBORAH: I'm very disappointed in Ethan. I thought he had more sense.

CLAUDE: Do you think I'm wrong?

DEBORAH: No, dear. He looks ridiculous with that long hair, and I've told him so.

CLAUDE: It's not his appearance I'm concerned about. I'm thinking of his welfare, and the welfare of all those boys who are following a way of life that's sick, that's degenerate. He made one mistake, that homosexual relationship he had with Carl, but I'm afraid that was only the beginning. He seems determined to defy all that's right and moral. He seems to have no respect whatsoever for what I have to say, for what's acceptable in our Society. It's as if the world is wrong, and he's the only one that sees things the way they should be. Religion, of course, is a personal thing. But one must believe in something. One cannot live like a pagan in a civilized Society.

DEBORAH: I quite agree.

THE HAIRCUT

CLAUDE: You seem to have more influence with him than I have.

DEBORAH: Not much more, I'm afraid. Why don't you eat some soup.

> (*CLAUDE takes a few spoons of soup, lays down the spoon and begins to weep.*)

DEBORAH: Oh, my dear. (*SHE clasps his head to her.*)

CLAUDE: I'm such a bloody failure.

DEBORAH: You're nothing of the sort.

CLAUDE: I'm a failure as an educator, I'm a failure as a husband, and I'm a failure as a father.

DEBORAH: Claude, you are a good man.

CLAUDE: I'm not really. I have such wicked thoughts, such terrible demons. If I were to tell you, you would find me disgusting. But I do my best to fight them, Debbie, I really do.

DEBORAH: I know you do, dear, and I respect you for it.

CLAUDE: Young people today, I feel that they're all against me, when, actually, I have nothing but their welfare in mind. Maybe I'm the one that's wrong. Maybe what I call sick and degenerate has become the norm. But it turns my stomach, it defies everything I was brought up to believe in, and I cannot give in. I cannot reject my faith, everything I've lived for, everything that I was taught was good and fine. I keep hoping...

DEBORAH: What, dear?

THE HAIRCUT

CLAUDE: Sinners sometimes see the evil of their ways. It's difficult, I know, but time and time again, the wicked have shed their blasphemous ways and walked in the steps of the righteous. I'm a perfect example. Ethan's a fine boy, I know that. But how can he not see the beauty of the sacrament? How can he reject Christ?

DEBORAH: He's at an age when he questions everything. And, in a way, that's healthy, don't you think?

CLAUDE: You think he'll come around?

DEBORAH: I think so, yes, eventually. But I do think we have to make some allowances. If we close our minds, we've lost him. Eat your food, dear. It's getting cold.

CLAUDE: *(HE eats, then stops.)* You think I ought to compromise. But don't you see? Compromise is...

DEBORAH: What?

CLAUDE: One step down the road to hell.

DEBORAH: I'll bet you, that if you told Claude he could continue to wear his hair long, he would turn around and get a haircut.

CLAUDE: You really think so?

DEBORAH: I do.

CLAUDE: You're the only one I can turn to.

DEBORAH: I'm here for you, Claude, you know that.

THE HAIRCUT

CLAUDE: You won't desert me, will you, because without you at my side...

DEBORAH: *(SHE embraces him.)* Shhhh.

(There's a knock at the door.)

DEBORAH: That must be Walter.

CLAUDE: What's he doing here?

DEBORAH: He brought me.

(Another knock is heard.)

DEBORAH: Aren't you going to open the door?

(CLAUDE goes off. WALTER enters followed by CLAUDE.)

WALTER: Are you locking yourself in, or everyone out?

DEBORAH: What took you so long?

WALTER: I ran into some of the students. *(HE turns to CLAUDE.)* You know, of course, that they're planning to take over the building. I said...

CLAUDE: I heard you the first time.

(CLAUDE returns to finish up his lunch. WALTER and DEBORAH exchange looks.)

DEBORAH: Claude...? The revolver's missing. Do you know what happened to it?

THE HAIRCUT

CLAUDE: What's that?

DEBORAH: The revolver. Do you know what happened to it?

CLAUDE: Yes. I brought it back to the store. There's something wrong with the firing pin.

WALTER: You're not really in danger, you know. The police have been alerted, and the students have no intention of harming you.

DEBORAH: As a matter of fact, dear, they think it would be better for all concerned if you left the building.

CLAUDE: I'm aware of that.

DEBORAH: You're not going to spend the night here, are you?

CLAUDE: Quite possibly.

WALTER: What do you hope to accomplish?

CLAUDE: I don't think you would understand.

WALTER: Try me.

DEBORAH: Walter's right, dear. Your presence here just aggravates the situation.

CLAUDE: I don't think Walter's in any position to give advice to anyone. Do you?

DEBORAH: Well, he is the head of the Board.

THE HAIRCUT

CLAUDE: Which I find rather ironic. An adulterer in charge of education. You know, of course, that Lily's divorcing him.

DEBORAH: Yes, he told me.

CLAUDE: You never mentioned it before.

DEBORAH: He just told me, a short while ago.

CLAUDE: You spoke to Lily over the week-end. You said nothing about the divorce.

DEBORAH: Lily never mentioned the divorce.

CLAUDE: I find that highly unlikely since the two of you are such great chums.

DEBORAH: Lily and I are not great chums. As a matter of fact, we have very little in common.

CLAUDE: On the contrary.

DEBORAH: What is that supposed to mean?

CLAUDE: Incidentally, what grounds is Lily using for the divorce?

DEBORAH: I don't know.

CLAUDE: Walter?

DEBORAH: I'm not quite sure. Incompatibility, perhaps.

CLAUDE: Or adultery, perhaps, with my wife as correspondent..

THE HAIRCUT

DEBORAH: Claude, dear, that is highly unlikely, and Walter's divorce is really none of our business.

CLAUDE: You think not? When he's the one you should have married.

DEBORAH: Darling, I don't think that this is the time.

CLAUDE: Why not, when all three parties are present, and the crucial moment is at hand. Everyone knows that if Walter hadn't knocked Lily up, to put it crudely, you and he would now be man and wife. Or are you prepared to deny it?

DEBORAH: Oh, Claude, please.

CLAUDE: This is your golden opportunity.

WALTER: Oh, Claude, for God's sake, don't be a fool.

CLAUDE: Isn't that what I've been all along? But maybe I'm not the fool you take me for. That evening you just happened to run into each other in the city. And that New Years Eve, when you used the midnight chimes to linger over that long passionate kiss.

DEBORAH: All right, Claude.

CLAUDE: Oh, come now, Debbie, you know perfectly well you would much have preferred that great stud, Walter Ambrose, in your bed, than that meek, mild Claude Fairchild.

WALTER: You're doing yourself a great injustice, Claude. You have never been meek, nor have you ever been mild. You're a cold, creepy, bigoted church-going prig. God knows what goes on in that

THE HAIRCUT

sick mind of yours. You are a miserable man, and you really don't deserve a woman like Debbie.

DEBORAH: Walter, that's enough.

CLAUDE: No, please. I find this very informative. It's refreshing to hear what Walter really thinks of me. The one friend I do have on the Board.

DEBORAH: Walter, I think you'd better leave.

CLAUDE: No, no. Let him stay. There's one more thing I'd like to clear up.

WALTER: And what might that be?

CLAUDE: Your relationship to the boy who's supposed to be my son.

WALTER: Go on. I can't believe this.

CLAUDE: That picnic last year.

WALTER: What about it?

CLAUDE: The way you were coaching my son to hold a bat, the way you had your arms around him. The way you held him close as you supposedly showed him the proper way to swing.

WALTER: You are sick.

CLAUDE: Or maybe you felt close to him because he wasn't my son, but yours.

THE HAIRCUT

WALTER: Debbie, have you heard enough?

CLAUDE: Go on, go on. Get out of here, the both of you. You're disgusting.

DEBORAH: Claude...

CLAUDE: Please go.

WALTER: I think we'd better leave.

CLAUDE: Get out? The both of you!

> (DEBORAH goes off, followed by WALTER. CLAUDE paces nervously. The chant outside grows louder. CLAUDE puts his hands to his ears. There is a knock at the door. The knock continues and grows louder. CLAUDE lowers his hands.)

CLAUDE: Who is it?

ETHAN: *(Offstage)* It's Ethan, Dad.

> (CLAUDE goes off. ETHAN enters followed by CLAUDE.)

ETHAN: Dad...

CLAUDE: Yes? What is it?

ETHAN: I think we ought to have a talk.

CLAUDE: Man to man?

ETHAN: Father to son.

THE HAIRCUT

CLAUDE: Isn't it a little late for that? Listen to them out there, your colleagues, the future of America, a gang of young hoodlums.

ETHAN: Did it ever occur to you that we have principles, too? Let me ask you this. Is this a personal thing between you and me, or are you really serious about my hair.

CLAUDE: What do you think?

ETHAN: I don't know, but I do think this is something so trivial, so unimportant to make a fuss about.

CLAUDE: I've just been called a fool. Do you think I'm a fool?

ETHAN: I'm trying to understand where you're coming from, Dad. Don't you think that people should be allowed to think for themselves.

CLAUDE: Don't you think it's foolish to ignore the wisdom and the experience of those who've come before us? Don't you think that I've had the same ideas, the same urges that you've had? But I was saved...

ETHAN: From what?

CLAUDE: From hell and damnation.

ETHAN: Do you really believe in hell and damnation?

CLAUDE: I believe there is a struggle going on within us, a struggle between good and evil. It's a struggle we cannot cope with alone. We need the help of those who came before us to help us distinguish between salvation and destruction.

THE HAIRCUT

ETHAN: You believe that my affair with Carl was evil.

CLAUDE: I'm not the only one, Son. Read your Bible.

ETHAN: There are lots of things in the Bible, Dad, many of them contradictory.

CLAUDE: I can't force you to think as I do. But I do know that my father was my salvation, and I had hoped that I would be yours.

ETHAN: I wish I'd known my grandparents.

CLAUDE: He was a fine man, Ethan, a fine man. And he saved my life. You see, I too, had my Carl. His name was Kenneth, and we had, what you might call a relationship. But my father showed me the evil of my ways. I put an end to my relationship with Kenneth. I told him that what we were doing, was wrong. He pleaded with me, he implored me to think it over. "But I love you, Claude," he said. But I was strong, you see, and I rejected him. I told him what we were doing was filthy, was twisted, was disgusting. And how right my father was, because Kenneth persisted in his sinful behavior, and six months later he took his own life.

ETHAN: How awful!

CLAUDE: And how lucky for me...that I had my father to guide me, for I'm sure that I would have ended up the way that Kenneth did. For Satan is always there, always there beckoning us, teasing us, but to this day I've continued to fight those evil thoughts, and I've prayed for you, Son, for you and Carl, and my prayers, I think have been answered, since you and Carl have discontinued this

THE HAIRCUT

perverted relationship. And, you see, Son, the way you wear your hair, it's the last vestige of this stage you've been going through.

ETHAN: You're afraid of affection, aren't you, Dad? You're afraid of yourself.

CLAUDE: True love is between a man and a woman, the straight and the narrow, and sometimes it may be difficult to follow, but in the end it's the only way.

ETHAN: Suppose I were to say that I would cut my hair, just to please you?

CLAUDE: No, no, no, Son. That would be meaningless.

ETHAN: What would have meaning for you?

CLAUDE: If you were to cut your hair because it was the right thing to do, because you've seen the evil of your ways.

ETHAN: I couldn't do that.

CLAUDE: Then you've chosen a path I cannot condone; and I mourn for you, Son. I mourn for you, the way King David mourned for Absalom.

ETHAN: I'm sorry. I really am. But I cannot believe that love, any kind of love, is evil.

> *(ETHAN kisses CLAUDE. CLAUDE flinches. ETHAN stands hesitant for a moment, sighs and walks off. CLAUDE stands lost in thought. HE sits, as if in a daze. After a moment HE rises, slowly gathers up the plates and the silverware and places them neatly in the basket, then sets*

THE HAIRCUT

the basket aside. Methodically HE straightens all the items on the desk, making it neat and organized. The chant outside grows louder and louder. CLAUDE then goes to the desk, opens the drawer and takes out the gun. HE shuts the drawer, stands in the center of the room, raises the gun and points it to his temple. The lights black out, and a shot is heard in the dark.)

A DARK CORNER OF AN EMPTY ROOM
(A Phantasmagoria in Three Scenes)

CAST OF CHARACTERS

Frank Carter (An African American)

Chloe Carter (His Mother; an African American)

Walter Carter (His Father; an African American)

Bea Carter (His Sister; an African American)

Hazel (A Lover: a Caucasian)

Rhoda Sanford (An Activist; an African American)

Benny Smith (A Friend; an African American)

Reverend Daniel (an African American)

Phil Ryder (An Activist; an African American)

A White Detective

Various Offstage Voices

SCENE
A room in an empty tenement apartment

TIME
1968

SCENE ONE

(As the lights in the theatre come down, gunshots are heard faintly, as if coming from the distance. The lights come up on the living room of an empty tenement apartment. It is a late summer afternoon. The windows are open and neighborhood noises can be heard; children playing, a radio, a Mother calling to her child. The door, which is ajar, is opened and FRANK CARTER, gun in hand looks in. Seeing the room is empty, he tucks the gun away and closes the door behind him. HE hops toward the window, wincing in pain.)

FRANK: Son of a bitch!

A WOMAN'S VOICE: Jerry, you come on home. You hear me? Jerry? What you doin' out there?

FRANK: He's playin' with himself, that's what he's doin'.

WOMAN'S VOICE: Jerry!!

FRANK: Jesus Christ, Jerry, why the fuck don't you go home?!

RADIO: "My baby don't care for clothes.
My baby don't care for shows.
My baby just cares for me.
My baby don't care for furs and laces..."

(FRANK returns to the door and locks it. HE notices a phone on the floor and hops over to it.)

FRANK: Oh, Baby, please! *(HE picks up the receiver, listens for a moment, then dials a number. HE waits impatiently, then slams the receiver.)* Shit! *(HE dials another number. No answer. HE hangs up and dials again.)* Hello, operator? Can you give me the

THE DARK CORNER OF AN EMPTY ROOM

number for Tom Fairchild on Foster Street? Right. *(HE hangs up and dials again.)* Hello? Mavis? This is Frank. I tried to get Rhoda but she's not home. If you should hear her come in would you have her call me? No, no. I'll give you the number. It's 617-8535. Thanks a lot. *(HE hangs up, limps to the window and looks out, careful not to be seen. HE listens to the street noises for a moment, then hops off into an adjacent room. HE returns dragging a mattress which he positions so that he can watch the window and the door. HE picks up the phone and dials, listens, then hangs up, sets down the phone and cries out in pain.)* Jesus! *(HE rubs his leg, then sits on the mattress, resting his head against the wall.)*

(The dusk deepens. The street noises dim. FRANK closes his eyes, and drifts off. There is a change in the atmosphere.)

FRANK: Mama, why are some people black and some people white?

(CHLOE appears.)

CHLOE: I guess some of us just faded, Honey.

FRANK: Why do we sleep at night and get up in the morning?

CHLOE: If you slept all day, you wouldn't be able to go to school.

FRANK: Why can't we have school at night?

CHLOE: Why don't you ask your father some of these questions?

(WALTER appears.)

FRANK: Papa, why don't they have school at night?

THE DARK CORNER OF AN EMPTY ROOM

WALTER: They do, but that's for grown-ups.

FRANK: How long does it take to be a grown-up?

CHLOE: Your father wouldn't know about that. Oh, come on, Walter, I was only kidding.

FRANK: You got a big mouth, woman.

(The phone rings. WALTER and CHLOE disappears. FRANK sits erect.)

FRANK: Huh! Ouch. *(HE looks about.)* What the heck? *(HE picks up the phone.)* Hello? Who? You got the wrong number. *(HE holds up his wrist to catch the fading light, and looks at his watch.)*

(The phone rings again. FRANK picks it up.)

FRANK: Hello? You got the wrong number. Yeah. Well, they moved. I don't know. Call information. *(HE hangs up and dials.)* Hello, Lily? Is Harry home? Yeah, well, Benny didn't make it. If you haven't heard anything, Harry must be okay. Look. Get in touch with Phil Ryder and give him this number. It's 617-8535. I'm holed up in this apartment, my leg is busted and there are cops all over the place. I don't know. Just tell him to call me.

(HE hangs up and leans back against the wall, closing his eyes, and drifts off. A radio in the distance is playing music softly.)

CHLOE'S VOICE: Now look, son, I've cooked this food and you're gonna eat it.

A WOMAN'S VOICE: Eat me, Baby. Tongue me.

THE DARK CORNER OF AN EMPTY ROOM

BEA'S VOICE: Daddy, Frank's playin' with himself again.

WALTER'S VOICE: Now how do you know that, young lady?

BEA'S VOICE: 'Cause he's locked himself in the bathroom and he won't come out.

FRANK: I was shavin'.

BEA'S VOICE: You ain't got nothin' to shave, unless you was shavin' down there.

CHLOE'S VOICE: Now what kind of talk is that?

WALTER'S VOICE: If Frank said he was shavin' then he was shavin'. You show a little respect for your brother, or you ain't gonna have any boyfriends.

BEA'S VOICE: I don't want no boyfriends.

FRANK: Any boyfriends. *(After a moment.)* What difference does it make? I'm fifteen. You want it or don't you? Five bucks. Watch your teeth. *(After a moment)* Hey, Dora, where you rushin' off to? You didn't charge Harry. *(After a moment)* Listen, Benny, watch out for Dora. I think she gave me the clap.

(REVEREND DANIEL appears.)

REVEREND DANIEL: No, my friends, it is not the things we can touch that are important in life. Money, flesh, cars, food... Temptation! That's what these things are. Temptations to betray our integrity. And what is integrity? Does anyone here know what integrity is? Oh yes, my brothers and sisters, we know, but have

THE DARK CORNER OF AN EMPTY ROOM

we the courage to listen, to listen to the still, small voice of our conscience, the voice that tells us what is right and what is wrong?

(BEA appears.)

CHLOE'S VOICE: Are you listening to this?

BEA: Yes, Mama, but I don't know about Frank.

CHLOE'S VOICE: Hush now.

(REVEREND DANIEL disappears.)

BEA: Frank? Have you been with a girl? Have you?

FRANK: Yeah.

BEA: Many times?

FRANK: A couple.

BEA: It don't mean nothin', does it? I mean...

FRANK: You mean...what?

BEA: Nothin'.

FRANK: Well, don't you go foolin' around. You hear me?

BEA: Yes, I hear you.

FRANK: And if anyone bothers you, you come to me. You hear me?

THE DARK CORNER OF AN EMPTY ROOM

BEA: Yes, yes. Okay.

(BEA vanishes. FRANK, bright and eager stands erect and recites.)

FRANK: "My Heritage by Frank Carter. I was born black. I don't look upon that as a handicap. I look upon that as a gift. I can look at the world without hypocrisy. Nobody thinks of putting on airs in front of a colored man. A colored man is part of the scenery, like a tree or a house or a street light, so I can see people as they really are, and I can see that my people, the black people, are truly beautiful." *(After a moment he looks puzzled.)* Mr. Walker?

MR. WALKER'S VOICE: Yes, Frank?

FRANK: Why did you give me a "C"?

MR. WALKER'S VOICE: It's an Uncle Tom composition, Frank. It's pretty, it's sweet and it's a lie. I think you've got more to offer.

(BEA appears.)

BEA: Well, I think it's an excellent composition. It's honest and...well, beautiful.

FRANK: Are you sure you haven't got a headache. *(After a moment)* Who's this cat you're seeing? Is it serious?

BEA: I don't know. Frank?

FRANK: Yeah?

BEA: What are you gonna do when you grow up?

THE DARK CORNER OF AN EMPTY ROOM

FRANK: I'm gonna be rich and famous.

(Music is heard.)

BEA: It must be wonderful to be able to compose music like that. Being a composer must be almost like being a God.

FRANK: Don't let Mama hear you say that.

BEA: Mama loves music.

FRANK: But she loves God better.

BEA: Do you believe in God?

FRANK: I think one day I may go into politics.

BEA: You have to be a lawyer to go into politics, don't you?

FRANK: I don't know, but civil rights is where it's at. I think I'd like to go to a white college, and learn all of Whitey's tricks.

BEA: Why would you wanna go where you're not wanted?

FRANK: Why shouldn't I be able to go wherever I wanna go? Why should a colored man have to be a singer or a writer to get somewhere. Why shouldn't a colored man be able to be president of the United States? Ralph Bunche won the Noble Prize, didn't he?

BEA: You could do it, Frank. I bet you could, if you really wanted to.

FRANK: Yeah, well, I'm not so sure that I want to. I don't even

THE DARK CORNER OF AN EMPTY ROOM

know if I wanna finish high school. Some of those classes are a pain in the ass.

BEA: But if you wanna get somewhere, you've gotta have an education.

FRANK: Colleges teach you how to be like Whitey.

BEA: You just said that you wanted to learn Whitey's tricks.

(BEA disappears and WALTER appears.)

WALTER: When I was your age, I coulda had a scholarship, but I never took advantage of it. Your Uncle Seymour, out in Detroit, now he's a big executive with a home of his own and a car. And don't make the mistake thinkin' you've got forever. You gotta grab the bull by the horns.

(WALTER pats FRANK clumsily on the shoulder and walks away, unsteadily as CHLOE appears.)

CHLOE: What's he been tellin' you?

FRANK: Nothin'.

CHLOE: Nothin' is right.

FRANK: Did Papa get fired?

CHLOE: Your father drinks too much. There's nothing wrong with a man drinkin', if he can afford it, and if he can hold his liquor, but your Pa don't qualify in either case. You might as well know the facts, Son, so's you can profit by his mistakes.

THE DARK CORNER OF AN EMPTY ROOM

(CHLOE disappears as BENNY appears.)

FRANK: I'm hungry, Benny. Let's get ourselves some grapes.

BENNY: I don't know, Frank. That old man Zacharias is carrying a gun.

FRANK: That's a lot of crap.

BENNY: Yeah, well, he shot somebody the other night. Some junkie tried to break in when he was closing.

FRANK: Okay, okay. If you're chicken I can go by myself. I just feel like having me some grapes.

BENNY: I didn't say I wasn't going.

ZACHARIAS'S VOICE: Hey, you kids! Stop or I'll shoot.

FRANK: He ain't gonna shoot.

(A shot is heard.)

BENNY: I don't know, Frankie, every time I listen to you...

(BENNY disappears as BEA appears.)

FRANK: Aw, come on.

BEA: Come on, where? Where are you heading for, Frankie?

FRANK: I only take what belongs to us.

BEA: Us? Who is us? You steal from colored as well as white.

THE DARK CORNER OF AN EMPTY ROOM

FRANK: It don't mean nothing.

BEA: If it don't mean nothing why do you do it?

FRANK: It's like making a statement. And a black man ain't colored, he's black.

BEA: I don't know anyone' that's black, except inside maybe. I'm a brown man...woman. And I ain't gonna visit you in reform school. And how do you think Mama's gonna feel? She's not a well woman, you know. I used to think you were gonna be something. You got a brain, Frankie, why don't you use it?

FRANK: It's easy for you to talk. You ain't had no cop beat up on you for nothing at all, for just hanging out.

BEA: So are you gonna spend your life getting even? Are you gonna give up before you've even started? How are you gonna be rich and famous?

FRANK: You're worse than Mama, you know that? You don't have anything to worry about. You're gonna find yourself some nice dependable cat, and stay home and raise a whole bunch of kids.

BEA: I'm not gonna have any kids.

FRANK: What are you gonna have, kittens?

BEA: Very funny.

> *(A church organ is heard. BEA vanishes as BENNY appears.)*

THE DARK CORNER OF AN EMPTY ROOM

BENNY: Man, he looked cold. Stiff and cold. And did you see the expression on his face?

FRANK: I thought he looked kinda peaceful like.

BENNY: He looked dead.

FRANK: Who do you think did it?

BENNY: Probably some junkie.

FRANK: I feel sorry for that kid of his, and Mandy. Why did he let her have it. She was just a kid herself.

BENNY: She was afraid of having it fixed. They had a doctor lined up and she chickened out.

FRANK: You think that's why he started pushing? To make money for the kid?

BENNY: He was selling the stuff before that.

FRANK: How come you knew, and I didn't?

BENNY: Well, you were always sounding off against pushers.

(REVEREND DANIEL'S VOICE is heard.)

REVEREND DANIEL'S VOICE: No man is an island. Ask not for whom the bell tolls, my brother, it tolls for thee.

BENNY: He's fuckin' all those women in the back of the church.

FRANK: I don't believe it.

THE DARK CORNER OF AN EMPTY ROOM

REVEREND DANIEL'S VOICE: God is everywhere. We are in God and God is in us.

BENNY: You can say that again.

REVEREND DANIEL: The Universe is one, and the Word is Love.

BENNY: He was fuckin's Jerry's sister.

FRANK: How do you know?

BENNY: 'Cause Jerry told me.

(BENNY disappears and FRANK approaches BEA.)

FRANK: He was fuckin' Jerry's sister.

BEA: I don't believe it. And don't you go spreadin' stories like that. And how do you know?

FRANK: Jerry told Benny.

BEA: Jerry's dead.

FRANK: Before he died. And why should anyone lie about a thing like that?

BEA: But you don't know for sure.

FRANK: Why are you defending him? What difference does it make to you? Unless....

BEA: Unless what?

THE DARK CORNER OF AN EMPTY ROOM

FRANK: Unless he's been fuckin' you too. Has he? I'll beat the shit out of him, that dirty old nigger. Why'd you let him?

BEA: Don't you say anything to anybody. I'll deny it if you do.

FRANK: Don't you go near him again.

BEA: I'm supposed to see him this afternoon, for my Bible lesson.

FRANK: I'll give him a Bible lesson he won't forget.

BEA: Don't you touch him, Frank. He's a preacher.

FRANK: Fuckin' little girls.

BEA: Frank, please. Don't make any trouble. I'll deny it. I swear I will. Frank, please don't make any trouble.

REVEREND DANIEL'S VOICE: No, boys...no..!

(WOMEN are heard screaming.)

REVEREND DANIEL'S VOICE: Help! Police!

(The sound of a police siren is heard. REVEREND DANIEL, CHLOE and WALTER appear.)

REVEREND DANIEL: I'm not gonna press charges, Sister Carter, but that boy is wicked. And he's got to be dealt with, for his sake, for your sake, for the sake of the whole community. Spare the rod and spoil the child.

(FATHER DANIEL disappears as WALTER appears.)

THE DARK CORNER OF AN EMPTY ROOM

CHLOE: Well, what are you gonna do about it?

WALTER: What do you mean, what am I gonna do about it?

CHLOE: You're his father, ain't you?

WALTER: And you're his mother. And if that boy beat up on that preacher, he must have had his reasons.

REVEREND DANIEL'S VOICE: Corruption is in the cradle, and the corruption is ours, for we are our children.

CHLOE: Oh Lord, Lord, Lord! Forgive me for my sins.

FRANK: He's a phoney.

(CHLOE disappears.)

WALTER: I don't wanna hear another word. You've gotta calm down, Son. You've gotta behave yourself, or you're gonna end up in prison. You hear me?

FRANK: It won't happen again.

WALTER: All right. Now try and do better, Son, you hear me?

FRANK: Yes, sir. I will.

(WALTER disappears and FRANK approaches BENNY.)

FRANK: Did you say anything?

BENNY: You told me not to.

THE DARK CORNER OF AN EMPTY ROOM

FRANK: It wouldn't have done any good. Everybody's chicken. They're afraid of making trouble.

BENNY: Yeah, well, they sure beat the shit out of me.

FRANK: It's good for your soul.

BENNY: It sure as hell ain't good for my ass. What about you?

FRANK: My father gave me a talking to.

BENNY: Yeah, well, you were lucky.

(BEA appears as BENNY leaves.)

BEA: The next time it won't be probation, Frank. They're gonna send you to prison.

FRANK: I didn't start that fight. I was just pulled into it.

BEA: And you sure finished it. Why don't you put all that energy to good use?

FRANK: Like what? Like your N-A-A-C-P and your F-U-C-K?

BEA: I am proud of being black, and I want to take my place in the world, just like everyone else. You used to feel that way, too.

FRANK: That was in my youth.

BEA: Your youth? You haven't reached your youth. You're still an infant.

THE DARK CORNER OF AN EMPTY ROOM

FRANK: And the only reason you're all worked up about saving your black brothers is because of this cat you're seeing and, man, is he a phoney.

BEA: I don't think he's phoney at all. And he doesn't waste his time being bitter.

FRANK: Woooooooooeee!

BEA: Well, you can make fun all you want to, but Harlan ain't going to spend the rest of his life in jail.

FRANK: And I am?

BEA: If you keep on the way you are. And you're gonna break Mama's heart.

FRANK: I think the world beat me to it.

BEA: The world, the world, the world. You keep complaining about the world. Why don't you stop complaining and do something? And I don't mean robbing stores and stealing cars and I don't know what else, and I don't wanna know.

(BEA disappears and CHLOE appears.)

CHLOE: Son, I don't know what to say to you anymore. You're getting too big to spank, and you won't listen to reason. Your father and I both work hard. There's always enough to eat, ain't there? Have you ever gone hungry? Answer me when I talk to you.

FRANK: No.

THE DARK CORNER OF AN EMPTY ROOM

CHLOE: Then why did you steal that fish? What did you expect to do with it? I'm asking you. What did you expect to do with that fish?

FRANK: Sell it, maybe.

CHLOE: Who's gonna buy a fish from some kid? And you ain't a kid anymore. You been to reform school once. You wanna go back there?

FRANK: No.

CHLOE: You takin' dope? Are you?

FRANK: No. I ain't takin' dope.

CHLOE: Then why did you steal that fish?

FRANK: Hell, Ma, you said yourself that old Jew was stealin' us blind, so why can't we steal from him? All those Jews are sucking us dry.

CHLOE: Two wrongs don't make a right. And I never said that all Jews are bad. People are people. Some are good and some are evil. Here you are stealin' fish. How would you like it if someone said that all colored boys are thieves. How would you like that?

FRANK: But it ain't true, and you know that all those Jews are stealin' us blind.

CHLOE: When did I ever say that?

FRANK: Well, it's true, and you know it. He's a dirty old Jew, I'm gonna steal from him any time I want.

THE DARK CORNER OF AN EMPTY ROOM

(CHLOE slaps FRANK across the face.)

CHLOE: Go ahead. Hit me back. Go ahead.

FRANK: You and Papa ain't nothing. You, and that Reverend Daniel fucking little girls, and Papa's always half loaded, and I <u>have</u> gone hungry. The only way to get ahead is to take what you want. And if I ever get married, I ain't gonna let my wife crawl on her hands and knees scrubbin' some white man's floor.

CHLOE: You ain't gonna live long enough to get married.

FRANK: And I ain't gonna take the jobs nobody else wants, just because I'm colored.

CHLOE: Once you get a record, you ain't gonna be able to get any jobs.

FRANK: Who cares? I'm gonna make it, and if I don't, I don't care. I don't care if I die in the electric chair. I'd rather be dead than live the way you and Papa are living. Hell, that ain't living. My friend, Jerry, made more money in one day than you and Papa put together in a month.

CHLOE: And where is your friend, Jerry, now?

FRANK: I don't care. I wanna have enough money to buy nice clothes and go to a good restaurant. And I wanna live in a decent house in a decent neighborhood.

CHLOE: You ain't even fit for this neighborhood. Then again, maybe you are, Son. Maybe you are.

(WALTER appears.)

THE DARK CORNER OF AN EMPTY ROOM

WALTER: Where am I gonna get money for a lawyer? Let him go to jail. That's where he belongs.

CHLOE: Calm down, Walter.

WALTER: I never stole a thing in my life, and nobody in my family ever stole anything. My cousin Seymour is a big executive in Detroit.

FRANK: I thought he was my uncle. And how come we never see this uncle or cousin...or whatever he is?

WALTER: Don't you give me any of your lip, boy.

FRANK: And don't you call me a boy. I ain't no boy.

WALTER: No, Son, you're not. What you are is a thief.

FRANK: You try to whip me like you did the last time, and you'll find out who I am.

WALTER: Get him out of here. You get him out of my house.

CHLOE: This is my house, too.

FRANK: Well, it ain't mine. And you can keep your house, 'cause I'm goin'.

(CHLOE and WALTER disappear. BEA approaches FRANK.)

BEA: But where do you sleep?

FRANK: Don't worry about me.

THE DARK CORNER OF AN EMPTY ROOM

BEA: Mama hasn't slept a wink, you know. Have you got any money?

FRANK: I make out.

BEA: I got twenty dollars that I saved up. Do you want me to bring it to you?

FRANK: No, you keep your money.

BEA: Mama's been talkin' to this lawyer, and I think he's gonna take your case. You are gonna show up for your trial, ain't you?

FRANK: I guess so.

BEA: If you come back, Papa wouldn't say a thing. I know it.

FRANK: Papa's an old blow-hard. I'm sick of his shit.

BEA: But we're still a family, Frank. We gotta make allowances. People need each other, Frank.

FRANK: I don't need anyone. I found myself an empty apartment, and I'm doin' fine. I come and go as I please. No one to tell me what to do and when to do it. Why should I go back? What for. I'm tired of getting pushed around.

(WALTER and CHLOE appear. CHLOE embraces FRANK.)

CHLOE: Three years ain't that long, Son, and maybe, if you behave yourself, maybe they'll let you out early.

WALTER: And maybe you can learn a trade while you're in there.

THE DARK CORNER OF AN EMPTY ROOM

FRANK: I'll be all right. Don't you worry about me.

CHLOE: Now you know we're going to worry, Son.

(BEA, WALTER and CHLOE disappear. Flashing searchlights are seen in the distance. FRANK sits up and looks around. An ANNOUNCER on a radio is heard.)

ANNOUNCER: The money has been recovered, and the police are combing the area for the two men who escaped. Officer Wilson died a few minutes ago.

(Someone has switched the station and music can be heard. FRANK sits lost in thought as the lights come down.)

SCENE TWO

(The action is continuous. The soft murmur of voices is heard. Music. FRANK is alert, listening. The phone rings. HE picks up the phone.)

FRANK: Hello? Oh, Honey. I'm holed up in this empty apartment. My leg's been hurt pretty bad, and the police are staked out all over the place. I've just got to wait it out. It's somewhere near Pontiac Avenue. I don't know the address. I don't know what he can do, but let Phil know. I'll be okay. Don't worry. Let Phil know. *(HE hangs up.)* Yeah, don't worry.

(HE relaxes and drifts off. PHIL RYDER appears.)

PHIL: Ryder. Phil Ryder.

FRANK: Oh, yes. I know all about you, Ryder.

PHIL: What it all comes down to is war, a war for survival. And you can't fight a war by yourself. You look skeptical.

FRANK: If you're not fighting alone, why are you in this joint?

PHIL: I'll be out in a couple of weeks. You got that list of books I sent you?

FRANK: Yeah, I got it.

PHIL: You may not be able to get them all.

FRANK: I may not be able to understand them either.

PHIL: You're a bright kid, Carter. Otherwise I wouldn't be wasting my time.

THE DARK CORNER OF AN EMPTY ROOM

FRANK: If organizing is the answer, how come you're in here in the first place?

PHIL: I was framed, but like I said, I'll be out in a couple of weeks. That's 'cause my brothers are out there fighting for me.

FRANK: How many brothers you got?

PHIL: Just read the books. You got plenty of time.

FRANK: Yeah, well, I'm not gonna be spending the rest of my life in this joint, I'll tell you that.

PHIL: You wouldn't be the first. You got someone waiting for you?

FRANK: You mean a woman? No. I don't want no old lady latchin' on to me. I wanna be free to come and go. What are you smiling at?

PHIL: Nothing, brother. But you can waste a lot of time chasing pussy.

FRANK: I don't have to chase it.

PHIL: You're a real stud. What are you in for?

FRANK: Armed robbery.

PHIL: What did you get?

FRANK: Three years. I'll be out in another year, if I stay clean that is.

THE DARK CORNER OF AN EMPTY ROOM

PHIL: You don't like me, do you?

FRANK: I just don't know where you're coming from. You got a good mind. I can see that. And you ain't no fag, but I can't see you with a woman either.

PHIL: I'm married, and I got two kids.

FRANK: Anyway, I've made up my mind. When I get out of here, I'm going to college. This teacher I know says he can get me a scholarship.

PHIL: Good for you. Let's keep in touch. My phone number's on that paper.

FRANK: Yes, I know.

(PHIL disappears as HAZEL appears.)

HAZEL: You don't trust anyone, do you?

FRANK: I have my reasons.

HAZEL: And you certainly don't think much of us, do you?

FRANK: Us? Who is us?

HAZEL: All the students on campus.

FRANK: There are some exceptions.

HAZEL: Meaning me? Why? Because I'm pretty.

THE DARK CORNER OF AN EMPTY ROOM

FRANK: There are lots of pretty girls on campus. And they may have the chassis, but there's no motor inside.

HAZEL: I guess I should be flattered. You sure are a mass of contradictions.

FRANK: In what way?

HAZEL: You make fun of the radicals on campus, and yet, in your heart, I think you're really one of them.

FRANK: You know something?

HAZEL: What?

FRANK: You think too much.

HAZEL: I thought that was what you liked about me.

FRANK: Yeah, well, I guess that's part of the white man's burden. We think too little; that's part of the black man's curse.

HAZEL: You know something, Frank? I think you're full of shit.

FRANK: A nice, respectable girl like you. Where did you pick up that kind of language?

HAZEL: I wonder.

FRANK: *(After a moment)* What's been bothering you, Honey? Something's wrong. What is it?

HAZEL: I've left home. I told my father I was meeting you, and we had a big fight, and I moved out.

THE DARK CORNER OF AN EMPTY ROOM

FRANK: Are you sure that's what you wanna do?

HAZEL: I love you, Frank. I've never loved anyone before, not like this.

RADIO: *(In the distance)* "My baby don't care for shows./ My baby don't care for clothes. My baby just cares for me."

(THEY embrace.)

HAZEL: Oh, Frank!

(THEY sit. SHE notices a book.)

FRANK: What are you reading?

FRANK: It's a book by William Du Bois. "The Souls of Black Folks."

HAZEL: Is it good?

FRANK: It's beautiful.

HAZEL: What was it like in prison?

FRANK: I wouldn't wanna go back.

HAZEL: I was speaking to Professor Gilbert. He thinks you have a natural talent as a writer.

FRANK: That's not what he told me.

HAZEL: He doesn't believe in flattering people.

THE DARK CORNER OF AN EMPTY ROOM

FRANK: It's all so phoney.

HAZEL: What is?

FRANK: Life here on campus. It has nothing to do with reality. I walk across the campus, and it's like being in another world.

HAZEL: But this world exists.

FRANK: I wonder. Some day, I think I'm gonna wake up, and this will all be gone, the school, the classes and you. I'm gonna wake up all alone, in a room just like this one, only the furniture won't be as comfortable and when I look out the window, I won't see the trees and the grass. I'll see the jungle I grew up in. The streets and the tenements, and I'll smell the piss in the hallway.

HAZEL: It doesn't have to be that way.

FRANK: You grew up white, Honey. Everything looks pink and rosy to you.

HAZEL: And everything looks dark to you.

FRANK: Being black is a burden. It's a load I've got to carry for the rest of my life.

HAZEL: Sometimes I think you're in love with your burden.

FRANK: I've never tried to forget it, and I never will.

HAZEL: What does that mean?

FRANK: It doesn't mean anything. It's a simple fact.

THE DARK CORNER OF AN EMPTY ROOM

HAZEL: It means it's a part of your life that I can never share.

FRANK: I love the way you ask a question, and then go right ahead and answer it.

HAZEL: It's the truth, isn't it?

FRANK: I think in every relationship there has to be some private areas.

HAZEL: You wouldn't say that to a black girl.

FRANK: What the fuck do you want? You want me to absolve you of your guilt?. Is that what you want?

HAZEL: In other words, our relationship's built on my assuming the white man's guilt. Is that what you're telling me?

FRANK: To some extent.

HAZEL: What nonsense! I love you...

FRANK: Why?

HAZEL: Because you're you.

FRANK: Because I've got a chip on my shoulder? I'm only kidding.

HAZEL: No. It's the truth. I love you for your animosity, and yet, somehow, I resent it. Oh, I don't want to think about all that. Why can't we just love each other? That's the important thing. *(After a moment)* Frank?

THE DARK CORNER OF AN EMPTY ROOM

FRANK: Yeah?

HAZEL: Would you take me to meet your family some time? You've met mine.

FRANK: That went over like a lead balloon.

HAZEL: Are you ashamed of them?

FRANK: No, I'm not ashamed of them.

HAZEL: Are you ashamed of me?

FRANK: What would you have to talk about?

HAZEL: You, for one.

FRANK: You might enjoy meeting my sister. We used to be close. She's pretty disgusted with me though, ending up in prison.

HAZEL: Do you still see her?

FRANK: Occasionally. She's married now, and I've been to visit her.

HAZEL: But you don't go there often.

FRANK: Her values, and mine, are not the same anymore. She's got a family now, and that's all that's important.

HAZEL: Isn't that natural?

FRANK: Don't ask me what's natural, Honey, 'cause natural, to me, ain't important.

THE DARK CORNER OF AN EMPTY ROOM

HAZEL: What is important to you, Frank?

FRANK: Catching up.

HAZEL: With what?

FRANK: With those years I lost in prison.

(HAZEL moves away and disappears, as CHLOE appears.)

CHLOE: Sure I want you to get an education. But that doesn't include getting involved with some white girl. I'm not sayin' anything against her. If you like her that much, then she must be nice. But she's white, and you're black, and some day she's gonna call you a nigger, and really mean it.

FRANK: So what?

CHLOE: Honey, it's hard enough when you're both the same color.

FRANK: Color, color, color. That's all you think about.

CHLOE: You're gonna change the world, you damn fool boy? You're gonna make believe that black is white, and white is black? You Carters are all alike. You live in a world of dreams. Your father thinks that he's really made it. Well, maybe he has. For a nigger to stay out jail is really makin' it.

FRANK: I don't think Papa's done too badly.

CHLOE: He don't play around, that I know of, and he don't beat up on me. He better not! And when it comes to talkin', he can take the prize, drunk or sober; and he'll go tellin' you to do what you

THE DARK CORNER OF AN EMPTY ROOM

wanna do. But when you're in trouble, what's he gonna do to get you out of it? And if you go into politics...

FRANK: Who said anything about going into politics?

CHLOE: No one's gonna look at you. Not the whites, not the blacks. So go on ahead and live with that white woman of yours if you want to, but just remember, when it does come to breakin' up, it ain't gonna be easy.

(WALTER appears.)

WALTER: Your mother'd be jealous of any woman you took up with, Son; white or black. Shit. A woman's a woman, and a man's a man. That's what this world's all about. Your mother's got white blood in her, and so have I. Those damn fool niggers who wanna shut themselves up in a ghetto, let 'em. I don't wanna go back to Africa. I'm an American. My father was born here, and so was his. This is my country, and I'm gonna fight for it.

CHLOE: You're gonna what?

WALTER: Don't you sass me, woman; not in front of my son.

CHLOE: Your son? You perform miracles now? You get sons all by yourself now?

WALTER: Isn't it time for you to take your nap?

FRANK: You takin' naps now?

CHLOE: It's the doctor's idea. Not that it does me any good. I'll just lie down for a few minutes. You stick around. *(SHE kisses him and goes off.)*

THE DARK CORNER OF AN EMPTY ROOM

FRANK: Is her heart getting any worse?

WALTER: It doesn't get any worse. It doesn't get any better. Talking about getting ahead. I could have worked with Louis Armstrong. I never told you that. I knew him once, him and his whole family. And there was a time, I was even thinking about going into politics.

FRANK: Why didn't you?

WALTER: I had too much integrity, that's why. I don't believe in kissing ass. But it's different today. A black man can make a place for himself without losin' his self respect.

CHLOE'S: *(Offstage)* I thought there was no such thing as a black man.

WALTER: There's lot of pure blooded blacks. You just ain't one of them, that's all. I thought you were taking your nap.

(WALTER goes off as BEA appears.)

BEA: So, what have you been up to?

FRANK: Studying.

BEA: You still seeing that white girl?

FRANK: I was thinking of bring her over to meet the family. What do you think?

BEA: Are you out of your mind?

FRANK: Why not?

THE DARK CORNER OF AN EMPTY ROOM

BEA: Because Mama's a sick woman, that's why. The doctor said she was not to be excited. You gonna marry this white girl?

FRANK: Who said anything about marriage?

BEA: Well, it's obvious she wants to get married. Why else would she want to meet the family?

FRANK: Wouldn't you like to meet her?

BEA: Not particularly. What is she? Jewish? Italian?

FRANK: She's a human being. What the fuck is the matter with you?

BEA: Not so loud. Mama's asleep.

FRANK: I'm surprised you bother coming around here anymore. You've gotten so high and mighty.

BEA: Why do you think Mama's sick?

FRANK: On account of me. I gave her a heart-attack.

BEA: She spends her whole life worrying about you. What have you ever done for her? Tell me one thing.

FRANK: Look, I come here to see my parents. If you want, I can arrange it that we don't come here on the same day. I'm not perfect. But neither are you. And now that you're married to some Uncle Tom...

BEA: Spencer's no Uncle Tom, and he's more of a man than you'll

THE DARK CORNER OF AN EMPTY ROOM

ever be. All of a sudden, you're going to college. I knew that was too good to last.

FRANK: I'm still there, ain't I?

BEA: Sure. And what are you doing there? Ballin' all the white chicks.

FRANK: I'm only ballin' one.

BEA: At a time. And you want Mama to meet that white trash of yours.

FRANK: You're just itchin' for a smack in the mouth.

BEA: Just go ahead an try it.

(CHLOE appears.)

CHLOE: What's goin' on in here? What are you two fightin' about? Where's Spencer?

BEA: He took the kids for a ride.

CHLOE: Did your father go with them?

BEA: No. He went for a walk. How are you feeling?

CHLOE: I'm feeling fine. What's eatin' him?

BEA: Maybe you oughta see another doctor.

CHLOE: What's eatin' him?

THE DARK CORNER OF AN EMPTY ROOM

FRANK: What are you asking her for? Why don't you ask me?

BEA: You don't have to snap at her like that.

FRANK: It's nothing important.

CHLOE: Than what are you making all this fuss about?

FRANK: I just thought it might be nice if you met Hazel.

CHLOE: Why? You planning to marry her?

FRANK: That's all you women think about. No, I'm not planning to marry her. I just thought you it might be a good idea for you to meet her.

CHLOE: Sure I'd like to meet her. Mind your own business, Bea. I know she's white but, like Frank said, he ain't planning on marrying her and, just in case it might cross his mind, it might be good for all of us to meet. Why don't you bring her over next Sunday.

FRANK: You don't have to fuss.

CHLOE: I don't intend to. *(SHE turns to BEA.)* Can you be here?

BEA: I don't know.

CHLOE: You be here.

BEA: I'll have to talk to Spencer.

FRANK: They don't have to be here.

THE DARK CORNER OF AN EMPTY ROOM

CHLOE: I'd like 'em to be.

BEA: You wanna go outside and sit on the stoop?

CHLOE: Maybe it's a little cooler out there. You wanna join us, Son?

FRANK: I'll be out in a little while.

(BEA and CHLOE go off as HAZEL appears.)

FRANK: Now there's nothing to be nervous about. They're people, just like you and me.

HAZEL: Like you, maybe.

FRANK: We're not gonna stay long. They don't expect us to.

(THEY approach CHLOE and WALTER.)

HAZEL: I'm so glad to meet you. I feels as if I know you all.

CHLOE: Frank never said much about you.

WALTER: And he never told us how pretty you were.

HAZEL: That's very kind of you to say so.

CHLOE: Do your parents know you're goin' with a black man?

HAZEL: Why, yes, they do.

CHLOE: And how do they feel?

THE DARK CORNER OF AN EMPTY ROOM

HAZEL: They don't approve.

CHLOE: And I suppose you expect us to be happy that our son's going with a white girl.

HAZEL: Must we always think in terms of black and white?

CHLOE: I didn't make the world.

HAZEL: But you approve of separating people according to color.

CHLOE: That's not me, my dear. I just try to live the best I know how. Frank is still young, and he's been enough trouble for a man twice his age.

HAZEL: Sometimes avoiding trouble can cause even more trouble.

CHLOE: I ain't got nothing against you. Not personally.

HAZEL: Doesn't that make it even worse? Condemning someone you don't even know.

CHLOE: We carry our color like the mark of Cain. Why shouldn't you?

FRANK: Mama knows her Bible.

CHLOE: Frank's over twenty one. He can do what he likes.

HAZEL: I just thought it might be easier on Frank if we could all be friends.

(BEA approaches.)

THE DARK CORNER OF AN EMPTY ROOM

BEA: I don't think you're the least bit concerned with what would be easier for Frank.

FRANK: This is my sister, Bea.

HAZEL: I gathered as much.

BEA: I don't know if Frank has told you, but my mother is not a well woman. She has a heart condition, and the doctor has warned us that she should not be upset.

HAZEL: You can't fight that, can you? Perhaps I'd better leave.

BEA: I think that would be a good idea.

HAZEL: I'm sorry.

(SHE walks away as BEA, CHLOE and WALTER disappear.

FRANK: Now look, Honey, this was your idea.

HAZEL: I know, I know.

FRANK: Incidentally, I may be getting back a little late tonight.

HAZEL: Oh? Anything special?

FRANK: Phil Ryder's in town, and we're supposed to get together.

HAZEL: I'd like to meet him.

FRANK: Not this time around. We've got some things I'd like to talk to him about.

THE DARK CORNER OF AN EMPTY ROOM

(HAZEL disappears as PHIL appears.)

PHIL: Well, look who's here. I thought you'd forgotten all about us.

FRANK: I haven't forgotten. I've just been thinking things through.

PHIL: And?

FRANK: I'm still thinking.

PHIL: Well, if you're lookin' for glory, forget it. Not only will the whites be down on you, but so will our own people...a lot of them. They're making a saint out of Martin Luther King, but it's our work that's getting the action. Might is right.

FRANK: But we ain't got the might.

PHIL: It doesn't come to you, Brother. You gotta reach out for it. How do you think the Israelis got to be where they are today? I'm talking about those Zionists. You don't hear anymore about the Stern gang or the Hagannah, but where would they be without them? Think about it. You still seeing that white girl?

FRANK: What difference does it make?

PHIL: Don't ask me.

(Soft music is heard as PHIL disappears and HAZEL appears.)

HAZEL: Look at that cloud floating in the sky. Look at that tree. Those are the things that are real. You're not listening to me.

FRANK: I'm listening, I'm listening.

THE DARK CORNER OF AN EMPTY ROOM

HAZEL: It's so easy to lose one's perspective, to bury oneself in problems we invent for ourselves.

FRANK: What about problems we don't invent for ourselves?

HAZEL: In either case, I think it's important to keep ones perspective. You don't have much of a sense of humor. It's one of your few faults.

FRANK: You think life is funny?

HAZEL: At times. You're so...

FRANK: So...what?

HAZEL: So somber.

FRANK: Black man, black thoughts. *(After a moment)* Hazel, honey, suppose we stopped seeing each other for a while.

HAZEL: Why? Is there someone else? Don't lie to me, Frank.

FRANK: There's no one else.

HAZEL: Then...?

FRANK: Because from here on in, things may be getting pretty rough.

HAZEL: Oh? And you think I'll fall apart?

FRANK: It isn't that.

HAZEL: What is it, then?

THE DARK CORNER OF AN EMPTY ROOM

FRANK: I just don't think you're prepared...to...

HAZEL: To what?

FRANK: To make the sacrifices I'm prepared to make. And there's no reason why you should be.

HAZEL: What am I supposed to say? "Bless you, my child? May you be happy with your black paramour?"

FRANK: I was afraid of this.

HAZEL: Isn't that rather a strong word to use, "afraid"? A big, strapping man like you, afraid of a fragile creature like me. We've never really been honest with each other, have we? It's been sex, hasn't it? Pure and simple. And we've both tried to pretend it's been more. Isn't that so?

FRANK: Our relationship has meant a great deal to me. It would be nice...if...

HAZEL: If what? If I could just slip away quietly, just disappear? Well, I'm afraid it's not going to be that easy, Frank. I've given up my family for you. You are my life, my breath. I'm not just another cunt, one more white pussy.

FRANK: *(Feverishly)* My leg, Hazel, it's killing me. It's broken, I know. And it's swelling up.

HAZEL: It's because of your family, isn't it?

FRANK: This has nothing to do with my family.

HAZEL: I'll fight for you, Frank.

THE DARK CORNER OF AN EMPTY ROOM

FRANK: With what? Emotional blackmail?

HAZEL: I'll kill myself.

FRANK: Don't talk like that, Hazel, please. Don't soil what we had.

HAZEL: No platitudes, please.

FRANK: I'm in a corner, Baby. Don't you understand?

HAZEL: I couldn't go on without you.

FRANK: *(Feverishly)* My leg is killing me!

REVEREND DANIEL'S VOICE: If thy eye offend thee, pluck it out.

FRANK: It's my leg. It's killing me! Look, we are both adults.

HAZEL: Another platitude.

FRANK: Stop it, Hazel, please.

HAZEL: My death is on your conscience, Frank.

(HAZEL disappears.)

FRANK: Hazel, don't be a fool. Hazel!

(A police car is heard very faintly in the distance. As the lights dim FRANK sits up and looks around.)

SCENE THREE

(The action is continuous. The faint sound of a police car is heard, then fades. Soft music from a radio is heard. FRANK sits, lost in thought.)

"My baby don't for care shows.
My baby don't care for clothes.
My baby just cares for me."

FRANK: I still can't believe it.

(HAZEL appears in a dim light, obviously nude.)

HAZEL: I warned you, didn't I?

FRANK: How could you, Baby?

HAZEL: It was easy, my dear. I just filled the tub with warm lovely water, slipped in under that cozy wet blanket and reached over for your razor. It was just a pinprick, if you'll pardon the expression. I closed my eyes, and I floated to heaven on a sea of blood.

FRANK: We were so good together, baby.

HAZEL: It was Shangri La.

FRANK: Oh, how we fucked.

HAZEL: Made love, my dear.

FRANK & HAZEL: We cried when we came.

HAZEL: And now you're mine, and I shall never let you go. La belle dame sans merci. Oh, my lovely lover with coal black arms

THE DARK CORNER OF AN EMPTY ROOM

and white flashing teeth. And look. I'm no longer white. The fires of hell are crimson, and see how they lick my body. Look. I'm crimson now.

(HAZEL vanishes as PHIL appears.)

PHIL: When are you gonna stop brooding about that white chick of yours?

FRANK: If only we could have spent our life in bed.

PHIL: You're a sentimental slob.

FRANK: Somebody else said that to me once. Actually he called me an Uncle Tom. an English teacher of mine, in grammar school, no less. He said I had no balls.

PHIL: There's something psychotic about a white girl that digs a black man.

FRANK: What about a black man that digs a white girl?

PHIL: It's natural for the lower economic class to reach up.

FRANK: You're a walking textbook, aren't you? Life isn't all theory, you know. What about people?

PHIL: People? Did you know that Afro-Americans have the lowest suicide rate. And do you know why?

FRANK: No, but I'm sure you're gonna tell me.

PHIL: Because you back someone up against the wall, and he has

THE DARK CORNER OF AN EMPTY ROOM

no where to go but forward. That girl of yours was not prepared for life, and it would have happened, sooner or later. It's been almost a year now. Don't you think it's time you pulled yourself together?

FRANK: Don't push me, brother. The fact of the matter is, I'm not so sure about this black power shit, like marching into a courtroom brandishing arms?

PHIL: When you carry arms, you've got power. And power is what people respect.

FRANK: And when you carry arms, sooner or later you're gonna use them.

PHIL: If we have to, sure.

FRANK: And you end up in jail, and they murder you there.

PHIL: And it only makes us push all the harder.

FRANK: Yeah, and we push harder and they push back even harder, and then what have you got? A bunch of corpses laying around.

PHIL: It's not a tea party, you dumb fuck. It's a revolution. *(After a moment.)* Have you been seeing Rhoda Sanford lately?

FRANK: What about it?

PHIL: She's not just an ordinary chick, you know.

FRANK: What are you, her father?

THE DARK CORNER OF AN EMPTY ROOM

PHIL: She's a valuable member of the organization, and I don't want to see her hurt.

FRANK: Why don't you just stick to your revolution, Sonny?

PHIL: Look, nigger, I've had my doubts about you from the very beginning. You're on an ego trip, and the last thing we need around here is a nigger that's out for himself. That white bitch of yours is dead.

(FRANK knocks PHIL to the ground. PHIL rises and rubs his jaw.)

PHIL: Stay out of my way, Carter.

(PHIL disappears as RHODA appears.)

FRANK: He likes to think of himself as some sort of a Robespierre. A Baudelaire, a poet of evil.

RHODA: He's a brilliant man.

FRANK: And talk about ego. For as long as I can remember, I've been pushed around. My parents, the other kids on the block; and then the "fuzz." They beat me up so bad I was in the hospital for almost a week. I was sixteen at the time.

RHODA: So you want revenge.

FRANK: No. Not anymore. If I've learned one thing, I've learned to mistrust all emotions.

RHODA: Yes, I've noticed that.

THE DARK CORNER OF AN EMPTY ROOM

FRANK: And I've been thinking, maybe the movement's really the answer. Its a revolution, like Phil says. It's a political act, and there's no place for emotion. I've got to recreate myself. A new mind, a new heart, a new body.

RHODA: You make it sound like Frankenstein's monster.

FRANK: I thought you believed in the movement.

RHODA: I happen to be black, and I happen to be political, but first and foremost, I am a woman. That's a fact of nature, Honey, and that's something that never changes. Are you disappointed in me, Brother? Are you disappointed that I'm just like your mother and your sister and your dead, white girl friend?

FRANK: You're not like any of them.

RHODA: I'm not like what you thought I was, and you can't be a machine with me.

FRANK: I just don't wanna be pushed around anymore, by anybody...not even myself.

RHODA: Then you won't be.

(FRANK kisses her.)

RHODA: I've gotta go.

FRANK: You coming to the rally tonight?

RHODA: Honey, I am the rally. I organized it.

FRANK: Phil's kinda sore at me.

THE DARK CORNER OF AN EMPTY ROOM

RHODA: Forget it. He likes you.

(RHODA moves away and disappears as WALTER appears.)

WALTER: I wish I were young enough, Son. I'd be right there with you. I did a lot of reading in my day, but the time wasn't ripe.

FRANK: Well, the time's right now. We're gonna rise up and take this country.

(CHLOE appears.)

CHLOE: And you think this country's gonna sit back and let you? This country's gonna squash you and your little movement like some little black bug. They got more guns than you got, they got more men, and they got plenty of prisons to hold the lot of you, the ones that they don't kill, that is.

FRANK: There's one thing you forget, Mama.

CHLOE: And what might that be?

FRANK: We've got right on our side.

CHLOE: I don't approve of no killing. Nothing can make it right, Son. Nothing makes it right to take a human life.

FRANK: What about war? Or suppose someone came at you with a knife?

CHLOE: Nothing.

FRANK: Now you know you don't believe that, Mama.

THE DARK CORNER OF AN EMPTY ROOM

CHLOE: Our Lord was nailed to the cross, and his dyin' words were, "Forgive them. They know now what they do."

FRANK: That was a white man talking, Mama.

CHLOE: According to Reverend Daniel, Jesus Christ was black.

FRANK: Then he was an Uncle Tom.

CHLOE: But he won out in the end, Uncle Tom or not.

FRANK: Religion is an opiate, just like heroin, Mama.

CHLOE: A human being has got to believe in something.

FRANK: How about another human being?

CHLOE: He's got to believe in something bigger.

FRANK: If we look after ourselves, God'll take care of the rest. He don't need our help.

CHLOE: But we need him, Son.

FRANK: Okay, Mama, you worship your idols, if that's what you need.

CHLOE: And what do you worship, Son? Your own strength? And when you get old and sick, what then?

(WALTER appears.)

WALTER: What are you trying to do to that boy? Take his manhood away from him?

THE DARK CORNER OF AN EMPTY ROOM

CHLOE: I'm trying to keep his manhood alive.

FRANK: And it's not all guns, Mama. We got all sorts of programs to help the black community. Free breakfasts for kids. We're providing health care for poor blacks. We're fighting to put an end to police brutality. We want a jury of our peers when there's a trial. You're not listening to me.

CHLOE: I'm listening to you, Son. I'm listening. But I gotta lay down for a while. *(SHE goes off.)*

FRANK: Is it still her heart?

WALTER: I'm afraid so, Son.

FRANK: What does the doctor say?

> *(Organ music is heard. FRANK and WALTER stand silently. BEA appears.)*

BEA: How dare you come here, you murderer?

> *(WALTER appears.)*

WALTER: Don't pay her any mind, Son. She doesn't know what she's sayin'.

BEA: She never had anything. In her whole life she never had anything.

FRANK: Everything I've done is for all of us.

WALTER: Your mother had a weak heart. It might have been anything that upset her.

465

THE DARK CORNER OF AN EMPTY ROOM

BEA: You let him in here?

WALTER: This is my house, and I don't wanna hear anything against my son.

BEA: He killed my mother.

FRANK: Why don't you turn me in?

BEA: Don't think I haven't thought about it, and I would have done it in a second, if it could have brought Mama back.

WALTER: Your mother died of a heart attack, and don't you go blaming your brother.

BEA: All those shoot outs, and God knows what else.

FRANK: It seems to me, when you were seeing that boyfriend of yours...what was his name?... Harlan, I believe, you were pretty hep on brotherly love and civil rights. Now it's just your precious little family. Well the day the world ends with my wife and child, they can take me out and shoot me. Come to think of it, they won't have to, because I'd be just as dead as you are.

BEA: Civil rights. That's a joke. He's in with a gang of murderers, Papa. He's worse than he ever was, and the sooner he's back in jail, the better off we'll be.

WALTER: I don't want you talkin' that way about your brother. He's doing his best to help our people.

BEA: He's a gangster, Papa. All he's doing is going out there and makin' trouble. Don't you read the papers? Don't you watch the news?

THE DARK CORNER OF AN EMPTY ROOM

WALTER: Now, let's just wait and see, child. Now look, Bea, I didn't invite you here.

BEA: Okay. If that's the way you feel, let Frank take care if you in your old age. *(SHE walks off.)*

FRANK: I don't want to come between you and Bea.

WALTER: She'll be back. Don't worry. Women think they know everything, but there's lots of things they don't understand, and that includes your mother, God rest her soul.

(WALTER disappears as RHODA appears.)

RHODA: Suppose I got in touch with her?

FRANK: What would be the point?

RHODA: She could cause a lot of trouble, if she wanted to. You've got a record, Frank. They could send you up for life.

FRANK: Bea ain't gonna cause any trouble. After all, I am her precious kid's uncle.

RHODA: There are a lot of people that feel the way she does.

FRANK: I'm never going back to prison. And as far as I'm concerned nothing is worse than life without hope. And speaking of life, how's my little son doing?

RHODA: Well, for one thing, it may not be a boy and, whatever it is, he's been doing a lot of kicking. Give me your hand. You feel it?

THE DARK CORNER OF AN EMPTY ROOM

FRANK: Son of a gun. The doctor said you were due by now. What's holding things up?

RHODA: Uh, oh! You said the magic word.

FRANK: What?

RHODA: Call a cab.

FRANK: Is it happening?

RHODA: I said, "Call a cab."

> (The sound of a car, a car horn, screeching wheels, and an infant crying.)

RHODA: It's a boy.

FRANK: He doesn't look like much, does he?

RHODA: Neither did you, when you were his age.

FRANK: If only Mama was here to see him. Do you think there's life after death?

RHODA: Right now, Honey, I'm concerned with life.

> (RHODA disappears as FRANK approaches WALTER.)

FRANK: Being part of a movement, being a father...suddenly I find that I'm at peace with myself. I never dreamed that the way to find ones identity was to lose it. Do you think Mama would have understood?

THE DARK CORNER OF AN EMPTY ROOM

WALTER: We all gotta find our own way, Son. I don't know what you're up to, but I believe in you, Son, and I'll do anything to help.

FRANK: As a matter of fact, I've been wanting to ask a favor. I'm going out on a job and, well, if anything should happen, I'd feel more secure if I knew that there was someone I could count on to look in on Rhoda and the kid...just in case.

WALTER: What do you mean...just in case?

FRANK: You never know, Papa. I ain't afraid of dying. I just wanna make sure my family's well taken care of.

WALTER: You be careful, Son. You hear me?

(WALTER disappears as RHODA appears)

FRANK: No, Honey, no. I've spoken to Phil, and Benny's gonna take your place. Staking out a place is one thing, but I don't want you getting shot. From now on, one of us stays at home. I don't want my son being raised by strangers?

RHODA: Okay, Frank, okay.

FRANK: You think I'm wrong.

RHODA: No, Honey, you're right, as usual.

FRANK: Don't overdo it.

(HE kisses her. RHODA vanishes as BENNY appears.)

FRANK: Come on, Benny, make up your mind. Are you in or are you out?

THE DARK CORNER OF AN EMPTY ROOM

BENNY: I'm in, I'm in. I told you I was in. Just don't say anything in front of Helen.

FRANK: It's a payroll, out in Brooklyn. There'll be just the three of us. You, me and Harry Lane.

BENNY: What do we need money for?

FRANK: Guns and equipment. It's an easy job.

> (We hear the sound of a car starting, motoring along. There's quiet. Then suddenly an alarm.)

FRANK: It's okay, it's okay. Just take it easy. We got time. (After a moment) Okay. Let's go.

> (We hear the sound of a car starting up, moving along, then suddenly speeding up. The sound of screeching wheels.)

FRANK: Take it easy, Benny. We don't want to attract attention.

> (The screeching of wheels.)

FRANK: Benny, what the fuck are you doing?

BENNY: It's not me. It's Harry. Harry, get your foot off the fuckin' gas!!

> (Gunshots are heard.)

FRANK: Harry! What are you doing? Are you nuts?

HARRY'S VOICE: They saw us. That police car.

THE DARK CORNER OF AN EMPTY ROOM

(An exchange of gunfire is heard, and the sound of a police siren. The sound of a car crashing.)

POLICE OFFICER'S VOICE: There were three of them.

(The sound of a chase. Panting. Footsteps on the stairs. Silence. The radio in the distance has changed stations and an ANNOUNCER is heard.)

ANNOUNCER: The police are combing the area for the two men who escaped. The dead suspect injured in the cross-fire has been identified as Benjamin Smith, aged twenty seven.

(BENNY appears covered with blood.)

BENNY: I don't know, Frankie. I'm always getting the shit end of the stick. I almost got shot by old man Zacharias. I got beat up on account of Father Daniel, and now I'm splattered all over the street.

FRANK: My leg is busted, Benny.

BENNY: Yeah, but you're still alive. Did you see me layin' there, covered with blood? And all you got is a busted leg I don't know, Frankie. Every time I listen to you...

FRANK: They're out to destroy us, Benny. Hoover, the FBI. It's a racist war, and it's taking place all over the world.

BENNY: And I'm dead, Frankie, dead.

FRANK: I'm not getting out of here, Benny. I can hear 'em closin' in on me.

BENNY: You gotta go out in style, Frankie, boy.

THE DARK CORNER OF AN EMPTY ROOM

(HAZEL appears.)

HAZEL: Oh, yes my darling. Do it gloriously.

FRANK: What does it feel like to die?

HAZEL: It's lovely, honey. It's like the ultimate orgasm.

BENNY: It hurt, Frankie. It hurt something awful.

(CHLOE appears.)

FRANK: Mama, what does it feel like to die?

CHLOE: It's different for everyone, Son.

FRANK: I would like to see my son grow up.

CHLOE: No one is ever really ready.

BENNY: You can say that again.

FRANK: I'm sorry, Benny.

BENNY: Don't say that to my old lady, Frankie. As a matter of fact, if I were you, I'd just keep out of her way. She thinks you're a bad influence on me and, well, I guess this sorta clinches it.

FRANK: Benny, tell me something.

BENNY: What?

FRANK: Have you any regrets?

THE DARK CORNER OF AN EMPTY ROOM

BENNY: Are you kidding? We had some good times though, didn't we, Frankie? Helen was jealous of you. Did you know that? She used to say that we were like a couple of fags. But hell, you were the only one I could say anything to, no matter how stupid, 'cause we had respect for each other.

(REVEREND DANIEL appears.)

REVEREND DANIEL: Frank Carter?

FRANK: Yes sir?

REVEREND DANIEL: Have you any last words?

FRANK: I wrote a composition once.

REVEREND DANIEL: And what was that about?

FRANK: I forget now. It was a long time ago.

HAZEL: You should have been a poet, Frank.

REVEREND DANIEL: Frank Carter do you regret all your crimes?

FRANK: I never looked on them as crimes.

REVEREND DANIEL: But we know better, don't we?

FRANK: Well, I'm not gonna beat my breast and shout mea culpa.

REVEREND DANIEL: Then there's nothing you regret?

HAZEL: *(Sings)* "You must remember this,
A kiss is still a kiss.

THE DARK CORNER OF AN EMPTY ROOM

A sigh is just a sigh.
Big romantic stuff, my darling.

FRANK: No one human being is completely responsible for another human being.

HAZEL: Aren't you contradicting yourself, my dear?

FRANK: You were dragging me down.

HAZEL: Was I...really?

(The phone rings. FRANK hesitates, then picks it up)

FRANK: *(He listens for a moment.)* Come and get me!

(WALTER appears.)

WALTER: Don't do anything foolish, Son.

FRANK: That cop was killed. It's Murder One, and I was the one that shot him.

WALTER: They've got to prove it.

RHODA: You're better off standing trial.

MAN'S VOICE: Come on out of there with your hands up.

FRANK: And what makes you think I have a choice? Those are pigs out there, and I killed one of them. The verdict is in.

REVEREND DANIEL: Guilty.

THE DARK CORNER OF AN EMPTY ROOM

BEA: Guilty.

CHLOE: Guilty, Son.

BENNY: Guilty.

HAZEL: Guilty as charged.

MAN'S VOICE: We'll give you three minutes. If you're not outside by then, we're coming in. We know you've been shot.

(FRANK rises and limps to the window.)

WALTER: Don't be a fool, Son.

(FRANK hears a noise. HE turns and faces the door. A volley of shots is fired through the door. FRANK falls to the floor. After a moment another volley is fired. The door is broken down. A WHITE DETECTIVE enters, gun in hand and walks over to FRANK and turns him over with his foot.)

WHITE DETECTIVE: *(Into a walkie-talkie.)* He's dead.

(RHODA, PHIL, BEA, CHLOE, WALTER, BENNY and RACHEL gather around FRANK.)

WHITE DETECTIVE: No, he's alone. Send up a stretcher. *(HE looks down at the body and shakes his head.)* They'll never learn.

(The WHITE DETECTIVE goes off. As the GROUP gathers closer around FRANK sounds are heard from the outside, and the lights begin to dim.)

THE DARK CORNER OF AN EMPTY ROOM

WOMAN'S VOICE: Jerry, where are you?

A RADIO: *(Softly in the distance)* "My baby don't care for clothes.
My baby don't care for shows.
My baby just cares for me."

(The lights are out.)

ABOUT THE AUTHOR

As an actor Norman Beim has appeared on Broadway in "Inherit The Wind" with the legendary Paul Muni, Off Broadway with Morgan Freeman at Joe Papp's Public Theatre, in various regional theatre productions and in film and on television. He is a director as well as a playwright and a novelist. His debut novel, "Hymie and the Angel," received excellent reviews.

His plays have been produced in Holland, Belgium and at theatres across the country and have won numerous awards. "The Wrath of God, Plus 5 Additional Dramas" is the tenth collection of Mr. Beim's plays to be published. Previous volumes, "Six Award Winning Plays" and "My Family The Jewish Immigrants" were used as textbooks at St. Olaf College in Minnesota.

He is a member of the Dramatist Guild, Actors Equity, the Screen Actors Guild and AFTRA.

He lives in New York City.